FREE-CHOICE
SCIENCE EDUCATION

How We Learn Science
Outside of School

EDITED BY JOHN H. FALK

with Elizabeth Donovan and Rosalie Woods

TEACHERS
COLLEGE
PRESS

Teachers College, Columbia University
New York and London

Published by Teachers College Press, 1234 Amsterdam Avenue, New York, NY 10027

Library of Congress Cataloging-in-Publication Data

Free-choice science education : how we learn science outside of school / edited by John H. Falk.
    p. cm. — (Ways of knowing in science and mathematics series)
  Includes bibliographical references and index.
  ISBN 0-8077-4065-9 (alk. paper) — ISBN 0-8077-4064-0 (pbk. : alk. paper)
  1. Science—Study and teaching. 2. Non-formal education. I. Title: How we learn science outside of school. II. Falk, John H. (John Howard), 1948–
III. Series.
  Q181.F8348 2001
  507′.1—dc21   00-068272

ISBN 0-8077-4064-0 (paper)
ISBN 0-8077-4065-9 (cloth)

Printed on acid-free paper
Manufactured in the United States of America

08 07 06 05 04 03 02 01   8 7 6 5 4 3 2 1

Contents

PART III. Looking to the Future

PART I

Theoretical Framework

CHAPTER 1

Free-Choice Science Learning: Framing the Discussion

John H. Falk

People utilize *free-choice* science learning resources, as well as free-choice science education venues, for many reasons. Adults go to science centers to satisfy their curiosity and to fulfill their needs for fun and intellectual stimulation (Falk, 1998b; Falk, Moussouri, & Coulson, 1998). They take their children because they feel that such experiences are worthwhile and educational, as well as fun. Children enjoy the opportunity to see and do new and interesting things (Falk & Dierking, 1992). Similar motivations are at work when individuals choose to watch nature specials on television or visit science informational sites on the Internet (Chadwick, 1998; Chadwick & Falk, 1999; Eveland & Dunwoody, 1997; Gross, 1997), or participate as part of a community group (Brice Heath & Smyth, 1999). Whether characterized as *entertainment* or *education*, learning is a prevalent motivation that underlies all science-oriented, free-choice experiences (Falk, Moussouri, & Coulson, 1998).

Although people rarely engage in free-choice learning to become experts in a subject, they invariably emerge more knowledgeable and more motivated to learn in the future (Falk & Dierking, 2000). People participate in free-choice learning to satisfy a personal sense of identity, to create a sense of value within the world, and to fulfill personal intellectual and emotional needs; what has come to be referred to as "meaning making" (cf. Brown, Collins, & Duguid, 1989). Families, schools, religious organizations, and government can no longer fully meet the learning needs of the society (Brice Heath & Smyth, 1999). During the past decade there has been a growing awareness that these learning needs are being met by a wide range of institutions and experiences variously described as the educational infrastructure (St. John & Perry, 1993).

SCIENCE LEARNING

Science, in particular, is a topic not easily confined to school hours and years. Both the process and content of science is ever-changing. Because of this constant, in fact ever-accelerating, rate of change, science is a subject that requires a lifelong commitment in order to remain literate and current. Fortunately, myriad resources committed to facilitating public understanding of science regularly provide current science information for public consumption.

Accordingly, the American public currently learns science from a wide range of sources, including the formal education system, libraries, museums (a generic term that includes natural history museums, science centers, zoos, aquariums, botanical gardens, arboretums, and nature centers), television programming (public, network, and cable), film and video, newspapers, radio, books, magazines, the Internet, community-based organizations (also a generic term meant to include organizations such as the YWCA, Boys and Girls Clubs, Scouts, 4-H, health-related organizations, and environmental organizations), and through conversations with friends and family (Brice Heath & Smyth, 1999; Caillot & Nguyen-Xuan, 1995; Crane, Nicholson, Chen, & Bitgood, 1994; Falk, Brooks, & Amin, 1998; Griffin, 1989; Hacker & Harris, 1992; Miller & Pifer, 1996; Rogoff & Lave, 1984).

Historically, disproportionate attention has been placed upon a single part of the infrastructure—formal education—for facilitating science learning. However, recent years have seen a growing appreciation for the important, in fact fundamental, role played by the vast array of nonschool science education institutions and sources listed above. The proliferation of science information, and its impact on virtually every facet of our lives, demands that those concerned with public understanding of science not only accept but directly support the expansion and improvement of these free-choice venues for acquiring science information and understanding.

Research strongly suggests that the more the separate influential spheres of family, school, work, and elective learning overlap in people's lives, the more likely they are to become successful lifelong learners (Brice Heath & Smyth, 1999; Epstein, 1995). The more these various components work together toward improving the quality of science education, the more likely all will be successful (Knapp, 1997).

ABOUT THIS BOOK

This book represents an effort to broadly describe the nature and extent of science learning in America with particular reference to the innumerable sources of science education that exist outside the formal education system. This work is a direct outgrowth of a national conference that was held in Los Angeles in November 1998.

The first Free-Choice Learning Conference was organized by the Institute for Learning Innovation with support from the National Science Foundation, the James Irvine Foundation, the California Science Center, and the Institute for Learning Innovation. The conference was designed to bring researchers concerned about assessing the structure and function of free-choice science learning across the various components of the infrastructure together with leaders in designing, facilitating, and managing free-choice science experiences. Represented were individuals from natural history museums, zoos, aquariums, botanical gardens, and science centers; the broadcast and print media; community-based organizations such as Cooperative Extension, Humane Society, and Boys and Girls Clubs; and the Internet. Also present were policy leaders concerned with supporting and implementing free-choice initiatives.

The conference was designed to facilitate a national dialogue about the strengths, weaknesses, and benefits of building a better national infrastructure for free-choice learning in general, and science learning in particular. The papers that were commissioned for this conference, and the discussion that was fostered, are captured and extended in this volume of contributed works. The intent, and hope, is that this collective work will support continued opportunities for information sharing, discussion, and networking between and among all the diverse constituencies that comprise the science education community, both formal and free-choice. Thus this book is designed to share current understandings and deficiencies in the workings of the infrastructure for free-choice science learning; it also is intended to encourage interactions and discussions and to propose future directions and policies.

In short, both the conference and this work were designed to catalyze significant interactions among leading researchers, practitioners, and policymakers who, despite sharing a common interest in promoting public understanding and awareness of science, historically have been unconnected and largely unaware of each other's efforts and influences.

This publication will accomplish the following:

1. Make a case for the existence of an infrastructure for free-choice science learning.
2. Highlight research studies that reveal the nature and function of the infrastructure for free-choice science learning.

3. Propose studies, policies, and approaches that would enable researchers, practitioners, and policymakers to better understand the nature, function, and effectiveness of the infrastructure for free-choice learning.
4. Encourage coalition building and collaborations across the infrastructure leading to better practice, greater resources, realistic assessments, and greater appreciation for the importance of free-choice science learning.

First, though, it is important to clarify a few terms and concepts used throughout this book, in particular *free-choice learning, public understanding of science, infrastructure*, and *learning*.

FREE-CHOICE LEARNING

Throughout this book, the term *free-choice* learning is used to refer to the type of learning that occurs most frequently outside of school; in particular, free-choice learning refers to the type of learning typically facilitated by museums, science centers, a wide range of community-based organizations, and print and electronic media including the Internet.

History of Terms

Historically, *formal* has been the term used to refer to school-based learning and *informal* the term used to refer to the type of learning that occurs outside of school. Why replace *informal* with the new term *free-choice*?

The distinctions between *formal, informal*, and *nonformal* go back nearly 50 years and were first developed by individuals working in the area of international development as a means to distinguish the kinds of educational experiences individuals in developing countries had in the absence of an established compulsory education system. In the 1970s, the terms were borrowed by museum professionals and environmental educators who were in search of a way to define and distinguish their activities from the activities of school-based educators. Since the 1970s, the terms *informal education* and *informal learning* have received increasing recognition within the educational community, as have the institutions and processes the terms purport to represent. However, Lynn Dierking and I have argued for a number of years that the term *informal learning* is problematic (cf. Dierking, 1987; Falk & Dierking, 1992, 1998, 2000).

Use of the Term *Free-Choice*

Clearly there are important distinctions between the educational experiences typically offered in school and nonschool settings, and a variety of individuals have enumerated their differences (e.g., Crane et al., 1994; Koran & Dierking Shafer, 1982; Ramey-Gassert, Walberg, & Walberg, 1994). However, the crux of the issue really is to find an appropriate term for characterizing the nature of the learning that occurs in these settings.

Problems arise when the terms *formal* and *informal* are used as modifiers of the word *learning*. Stated simply, there is no convincing evidence that the fundamental processes of learning differ solely as a function of the physical setting. Learning is influenced by many factors, one being the physical context—but physical setting alone is unlikely to influence the type of learning that occurs there. Making the point by extremes, it is clearly absurd to suggest that seating children in a museum auditorium and requiring them to hear a lecture is somehow different from seating children in a school auditorium to hear a lecture. At the other extreme, there is no basis to assume that open-ended, optional, inquiry-based experiences within a school setting are somehow fundamentally different from open-ended, optional, inquiry-based experiences within a museum setting. What makes learning different is partially the physical setting but equally important—perhaps more so—are the social context and the underlying motivation of the learner. Hence Dierking and I have argued for use of the term *free-choice learning*.

Free-choice learning is a term that recognizes the unique characteristics of such learning: free-choice, nonsequential, self-paced, and voluntary. It also recognizes the socially constructed nature of learning—the interchange that goes on between the individual and his or her sociocultural *and* physical environments. The vast majority of the learning that occurs outside of school involves free-choice learning—learning that is primarily driven by the unique intrinsic needs and interests of the learner. By contrast, the vast majority of the learning that occurs within formal education settings involves compulsory learning—learning that is driven by a predetermined set of requirements dictated by externally imposed authority. *Free-choice* thus emerges as a more descriptive, more accurate modifier for the term learning; it also has the advantage of being a neutral term, largely independent of the positive and negative biases that surround schooling.

Concerns About the Term *Free-Choice.* Of the several issues or concerns that have been raised about the use of *free-choice* as a construct for considering learning, two are particularly worth discussing. The first is the assumption that most subjects, science in particular, are sufficiently complex and abstract that they must be taught in order for prospective learners to achieve any reasonable understanding of them: Free-choice appears to exclude the teacher and our traditional notion of teaching. Such a perspective ignores the carefully crafted pedagogy and socially facilitated nature of virtually all free-choice learning. Whether a museum exhibition, an educational television show, a popular science book, a newspaper article, or an informational Web site, most free-choice learning is facilitated by carefully crafted educational media designed to achieve specific educational goals. Although the facilitator may not be the traditional standing-in-front-of-you schoolteacher, most free-choice learning is facilitated.

A second important issue is how *free* is free-choice learning really? Where do we draw the boundaries? For example, many schoolteachers give their students a choice of assignments to complete, whereas many media, such as television, afford relatively little choice other than whether to watch or not. What, then, are the boundaries of free-choice?

Arguably, free-choice learning is a relative rather than an absolute construct. The operative issue is *perceived* choice and control by the learner. To qualify as free-choice learning, the learner must perceive that there are reasonable and desirable learning choices available (reasonable and desirable as defined by the learner) and that he or she possesses the freedom to select or not to select from among those choices. Because school choices are typically defined by the instructor rather than by the student, and the student is obligated to select from these in order to satisfy an externally imposed goal (e.g., a grade or "extra credit"), the result is something short of "free-choice." By contrast, even the limited options afforded by television are totally within the discretion of the viewer. The decision between changing channels or turning off the television is always available, and normally a person makes that decision purely on the basis of internally derived, personal goals; hence television-viewing qualifies as free-choice. Ultimately, though, one person's "choice" may be another person's "necessity"; only the context reveals the reality.

Final Note on Free-Choice Learning. The first free-choice conference—and by extension this book—was designed in part as a device for beginning to move the educational community toward a rhetorical transition to the term *free-choice learning*. Not all participants at the conference, nor all contributors to this work, agree with either the need for or wisdom of such a transition (cf. Luke, Camp, Dierking, & Pearce, Chapter 9). However, the reader should be aware that throughout this work, except in cases of direct quotes or in reference to formal names of organizations, *free-choice education* is the term used to describe out-of-school educational efforts, and *free-choice learning* is the term used to describe the learning that results from these and the myriad of other free-choice experiences.

PUBLIC UNDERSTANDING OF SCIENCE

If the twentieth century was characterized as the century of science, the twenty-first century promises to be only more so. Science, both as a way of thought and as a cultural tool, has grown to dominate our daily lives. As Crane (1994) has stated,

> Few of us can escape the science and math in our lives even if we work hard to do so. When a family member becomes ill with debilitating back trouble, a heart attack, a stroke or cancer, what kinds of science information does the family seek or want to know? When a toxic waste dump is reported in your area, what steps do you take to learn more about what this means? (p. 5)

For the benefit of clarifying what is meant in this work by *public understanding of science*, the government's *Federal Coordinating Council on Science, Engineering and Technology, Committee on Education and Human Resources*, Public Understanding of Science Working Group's definition will be used. This definition, though not perfect, represents a reasonably operational definition for the discussions that follow:

> Public understanding of science empowers people of all ages to enhance the quality of life for themselves, their families, and society through science (Implementation Plan, 1995–1999). (Public Understanding of Science Working Group, 1993, p. 1)

In this definition, *public* refers to people of all ages; *understanding* is a four-part concept that includes appreciation, access to information, ability to analyze, and ability to take appropriate action; and *science* includes all the natural and social sciences, including engineering, mathematics, and health. As part of this definition, this government working group explicitly described *science literacy* as a threshold level of knowledge of basic principles of science and considered it as a subset of the broader, multidimensional concept of *public understanding of science*.

The Royal Society of London (1985) lists a number of reasons that *the public understanding of science* matters, including the following:

1. Improving the public understanding of science is an investment in the future.
2. There is a link between the public understanding of science and national prosperity.
3. The competitive edge of companies would be enhanced by the public understanding of science.
4. Nearly all public issues require a public understanding of science for their resolution.
5. Science and technology should be major considerations in public policy, and therefore public understanding of science would enhance the quality of decisions.

6. In a democracy, public opinion is a major influence in the decision-making process, therefore, there is a need for the public understanding of science.
7. A public understanding of science is important for individuals' private lives.
8. The major findings of science, about cosmology, for example, or about evolution, profoundly influence the way we think about ourselves, therefore, a public understanding of science is of value to our culture.

Despite the growing importance of the scientific enterprise, many, if not most, of the public seem only tacitly aware of this enterprise and only cursorily comprehend the most fundamental principles and concepts of science (Miller & Pifer, 1996). As efforts to rectify the growing chasm between the scientifically literate "haves" and the scientifically illiterate "have-nots" mount, the free-choice learning community stands poised to play a fundamental role. As St. John and Perry (1993) observe,

> One role of the [free-choice learning] infrastructure is to bridge critical disjunctions. Today, one can argue, such a disjunction exists in the way science is portrayed, on the one hand, in popular culture, and, on the other, in schools. Science museums and other [free-choice] science education institutions are places where people can meet science—informally, directly and on their own terms. In contrast, in schools, people encounter science formally, indirectly and on the school's terms. [The free-choice learning sector] thus serves as a bridge between the everyday world of the [public] and the world of science and natural phenomena. In connecting the everyday world with the world of science [free-choice education institutions] afford a wide range of people a chance to develop personal relationships with science. (p. 62)

Thus the free-choice science education community should be striving to facilitate the public's ability to negotiate between the needs and realities of their daily lives and the needs and realities of the scientific enterprise. The free-choice learning community, in measures equal to or greater than the formal education community, acts as the public's primary source of information about science (Falk, Brooks, & Amin, 1998, chap. 7).

AN INFRASTRUCTURE FOR FREE-CHOICE SCIENCE LEARNING

It is becoming more widely appreciated that narrowly focused and limited views of the science learning enterprise limit both the understanding of the enterprise and a meaningful assessment of its impact. This is equally true whether one is focusing upon formal or free-choice learning. In the latter case, Falk and Dierking (1992, 1997, 2000) have repeatedly argued that it is impossible to understand a science museum visitor experience within the limited confines of a science museum visit. Only by framing the science museum experience within the larger context of an individual's life can one begin to truly understand the nature and impact of that experience. Recent research confirms this view, both within the narrow viewpoint of efforts to assess how science information gained at a museum is used by visitors (Falk, 1998a; Falk & Dierking, 1997) and from the larger viewpoint of what resources the public utilizes to stay current in science (Falk, Brooks, & Amin, 1998).

In the latter case, research on residents of greater Los Angeles indicates that they piece together their scientific understanding from contact with a wide range of resources, including nonacademic books, television (public, commercial, and cable), newspapers and magazines, on-the-job experiences, museums, and, to a more limited degree, radio and the Internet. Thus an effort to assess the science learned as a consequence of using any one component, for example, a science center, requires knowledge of how that one component synergistically interacts with other components in the community. Recent research by Anderson (1999) reinforces that these same principles are equally true for formal learning. Research on student knowledge of electricity and magnetism revealed that much of the students' conceptual understanding of this school-presented topic was built upon, reinforced by, and/or altered by experiences occurring outside of school.

Mark St. John proposed nearly a decade ago that we should rethink how we look at the entire learning enterprise. He suggested that both the formal educational system and the broader free-choice learning sector be considered as parts of a single, larger educational infrastructure. By this thinking, the word *infrastructure* refers to something that "lies below the surface and provides critically important support to a wide range of economic and social activities" (St. John & Perry, 1993). In this view, infrastructure represents the essential undergirding for a variety of other activities; for example, the highway infrastructure facilitates transportation, and an infrastructure of community services such as a fire and police department and waste removal permits a community to support a growing population. Infrastructure investments help provide structures, create conditions, and develop capacities that are prerequisite to the functioning of daily life.

Of particular importance to this concept is the political value in defining learning as part of the infrastructure of the country. In the current information/knowledge economy, learning represents a fundamental source of capital, perhaps even superseding the industrial revolution triumvirate of money, labor, and land. From this perspective, the learning infrastructure is vital to the nation's economic as well as intellectual and spiritual well-being. The educational institutions that help to provide citizens with current and accurate knowledge and information, whether it is about health, politics, economics, or science, form the fundamental backbone of the knowledge economy. The explosion of the Internet, and the World Wide Web in particular, provides significant testimony to the perceived value of having a readily accessible tool that can provide virtually anyone with virtually any information, virtually any time. The Web, though, is just one part of an ever-expanding and, it's to be hoped, improving network of learning resources available to the general public.

Thus the learning infrastructure is supplying something of fundamental value to the nation. Important, though, is that the value an infrastructure affords is often indirect. For example, infrastructures such as the banking system, roads and bridges, power grids, and water systems create a substructure for many kinds of commercial and domestic activities and thereby both directly and indirectly contribute to a wide range of social and economic benefits—benefits that are collectively much greater than the value of any single component viewed in isolation. Most important, a viable infrastructure makes possible a wide range of other human activities that are productive in and of themselves. Thus the assessment of the value of the learning infrastructure must be predicated on how it collectively builds capacity and supports value across a broad range of outcomes, not just, for example, something as narrow as school test scores.

Free-choice science education facilitators such as science centers, zoos, aquariums, youth groups, health and environmental organizations, the Internet, public television, and libraries can thus be viewed as part of the nation's infrastructure for science education. Learning goes on both in institutions and at home, driven by curiosity, by need (e.g., a relative becomes ill, a new computer is bought), or by sociocultural demands (e.g., a parent helping a child with a school assignment or hobby). There are many in the science education community, though, who still question whether these experiences make a significant contribution to the science literacy of the society.

St. John and Perry (1993) argue, for example, that just as the economic health of a nation depends on the strength of its infrastructure, so too does the scientific and educational literacy of the nation depend on its educational infrastructure. They state,

> It is very important to note that the educational infrastructure is not only, or even primarily, made up of physical resources. Rather than being composed of bridges, highways and water systems, the educational infrastructure can be thought of as an interwoven network of educational, social and cultural resources. (p. 60)

As stated earlier, the public regularly and systematically derives their understanding of science from many sources. It is becoming increasingly clear that these myriad sources work synergistically to affect what the public does and does not know about science. Consequently, practitioners and policymakers charged with facilitating the public's understanding of science, as well as those researchers wishing to assess the impact of those efforts, are ill-served by efforts to consider science learning as a singular process. Those concerned with science learning need to fully appreciate and accommodate the full complexity of the science learning infrastructure, particularly the considerable indirect contributions made by the free-choice science learning sector. More recently, St. John (1998) stated:

> Too often we tend to see all of our investments in science education as providing programs that directly and immediately have a uniform and predictable impact on the "learning" of students. . . . This might be a reasonable expectation if a strong learning infrastructure already existed, if the system was already rich in capacity, but such is not the case, and increasingly it is less so. More and more our public educational investments will have to go to creating infrastructure resources that can help provide the conditions in which improvement is possible. (p. 6)

Defining and building the capacity of the science education infrastructure, particularly that part supported by free-choice experiences, is in fact the goal of this book. Although some might argue that such an infrastructure does not exist or that infrastructure is an inappropriate term to describe the free-choice learning sector (cf. Chapters 2 and 9). However, as described above, I, as well as the majority of individuals writing in this book, believe that an infrastructure is a useful way to conceptualize the myriad learning resources that exist in our society and that, in fact, such an infrastructure already exists. That this infrastructure, particularly the part that includes the free-choice science learning sector, is poorly developed, poorly understood, and rarely appreciated is why this volume, in large part, was written.

ON THE NATURE OF LEARNING

Finally, we come to perhaps the most difficult definitional challenge of all, defining for the purpose of this book what is meant by learning. Contributing to the complexity of the problem is the rapidly changing understanding of the nature of the learning process itself. Falk and Dierking (2000) recently summarized this changing understanding as follows:

> People make meaning through a constant process of relating past experiences to the present, connecting what is happening in the present to what has happened in the past. . . . Learning is a dialogue between the individual and his or her social/ cultural and physical environment; learning is a contextually driven effort to make meaning in order to survive and prosper in the world. (p. 136)

The Process of Learning

This view of the nature of learning is very different from traditional views of learning that basically treat learning as a linear and predictable accumulation of knowledge (cf. Roschelle, 1995). This model, often characterized as the transmission-absorption model of learning, operated as if learning was a process of filling up identically empty minds as they moved past on the educational assembly line. Brain research shows that this model is erroneous. Learning is revealed to be a uniquely personal, contextual experience, constructed from both internal (head and body) and external (physical world and social contacts) experience (Damasio, 1994, 1999; Restak, 1994; Rosenfield, 1988).

Consequently, learning is rarely linear and always highly idiosyncratic. What a visitor learns while engaged with a museum exhibition, for example, is determined first and foremost by the individual's prior experiences. Which prior experiences are called forth, though, are determined by a complex mix of factors that includes not only the content and presentation of the exhibition but also the conversations that occur between the visitor and his or her companions and whatever may have been on the individual's mind when he or she walked into the museum that day (e.g., the television show seen last week, the news bulletin heard on the radio that morning, etc.). Learning can even be affected by what an individual had for breakfast that day or whether or not he or she has a cold.

Learning researchers have come to more fully appreciate that learning is rarely an instantaneous event but rather a time-consuming, cumulative process. Typically, individuals acquire an understanding of scientific concepts through an accumulation of experiences, normally deriving from many different sources at many different times (Anderson, 1999; Anderson, Lucas, Ginns, & Dierking, 2000; Crane, 1994; Falk & Dierking, 2000; Gambone & Arbreton, 1997; Medrich, 1991). So, for example, an individual's understanding of the physics of flight might represent the cumulative experience of completing a classroom assignment on Bernoulli's principle, reading a book on the Wright brothers, manipulating a science center exhibit on lift and drag, and watching a television program on birds. All of these experiences are combined, often seamlessly, by the person to construct a personal understanding of flight; no one source of information was sufficient to create this understanding, nor was one single institution solely responsible.

Sociocultural View of Learning. Other investigators come at learning from a different tack and emphasize the collaborative, social nature of learning, thinking of learning not as primarily the process of accumulating knowledge but rather as a process of becoming enculturated into a community of learners. In this view (cf. Chapter 12), learning is best defined in terms of a learning community or exchange where the building blocks of understanding are put together through dialogue with others. In this case, understanding of science is only detectable through the dialogue and activities of individuals with others. In this case too, multiple sources of experience and information contribute to knowledge construction, but even more so than in the previously described framework, knowledge is conceived as being strongly situated within unique and specific sociocultural contexts.

Each of these two perspectives reveals that the traditional way of framing research on learning is flawed. In effect asking the question, *What did an individual learn as a consequence of this educational experience?* is likely inappropriate. A more appropriate way to frame questions of learning would be to ask, *How did this educational experience contribute to an individual's understanding?* In this view, research on learning in general, and science learning in particular, needs to account for the fact that learning is always a highly personal process, highly dependent upon prior experiences, occurring within a highly situated sociocultural context and involving multiple sources of experience and information, which collectively contribute to knowledge construction (Anderson, 1999; Anderson et al., 2000; Gambone & Arbreton, 1997; Griffin, 1989; Hacker & Harris, 1992; Rogoff & Lave, 1984; Roschelle, 1995).

DEFINING AND BUILDING AN INFRASTRUCTURE FOR FACILITATING FREE-CHOICE SCIENCE LEARNING

With these understandings as background, stakeholders can begin to more critically explore the nature of the infrastructure for free-choice science learning. Significantly, despite a growing appreciation for the fact that the public commonly utilizes sources of free-choice learning to understand more about science, relatively little is known about the structure and function of this vast infrastructure for free-choice learning. In particular, the following questions can be asked:

1. How effective are free-choice experiences/institutions individually or collectively in facilitating public understanding of science?
2. How and why does the public utilize some parts of the infrastructure for free-choice science learning and not others?
3. How do the various pieces of the infrastructure for free-choice learning interact to reinforce or contradict each other or formal schooling?
4. What strategies would best maximize the potential of the infrastructure for free-choice learning?

These are the issues, then, that are addressed in this work. The book is organized into three sections: Theoretical Framework, Research Case Studies, and Looking to the Future.

Theoretical Framework

The first of these sections, including this introductory chapter, attempts to lay out some of the key terminology, background, and issues necessary for understanding the infrastructure for free-choice learning. Bruce Lewenstein's chapter picks up where this chapter ends by making the case for an infrastructure for free-choice learning. In particular, Lewenstein addresses the questions (a) What are the sources of free-choice science information available to the public? and (b) What is the scale of resources invested in those sources. Rodger Bybee's chapter takes a very different tack. Representing the formal education perspective, in his chapter Bybee attempts to reconcile what he believes is a major divide between the formal and free-choice education worlds. He makes the case that both formal and free-choice education are important, that the National Science Education Standards can and should provide the common intellectual ground upon which both should operate, and that by doing so the current divide would be bridged. Finally, Geoffrey Godbey frames the issue of free-choice learning within the larger context of leisure in America. Arguably, because most free-choice learning occurs in the public's leisure time, Godbey's presentation on free time in America represents a fundamental baseline for understanding free-choice learning.

Research Case Studies

The second major section of the book is devoted to four research case studies. Each of these four chapters summarizes research efforts designed to better measure and understand the nature and function of the infrastructure for free-choice learning. The first of these chapters, written by John Wright, Daniel Anderson, Aletha Huston, Patricia Collins, Kelly Schmitt, and Deborah Linebarger, describes a landmark effort to investigate the long-term impact of children's television viewing on educational achievement. Along the way, Wright et al. deal with the many prevailing hypotheses and myths about the effects of television viewing on young children.

The next chapter features an important new research study by Jon Miller. Miller has been investigating public understanding of science in America for nearly 20 years but has only recently directed his energies toward quantifying the role that free-choice learning contributes to this understanding. In this chapter Miller presents new data on this question that supports the important but, according to Miller, limited role of free-choice science learning in public understanding of science.

Next, Pauline Brooks, Rinoti Amin, and I set out to accomplish a similar task but take a different approach. Falk, et al.'s chapter highlights an ongoing investigation to determine in what ways and to what extent a specific free-choice learning institution, the California Science Center in Los Angeles, contributes to the scientific understanding, appreciation, and behaviors of local citizens. The findings reinforce the complex, synergistic nature of science learning. Finally, the last chapter in this section, authored by Robert Lebeau, Phyllis Gyamfi, Karen Wizevich, and Emlyn Koster, describes an attempt to better understand how freedom of choice functions as a learning variable. LeBeau et al. describe initial efforts at manipulating freedom of choice at a science center, and they measure how that variable affects science learning.

Looking to the Future

As suggested by the section title, the final five chapters of this volume, each in its own way, provide both an assessment of where we are today and a view of where we can and should be tomorrow. The 1998 Free-Choice Learning Conference was the catalyst for this book and thus it is appropriate that some effort be made to provide readers with a sense of that meeting.

In their chapter, Jessica Luke, Betty Dunckel Camp, Lynn Dierking, and Ursula Pearce summarize what occurred at that meeting with particular reference to the major issues, debates and recommendations for future actions that emerged at the meeting. Diane Frankel's chapter appropriately follows next. Frankel argues from her perspective as former director of the Institute for Museum and Library Services the importance of moving beyond individual, local interests of museums, libraries, or media to a shared, national interest of a larger free-choice learning sector. She articulates specific steps and strategies that she feels would facilitate this effort. Frankel gave a similar presentation at the Free-Choice Learning Conference and, as they do here, her comments served as a call-to-arms for those in attendance.

Anchoring the middle of this section is a chapter by Charlie Walter and Vanessa Westbrook. Their chapter is not a "what if" but rather a "here's how." Walter and Westbrook describe on-going efforts in Texas to build a more robust, more inclusive infrastructure for science learning, an infrastructure that represents a true partnership between the formal and free-choice learning sectors.

Few would disagree that a key to the future of science education in general and free-choice science education in particular lies in developing better methods and approaches to documenting the impact of educators' efforts. Laura Martin's chapter makes an effort to address this issue directly, asking how best to investigate and document free-choice learning now and into the future. Martin makes the case that current efforts have been severely hampered by inadequate models, and she proposes several models that she believes will lead to a better, more accurate understanding of free-choice learning.

Finally, Ann Muscat concludes the book with a summary of where the science education field is currently and offers a series of challenges to the field for the future. Muscat recommends a number of actions, including greater collaboration and political action among institutions for free-choice learning, which would lead to a stronger, more viable infrastructure for science learning. In fact, Muscat argues that an agenda centered on lifelong learning and a more strategic, coordinated, and successful free-choice science learning infrastructure are essential for insuring that free-choice learning institutions emerge as powerful, co-equal players in the effort to promote public understanding of science.

CONCLUSION

As a whole, this book provides a rich starting point to what I believe will be the defining educational effort of the next 20 years—the broadening and enriching of educational roles and responsibilities. As the United States and other developed countries make a full transition into a "learning society," the myriad constituents of the science education infrastructure will all need to play an ever-greater, more coordinated role in facilitating public understanding of science. In the future, the free-choice learning sector, as a major part of this broader education infrastructure, can be expected to command an ever-greater share of the resources, responsibilities, and credit for the educating of America. The chapters in this book provide an intellectual starting point for better defining and building the infrastructure for free-choice science learning necessary for accomplishing this task.

REFERENCES

Anderson, D. (1999). *Understanding the impact of post-visit activities on students' knowledge construction of electricity and magnetism as a result of a visit to an interactive science centre.* Unpublished doctoral dissertation, Queensland University of Technology, Brisbane, Australia.

Anderson, D., Lucas, K. B., Ginns, I. S., & Dierking, L. D. (2000). *Development of knowledge about electricity and magnetism during a visit to a science museum and related post-visit activities. Science Education, 71,* 658–679.

Brice Heath, S., & Smyth, L. (1999). *ArtShow: Youth and community development.* Washington, DC: Partners for Livable Communities.

Brown, J. S., Collins, A., & Duguid, P. (1989). Situated cognition and the culture of learning. *Educational Researcher, 18*(1), 32–42.

Caillot, M., & Nguyen-Xuan, A. (1995). Adults' understanding of electricity. *Public Understanding of Science, 4*(2), 131–152.

Chadwick, J. C. (1998). A survey of characteristics and patterns of behavior in visitors to a museum web site. *Dissertation Abstracts Online.* (University Microfilms No. 9839201)

Chadwick, J., & Falk, J. H. (1999). *Assessing institutional websites* (Tech. Rep.). Annapolis, MD: Institute for Learning Innovation.

Crane, V. (1994). An introduction to informal science learning and research. In V. Crane, H. Nicholson, M. Chen, & S. Bitgood (Eds.), *Informal science learning: What the research says about television, science museums, and community-based projects* (pp. 1–14). Ephrata, PA: Science Press.

Crane, V., Nicholson, H., Chen, M., & Bitgood, S. (Eds.). (1994). *Informal science learning: What the research says about television, science museums, and community-based projects.* Ephrata, PA: Science Press.

Damasio, A. R. (1994). *Descartes' error: Emotion, reason and the human brain.* New York: Avon Books.

Damasio, A. R. (1999). *The feeling of what happens: Body and emotion in the making of consciousness.* New York: Avon Books.

Dierking, L. D. (1987). *Parent-child interactions in a free choice learning setting: An examination of attention-directing behaviors.* Unpublished doctoral dissertation, University of Florida, Gainesville.

Epstein, J. L. (1995). School/family/community partnerships: Caring for the children we share. *Phi Delta Kappan, 79*(9), 701–711.

Eveland, W., & Dunwoody, S. (1997). *Communicating science to the public via "The Why Files."* Paper presented at the International Conference on the Public Understanding of Science and Technology, Chicago.

Falk, J. H. (1998a). Pushing the boundaries: Assessing the long-term impact of museum experiences. *Current Trends: Vol. 12.* Washington, DC: American Association of Museums.

Falk, J. H. (1998b). Visitors: Who does, who doesn't, and why? *Museum News, 77*(2), 38–43.

Falk, J. H., Brooks, P., & Amin, R. (1998, March). *The Los Angeles science education research project: Quarterly report* (Tech. Rep.). Annapolis, MD: Institute for Learning Innovation.

Falk, J. H., & Dierking, L. D. (1992). *The museum experience.* Washington, DC: Whalesback Books.

Falk, J. H., & Dierking, L. D. (1997). School field trips: Assessing their long-term impact. *Curator 40*(3), 211–218.

Falk, J. H., & Dierking, L. D. (1998, July). Free-choice learning: An alternative term to informal learning? *Informal Learning Environments Research, 2,* 2.

Falk, J. H., & Dierking, L. D. (2000). *Learning from museums: Visitor experiences and the making of meaning.* Walnut Creek, CA: AltaMira Press.

Falk, J. H., Moussouri, T., & Coulson, D. (1998). The effect of visitor's agendas on museum learning. *Curator, 41*(2), 106–120.

Gambone, M. A., & Arbreton, A. (1997). *Safe Havens: The contributions of youth organizations to healthy adolescent development.* Philadelphia: Public/Private Ventures.

Griffin, R. J. (1989). Communication and the adoption of energy conservation measures for the elderly. *Journal of Environmental Education, 20,* 19–28.

Gross, L. (1997). *The impact of television on modern life and attitudes.* Paper presented at International Conference on the Public Understanding of Science and Technology, Chicago.

Hacker, R., & Harris, M. (1992). Adult learning of science for scientific literacy: Some theoretical and methodological perspectives. *Studies in the Education of Adults, 24*(2), 217–224.

Knapp, M. S. (1997). Between systemic reforms and the mathematics and science classroom: The dynamics of innovation, implementation and professional learning. *Review of Educational Research, 67*(2), 227–266.

Koran, J. J., Jr., & Dierking Shafer, L. (1982). Learning science in informal settings outside the classroom. In M. B. Rowe (Ed.), *Education in the 80's: Science.* Washington, DC: National Education Association.

Medrich, E. A. (1991). *Young adolescents and discretionary time use: The nature of life outside of school.* Paper commissioned by the Carnegie Council on Adolescent Development for its Task Force on Youth Development and Community Programs.

Miller, J., & Pifer, L. (1996). Science and technology: The public's attitudes and the public's understanding. *Science and Engineering Indicators* (pp. 7.1–7.21). Washington, DC: National Science Board.

Public Understanding of Science Working Group. (1993, July 30). *Committee on education and human resources, implementation plan for public understanding of science, fiscal year 1995–1999.* Washington, DC: U.S. Government Printing Office.

Ramey-Gassert, L., Walberg, H. J., III, & Walberg, H. J. (1994). Reexaming connections: Museums as science learning environments. *Science Education, 78*(4), 345–363.

Restak, R. (1994). *The modular brain.* New York: Simon & Schuster.

Rogoff, B., & Lave, J. (1984). *Everyday cognition: Its development in social contexts.* Cambridge, MA: Harvard University Press.

Roschelle, J. (1995). Learning in interactive environments: Prior knowledge and new experience. In J. Falk & L. Dierking (Eds.), *Public institutions for personal learning* (pp. 37–54). Washington, DC: American Association of Museums.

Rosenfield, I. (1988). *The invention of memory: A new view of the brain.* New York: Basic Books.

The Royal Society. (1985). *The public understanding of science.* London: Author.

St. John, M. (1998). *Measuring the interim performance of the Regional Educational Laboratory in the educational research development and dissemination infrastructure: What are the benchmarks and indicators of success?* Unpublished manuscript.

St. John, M., & Perry, D. (1993). A framework for evaluation and research: Science, infrastructure and relationships. In S. Bicknell & G. Farmelo (Eds.), *Museum visitor studies in the 90s* (pp. 59–66). London: Science Museum.

CHAPTER 2

Who Produces Science Information for the Public?

Bruce V. Lewenstein

Public communication about science permeates many aspects of daily life in the United States. Science news is available in newspapers and from radio and television programming, in museums, science centers, and from community groups—a wealth of information delivered by a myriad of sources. Various terms have been proposed to describe these science education efforts. Options include:

- Informal science communication
- Public communication of science and technology
- Popularization of science
- Public understanding of science
- Public understanding of science and technology
- Public understanding of science, engineering, and technology

Free-choice learning is another, recent introduction.

Although each of these terms carries a different meaning, a more fundamental issue is whether all the educational activities embraced by these terms should be considered as falling within a specific sector. Are the interconnected activities that comprise informal learning experiences in America part of an *infrastructure* for free-choice learning? Are they simply a set of sources that some people see as similar and yet others see as dissimilar? By infrastructure, I mean a pattern of connections that provide for interaction, communication, and progress—connections that help each of the sources accomplish things that otherwise could not be accomplished. Infrastructure provides for new initiatives.

THE QUESTION OF INFRASTRUCTURE

I assume that the range of organized activities in the United States that contribute to the process of free-choice science education do constitute an infrastructure and that these activities are distinct from formal education programs. The infrastructure includes the sponsors of activities, displays, and information such as those offered by zoos, botanical gardens, science museums, extension programs, science journalists, activist groups (environmental organizations and animal welfare groups), science clubs, and various government organizations.

At the first Free-Choice Learning Conference held in Los Angeles, California, in 1998 many people argued against my basic assumption. Even if practitioners within individual field sources do know each other and sometimes collaborate, those connections could hardly be called an infrastructure. The links are too tenuous, they argued, too dependent on individual connections, too unconnected from institutional imperatives. Those criticisms are valid, but I believe the connections exist and can be nurtured into a more stable, institutionalized interconnectedness that advances the field (in both self-understanding and in successful practice).

Certainly, some evidence argues against the idea of an existing infrastructure. Few training programs are available that allow young people to move into the broad field of free-choice science education; those programs that do exist are almost all targeted at just one part of the community within the field (such as science journalism or museum studies) without recognizing or promoting the connections between them. At the more advanced level, relatively few people move among the sources within the field; journalists rarely work for museums and community activists do not become museum directors. Research into the free-choice science learning sector is splintered into subfields (with a few exceptions, such as work published in the journal *Public Understanding of Science*). Perhaps most important, very few practicing scientists realize that a community exists of professionals committed to public communication of science and technology. Because scientists are one of the major groups concerned about public understanding of science and technology, their lack of knowledge is itself something that needs to be addressed.

On the other hand, some evidence indicates an existing infrastructure for free-choice learning. The most prominent is the National Science Foundation's Informal Science Education program (which provided funding for the first Free-Choice Learning Conference). NSF's program explicitly provides support to a range of interconnected activities, including television programming, museum exhibits, community groups, and science journalism. Within each community is a large part of the infrastructure, such as the traveling exhibition networks among science museums and the Internet listservs and newsletters circulated among science journalists. Some listservs, for example, ISEN-ASTC-L, run by the Association of Science-Technology Centers, appeal across a variety of activity sources. At-large institutions collaborate with each other in developing exhibitions or sharing resources among community groups and local institutions like museums or libraries. And within the research community, a growing body of interrelated literature on free-choice learning is appearing. Finally, a series of conferences and meetings suggest that connections are being sought between various proponents of the free-choice or informal science education sector.

Why does this question of infrastructure matter? The primary issue is local knowledge versus broad expertise. If no infrastructure exists and, more important, if no infrastructure is possible, then each group interested in public communication of science will have to create its own programs, its own materials, its own systems for dealing with the local context. Local knowledge will be all important. On the other hand, if an infrastructure exists for sharing information and resources, and if that information and those resources turn out to be useful in multiple contexts, then the creativity and energy of individuals in the field can be directed at creating new programs, new approaches, new connections that will serve the ultimate goal of increasing public understanding, appreciation, and participation in science. In other words, building an infrastructure or strengthening an existing infrastructure will avoid reinventing the wheel.

In this chapter, I provide detail about the many activities that already exist in the field of free-choice learning and explain why I think they add up to a larger infrastructure, which includes and provides an infrastructure for free-choice science education. A schematic diagram of the infrastructure I envision appears in Figure 2.1.

THE FREE-CHOICE SCIENCE EDUCATION INFRASTRUCTURE

Since the early 1900s, the American scientific community has initiated and supported a vast array of activities intended to communicate the essence of science to the American public. Those activities supplemented, and sometimes sustained, independent efforts for science education initiated by journalists, public health officials, museum benefactors, and indeed the formal education sector itself. Today there exists a greater enterprise than ever before of organizations and public and private dollars that together constitute an infrastructure for free-choice science education.

The defining characteristic of these activities is that they are conducted at

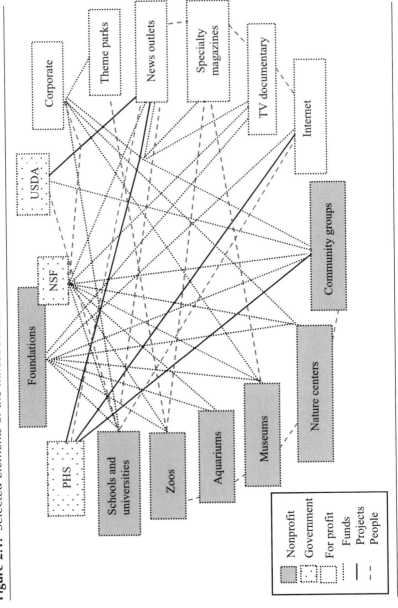

Figure 2.1. Selected Elements of the Infrastructure for Free-Choice Science Education.

free-choice learning settings or venues. Unlike in the formal school system, no regulation or power of the state requires people to attend to the information presented through the infrastructure of public communication of science and technology. No tests, no assessments, no filters judge whether people have heard the messages in these communications. Access to the information is *free-choice*. This chapter focuses on understanding the context in which any potential learning occurs, specifically, on setting the scene and describing the infrastructure. What do people have access to? Where does it come from? I am deliberately limiting my survey to the United States. Although public communication of science happens everywhere, and many of the relevant issues (such as how people gather information and mentally process it) do not depend on national or regional context, the details I want to give are better handled in a specific context. I invite readers to consider how the context described herein might be extended to other geographic locations.

HISTORY OF THE POPULARIZATION OF SCIENCE

Public communication of science and technology has a long history in the United States, taking root as an active enterprise around 1800 (Lewenstein, 1994). At least four different strands of scientific popularizing can be identified during the nineteenth century:

1. Leading scientists wrote clearly and persuasively about science, sometimes to explore philosophical issues raised by the technicality of their work, and sometimes to proselytize a scientific rather than superstitious approach to the world.
2. Efforts were made to educate the lower classes during the industrial revolution to create a work force inculcated with both the means, and the ideology, of a modern, technological world.
3. Itinerant lecturers and public demonstrations addressed the masses, again for both educational and entertainment reasons.
4. Museums displayed curiosities intended to appeal both to educated elites and to the masses, ostensibly to educate but more commonly to entertain.

Although many of these activities were based on activities in Great Britain, which in the early 1800s had only recently ceased to rule the United States, distinctively American styles had emerged by the end of the nineteenth century. By then, the United States had established widespread mechanisms for providing scientific information to the general public. These systems were largely controlled by people without any official responsibility for science policy, such as museum benefactors, industrialists, and itinerant lecturers. At the same time, these people were sympathetic to science.

The Twentieth Century and the Rise of Public Communication

In the twentieth century, the shape of public communication of science and technology was altered by new technologies and by the changing nature of science itself. Among the most important trends in the new century were the following:

1. The rise of scientific societies and disease-oriented voluntary associations with commitments to publicizing particular issues in science and technology.
2. Increasing specialization in both science and other professional activities, leading to decreased ability on the part of scientists to speak about science broadly and increased ability on the part of educators and journalists to write about science.
3. The development of new forms of media, such as radio, television, movies, industrial museums, science centers, and the Internet each of which contributed new opportunities tied to new constraints on how science might be communicated to the public.
4. Increasing public interest (and often concern) about the implications of scientific progress, as exemplified by excitement and dismay at the development of nuclear weapons and by widespread activism involving environmental issues.

By mid-century, these new initiatives had led to a broad, variegated system for public communication of science and technology. That system served multiple goals—education, information, proselytization, and recruitment for science. Various components of the system complemented and intersected each other: Books and lectures directed at elites were both emulated and reshaped for broader audiences; writers moved back and forth between pulp magazines, educational institutions, museums, and public-information campaigns; and audiences partook of different aspects for multiple reasons.

The contemporary infrastructure for public communication of science and technology is conventionally described as having been spurred by World War II. Recognizing the role in winning the war of the atomic bomb, jet engines, radar, penicillin, and a host of other scientific and technological achievements, the public demanded more information about science and technology—or so claimed leaders of the scientific community (Lewenstein, 1987a). Whether or not the demand existed, in the United States, people and institutions were ready to participate in new opportunities for public communication of science and technology after the war.

Science journalists, who were devoted to improving the public understanding of science, were among the first to respond to the postwar cries from the scientific community for more information about science. Their efforts were largely supported by the American Association for the Advancement of Science (AAAS), the new government agencies devoted to science (such as the Atomic Energy Commission and the National Aeronautics and Space Administration), and private philanthropic foundations linked to the scientific community. Science writers were some of the most vigorous supporters of the idea that public understanding of science should be interpreted to mean public appreciation of the benefits that science provides to society (Lewenstein, 1992).

The other forms of public communication had become so institutionalized that they lost some of their sheen, yet they continued in great force. Lecture series, new museums, books by prominent scientists, and public information campaigns by health organizations—all were part of the background cultural activity involving science and technology throughout the postwar years. Especially after the Russians launched Sputnik, new emphases did get placed on formal science education, with some spillover to free-choice science education (Lewenstein, 1992).

One new aspect of public communication of science and technology was the rise of environmental concerns. By the late 1950s, organized antinuclear activists were beginning to publicize the dangers of radioactivity. In 1962, Rachel Carson published her indictment of DDT, *Silent Spring*. Throughout those decades, a middle class with newly available leisure time began to acquire new concerns for open space and clean environments, which was demonstrated by new magazines, newsletters, and reporting devoted to environmental issues (Carson, 1962; Hays, 1972, 1987; Katz, 1987; Lewenstein, 1992). During the 1970s, science journalism became more critical of science, reflecting general social concerns about pollution, the environment, nuclear power, concentration of social authority, and other issues (LaFollette, 1990; Nelkin, 1987).

By the 1980s, however, the excitement of biotechnology, personal computers, and other topics led to new enthusiasms for science. That excitement was most evident in the United States, where the American public experienced a popular science boom, consisting of a new wave of museums, magazines, books, and newspaper sections devoted to science. Despite some setbacks, that boom continues today, the details of which will be discussed further here (Goodall, 1980, 1986; Lewenstein, 1987b).

INSTITUTIONAL SOURCES OF PUBLIC COMMUNICATION OF SCIENCE AND TECHNOLOGY

Although there are many possible ways to categorize science information that is available to the public, I have chosen to focus on *producers* (Lewenstein,

1994). In this survey, I have listed producing organizations as sources of science information for learning, along with a description of the size and character of their activities. In a few cases, I also have listed funding agencies, whose activities are of major significance. The major categories are government, mass media, museums, community organizations, industry, nongovernmental organizations (NGOs), and nonprofit foundations.

Government

The complexity of American government structure—with independent initiatives emerging from federal, state, regional, and local governments—makes an assessment of the government's overall commitment to public communication of science and technology difficult. However, it is possible to look at an overall federal picture. The last systematic data were collected in the early 1990s by the Federal Coordinating Council on Science, Engineering and Technology, Committee on Education and Human Resources, Public Understanding of Science Working Group (*FCCSET/CEHR PUNS working group*) (National Performance Review, 1993; Public Understanding of Science Working Group, 1993a).

The PUNS data reveal some of the conceptual problems that face the definition of what constitutes the infrastructure for free-choice learning. For example, some agencies considered activities that reached anyone outside the formal educational system to be part of the public understanding system. Other agencies believed that activities focused on adults alone should be counted. Thus the data still are not entirely comparable across agencies.

The PUNS working group explicitly labeled science literacy, defined as a threshold level of knowledge of basic principles of science, as a subset of the broader, multidimensional concept of public understanding of science.

Despite the limitations noted above, the PUNS working group data provides a useful benchmark for others interested in public communication of science and technology activity. In the 1993–1994 fiscal year, federal expenditures on PUNS activities were in the range of $75 million. The figures that follow are drawn from that estimate.

Together, two categories of activities account for about 80 percent of the federal expenditures: (a) public and community-linked projects—programs that incorporate science education into activities of daily life and (b) public service education/information resources—segments of public information campaigns, including hot lines and information clearinghouses, specifically directed toward scientific knowledge (Public Understanding of Science Working Group, 1993b).

Two other categories receive much less money: (a) media resources—using diverse media, including print, broadcast, film, computer, and other technologies to provide scientific information for the public (about 15 percent of expenditures) and (b) education programs for decision makers—programs aimed at educating government, educational, corporate, and media decision makers about scientific concepts, principles, and issues (about 6 percent of expenditures).

More than half of all the expenditures were attributed to the Department of the Interior, which includes both the National Park Service (which produces interpretive exhibits for most national parks) and the National Oceanographic and Atmospheric Administration (which produces weather information). The Department of Energy, which operates some museums and programs for media personnel and for decision makers, was responsible for about 20 percent of the expenditures, although some commentators have put the Department of Energy's budget at only about $1 million. The Smithsonian Institution was responsible for about 10 percent of the expenditures.

The definitional problems that plagued the PUNS working group's data collection are evident in these numbers. According to the numbers, the National Science Foundation provides less than $5 million for public understanding activities. But the annual expenditures of the National Science Foundation's *Informal Science Education* program, which most practitioners of public communication of science and technology outside the government consider the main source of federal funds, were then about $35 million. The discrepancy is apparently linked to the question of how to categorize programs that involve school-aged children, but outside formal classroom situations.

Another lacuna in the PUNS data is the absence of information on the cooperative extension system run by the U.S. Department of Agriculture. The extension system, established in the late 1800s, consists of university-based communication experts charged with extending university-based knowledge to the general community. Originally focused on agricultural and farming information, the extension system today includes everything from youth groups (known as 4-H, for Head, Heart, Hands, and Health) to programs for addressing urban poverty. The overall budget for the extension system is more than $1 billion. About 30 percent of the funds comes from the federal government, about 50 percent from state governments, and the rest from local governments or private sources. The 4-H clubs reach nearly 6 million children, ages 5 to 19, each year. And one of the largest individual extension programs at the federal level is a health and nutrition education campaign that targets low-income youth and families; working with as many as 50,000 volunteers a year, the program has an annual budget of about $60 million (Rasmussen, 1989; U.S. Department of Agriculture, personal communication, Public Affairs Office, November, 1993).

Despite these definitional problems, the message is clear: The federal government spends at least $100 million a year, and perhaps much more, on activities related to public communication of science and technology. But an exact statement of the programs and budgets included in that total requires both more work on definitions and more data from the federal system.

Mass Media

Traditionally, commentators have pointed to the mass media—newspapers, magazines, radio, television and now the Internet—as sources within the infrastructure from which most information is made available to those interested in free-choice learning. These forms of mass media are explored here in further detail; however, in-depth studies are only now being created to gauge the Internet's effects on free-choice science learning, so no data are available to report at time of press. However, the underlying assumption is that the mass media, taken as a whole, are the most important sources of information for the general public. Although some communication theorists are beginning to question this underlying assumption, the mass media are clearly the most easily accessible sources of science information to the general public. According to 1995 National Science Board figures, each year American adults watch more than 400 hours of TV news and more than 80 hours of TV science, listen to more than 200 hours of radio news, and read 200 newspapers, three news magazines, and two science magazines (National Science Board, 1996).

Newspapers. In 1978, the *New York Times* introduced a weekly section devoted to science. By 1989, another 95 daily newspapers had added similar sections, and an additional 100 newspapers or so (out of about 1,600 daily newspapers in the United States) had weekly science pages—a smaller space commitment, but still noticeable (Jerome, 1984, 1986, 1992b; Lewenstein, 1987b).

By the mid-1990s, however, the trend had reversed. Only 47 newspapers had a separate science section, and these were often smaller and less prominent than they had been. What's more, the trend in all the sections was away from science news, and toward health and fitness information. Although the earlier sections had been praised as tools that could be used for learning by teachers and consumers of science education, the newer sections are much more oriented toward entertainment. The tension among information, education, and entertainment has long been a key issue for science journalism (Jerome, 1992a; Siegfried, 1992).

But the dramatic decline in the number of science sections may not be completely indicative of how science is being covered by newspapers. Some science journalists have always thought that science sections do not serve science, because they might tend to create a science ghetto of sorts; general news editors might feel that they could ignore science because it was being covered elsewhere in the paper. A better strategy, these writers argued, would be to try to get more science-oriented studies mixed into the general news sections of newspapers.

Although the evidence is not clear, one study suggests that the primary effect of science sections is to lead to longer stories about science throughout the newspaper and to increase the segregation between basic research stories, which move to the science section, and medical or environmental stories, which appear throughout the paper. However, in the case of newspapers without science sections, readers who might skip over these sections would be more likely to find basic research stories in the sections of the paper they do read, though the stories are more likely to be shorter and less heavily illustrated (Bader, 1990).

A second reason for questioning the significance of the decline in science sections is that most of the sections relied heavily on the national wire services for their copy. Reducing the space allocated explicitly to science is not the same as reassigning staff to other duties. Because many of the newspapers may continue to publish wire service stories within the paper, it's difficult to judge whether the newspaper editors' commitment to science has changed. The papers may simply be allocating science-oriented resources in a different way.

Another confounding factor that makes the decline in science sections less easy to interpret is the general decline in newspapers in the United States. For more than 30 years, most Americans have claimed to receive most of their news from television rather than from newspapers. Today only about 50 percent of the public reads a newspaper every day. The newspaper industry in general is in a decline, with readership and circulation dropping each year. Although some data show that as in the past Americans read a newspaper at least once a week, the central role of newspapers in American life clearly is declining (Yarbrough & Scherer, 1991).

Magazines. Popular science magazines have been published in the United States for more than 100 years. A few, notably *Scientific American* and *Popular Science*, have lasted over much of that time, though sometimes in dramatically changed formats. Then, in the early 1970s, a new series of popular science magazines emerged. Some were devoted to environmental themes, others to psychology or popular medicine. A few focused on pure science. By the end of the decade, as part of a "popular science boom," nearly a dozen new magazines had been created (Burnham, 1987; Lewenstein, 1987b, 1988).

But, by the middle of the 1980s, many of the ambitious science magazines had failed. The ones that survived were of two types: (a) magazines that targeted a specific audience, such as *Astronomy* or *Oceans*, and (b) more general magazines, such as *Popular Science* and *Discover*. The survivors among the more general magazines were those that mixed pure science with information of more immediate concern to general audiences. *Popular Science* retained a strong focus on how-to stories and *Discover* featured a mix of stories on differing scientific topics. Today the mix of magazines remains largely split between many small ones devoted to specific subjects and a few general-interest publications with circulations of 1 to 2 million. In addition, many very large magazines, such as *Reader's Digest* and *Smithsonian*, and news magazines such as *Time* and *Newsweek*, include science among the mix of topics covered. Because of the commercial climate in which magazines exist, this is likely to remain the situation for some time to come.

Radio. Radio is a ubiquitous medium. Virtually anywhere in the country, one can tune in to a variety of stations, ranging from all-news programming to music-only stations that specialize in one of a variety of musical genres, to talk-radio stations featuring hosts who engage in live conversation with callers. As with all media, most stations are commercially supported by advertising. Although many stations are independently owned and operated, many others are part of networks. Whether locally owned or network-owned, most stations get their news programming from one of a few national syndication services.

Prepared stories about science appear on most commercial radio stations only as bits of news taken from the syndicated news services. Some stories may be read by the local broadcaster, others by the national correspondents. Only one commercial network has a dedicated science section, and that is a 90-second *Science Update* broadcast each day during the morning news shows of nearly 500 stations. Ratings information suggests that this broadcast is heard by more than a million people each day, Still, a million is a small number in a country with a population of more than 250 million, where radios outnumber people. Demonstrating the close connections between the many components of the public communication of science and technology system, the broadcast is produced and funded by the nonprofit AAAS (B. Hirshon, AAAS, personal communication, November 1993).

Although the AAAS's *Science Update* is the only regular journalism spot on commercial radio, many stations sometimes air similar programs on earth science, chemistry, and physics produced by other professional societies, by local universities, or by other organizations, often supported with funds from the National Science Foundation.

Many of these brief radio broadcasts air on National Public Radio (NPR). Although NPR was established by the government, nearly 70 percent of its funding comes from membership dues paid by NPR member stations, which tend to be small stations located in urban areas or on college campuses. Only 3 percent of the funds comes from the government, with the remainder derived from philanthropic grants. The member stations, in turn, receive funds from their members, from state or local governments, and from corporate donations (National Public Radio, personal communication, Public Affairs Office, December 1993).

Science and environmental topics are frequently covered by NPR, which has an excellent science unit consisting of about a half-dozen reporters and producers. In addition to the regular news programs, NPR also broadcasts a weekly show on environmental issues and hosts a weekly talk show on science. NPR's audience consists primarily of well-educated, politically active, wealthy individuals. Its programs, therefore, are influential. But the actual number of people who listen to NPR is extremely small compared with the number who listen to commercial radio. By some estimates, only about a quarter of the American radio audience ever listens to NPR ("NPR's Saddest Story," 1983).

Much more common among audiences is talk radio. Clearly, a great many topics that appear on talk radio involve science: abortion, drug control, AIDS, cancer and carcinogens, diet, food additives, and so on. These topics are often not explicitly identified as "science," however. To date, no comprehensive study has been made of science on talk radio.

Television. Television in the United States is dominated by commercial systems, which receive their revenue from advertising. By the end of the twentieth century, the structure of television in the United States had changed dramatically. Originally dominated by three national commercial broadcast networks, television now is fragmented between the major networks and a host of channels available only via cable systems. About two thirds of American homes are now linked to cable systems that offer them choices of 30 to 50 channels at any time, and many people have access to systems with many more choices, ranging into the hundreds of channels. Interactive capability and other technological wizardry are rapidly becoming routine elements of American media consumption.

These new systems put a premium on *narrowcasting* rather than broadcasting—that is, they produce programs that appeal to specific market segments rather than to the broadest possible audience. Science programming has been perceived as potentially benefiting from the developments. And, indeed, several of the major cable stations (such as CNN and the Discovery Channel) have science professionals on board and frequently present science-, medical-, or nature-oriented shows. Unfortunately, because of the proprietary nature of these commercial organizations, little information is available regarding budgets, viewership, or other measures of size.

In addition to the commercial networks, a major broadcaster of popular science programs in the United States is the Public Broadcasting System (PBS). Like NPR, this network is coordinated by a government-sponsored agency and is partially funded by federal dollars. But local stations are funded by state money, with major funding coming from individual viewers who make voluntary donations to the local station. Individual programs or series of programs are underwritten by private philanthropic foundations or corporate donors and often are produced by single stations within the public broadcasting system, then distributed via the national network to other stations. Indeed, many programs are also coproductions with public broadcasting systems in other countries, especially the British Broadcasting Corp. (BBC). Like the NPR system, the Public

Broadcasting System is often most appealing to wealthy, well-educated audiences.

The effect of television on free-choice learning is difficult to assess. The last systematic collection of data was made more than a decade ago, before the rapid development of cable systems, and is clearly out of date (Lewenstein, 1987b; National Science Foundation, 1992). Specific case studies have shown that television shows can have an effect, especially when there is interaction between formal and free-choice science education. Here, of course, the question of the definitional problems discussed above come in: Are children's television shows, with their potential for integration into the formal school curriculum, part of the free-choice science education system? Some data appear in a study commissioned by the National Science Foundation in the early 1990s (Crane, Nicholson, Chen, & Bitgood, 1994).

Nor are major shows the only way in which television reaches people. Public health authorities have long recognized television as an important tool for conveying science-based ideas, such as campaigns for the use of seat belts, against the use of tobacco, and for awareness of AIDS (Marchman & Jason, 1992). Given the widely recognized effect of television on American life today, much more work needs to be done to catalog public communication of science and technology activities on television and assess their influence.

Museums

After the mass media, science museums are traditionally considered one of the most important institutions in the public communication of science and technology. Science museums have existed in the United States for more than a century. Most of the early museums were traditional *cabinets of curiosities*, collections of animals and plants brought back from overseas expeditions. These museums were often established in cities as a sign of progress, funded by wealthy industrialists or other benefactors as ways of establishing the local commitment to learning, scholarship, and other activities considered to be of high status (Alexander & Alderson, 1996; Hudson, 1987).

Although there are about 80 traditional natural history museums in the United States, the greatest growth in museums in recent years has been in the area of *science centers*. These centers are characterized by their attention to hands-on, interactive exhibits. Although the line between science centers and museums is difficult to draw, most science centers are focused on providing exciting experiences for their visitors rather than on creating or maintaining collections of objects (as traditional museums do). Since 1977, the number of annual visitors to science centers has nearly doubled, from about 31 million visits per year to nearly 60 million per year. The vast majority of science centers are private, nonprofit institutions; other science centers are government units, part of a public school system, or a section of a national laboratory (Association of Science-Technology Centers, 1993).

According to figures collected in a series of studies for the National Science Foundation, each year since 1983 about 25 percent of American adults have visited a science or technology museum (including zoos, aquariums, natural history museums, and "hands-on" science centers). In 1997, 60 percent of all adults claimed to visit a science museum at least once a year. Of those visits, about half were to zoos and aquariums, the other half to science-technology museums and natural history museums (Miller & Heltne, 1992; National Science Board, 1998).

Science museums and science centers receive their funding from a wide range of sources. Budgets for science museums range from less than $50,000 to more than $10 million, with the majority of museums having budgets between about $250,000 and $5 million (St. John & Grinell, 1989). Figures from surveys of Association of Science-Technology Centers (ASTC) members suggest a total budget for more than 300 science centers of more than $500 million. Although the percentage of budgetary funds devoted to educational or public outreach programs is not known, a conservative estimate of 20 percent still yields a figure of $100 million devoted to public communication of science and technology.

In addition to the exhibitions and traveling exhibits associated with traditional museums and science centers, many smaller exhibitions are created and maintained by corporations or local societies. Virtually no numbers are available on these types of exhibits. But they may play a major role in the everyday public communication of science and technology, because these exhibits are often on display in shopping malls, airports, and other facilities through which people flow when they are not explicitly seeking out scientific or technical information. Another growing area of activity is *science theater*—plays and skits produced and performed for visitors to science museums, for use in classrooms, and for a variety of other settings.

Community Organizations

One of the most important trends in recent years has been the growth of science education activities among youth groups and community-based organizations. These groups—including the Boy Scouts, Girl Scouts, and local science and environmental clubs—are beginning to integrate science activities into the general recreational programs that they administer for youth throughout the country. Although some of the funding for these activities comes from the federal government (especially the National Science Foundation), other funding comes from private foundations and from local community groups. According to some estimates, nearly $20 million dollars annually is devoted to youth group activities (Inverness Research Associates, 1993).

The range of activities undertaken by these groups is tremendous. Some groups offer field trips for disadvantaged children. Others provide after-school programs that encourage girls to explore science or math. Girls often move away from science and, although the reasons are not clear, many experts believe that cultural barriers against getting involved in science can be overcome by providing specialized, targeted programs (National Science Foundation, 1992).

Funding agencies, including both government agencies and private foundations, have been especially eager to see new initiatives in the area of community organizations. Part of the reason is the high value that we Americans put on any program that is initiated, organized, supported, and undertaken on a local basis. Another aspect is the ability of local groups to target their actions toward specific audiences that have traditionally been under-represented in science, such as women or racial minorities. Thus it seems likely that the interest in community organizations as a site for public communication of science and technology will continue.

Industry

Given the American commitment to commercial activities, no discussion on public communication of science and technology in the United States would be complete without mentioning the role of private industry. Many companies provide a great deal of information about science and technology, for altruistic reasons and also because it is good for business. These activities range from small museums in corporate headquarters focusing on science or technology (for example, initiatives by AT&T, the telecommunications giant, or Merck, the pharmaceutical company) through massive public relations exercises, such as the flood of information on the health care system produced by companies concerned about the debate over a national health care plan in the United States. This material appears in advertisements, as direct-mail pieces, on billboards, and in other media.

However, given the size of the American corporate community, it is impossible to make any estimate of the size of this contribution to public communication of science and technology. Looking at just the public outreach budgets of a few organizations (some of which money goes to support media, museum, and community outreach activities), the corporate contribution must total tens of millions of dollars.

Nongovernmental Organizations (NGOs)

A key cultural value in the United States is the commitment to private initiative. This value has important implications for the infrastructure for free-choice science education, given the coherence between commitments to private enterprise and free-choice ideals in American culture. One result is that people, companies, and other organizations frequently come together in private associations to further particular social, economic, or cultural goals. In the area of science, these associations include ones devoted to conservation and environmental issues, to health issues, and to the interests of particular scientific disciplines or trades. A few of these organizations are even devoted explicitly to public communication of science and technology. What we do not know is how the information provided by these organizations is perceived by audiences—Does it have the same character as information in museums or news stories in the mass media? In the context of questions about free-choice learning, how is this information used?

Conservation and Environmental Groups

Because of the scientific base of so many environmental issues, education about scientific and technological topics related to the environment is often part of the public outreach programs of conservation and environmental organizations. More than 15 million people belong to environmental organizations. Together, these organizations have total budgets upward of $500 million, of which about 20 percent (at a very rough estimate) is devoted to educational activities. These activities range from publishing magazines to canvasing local communities to building support for political objectives by sharing technical information.

Voluntary Health Organizations

Beginning early in this century, a series of independent associations known as voluntary health organizations emerged to deal with widespread problems such as heart disease, cancer, and tuberculosis. Because these organizations have been so successful at attracting resources for research, treatment, and public education, they have been emulated on a wide scale, and dozens of health organizations now exist to target nearly every imaginable disease. Although many of the health organizations focus their efforts on research and treatment, most of them also operate media campaigns. Some, like the American Heart Association and the American Cancer Society, have sponsored seminars for science journalists for several decades. Many of these organizations also maintain media relations offices to help journalists working on stories that touch on the various diseases (Wax, 1993). In addition, large numbers of these organizations undertake major public education campaigns, often linked to lobbying or fundraising drives intended to raise money for research and treatment from government or private donors.

No information is available about the size or budgets of the public communication of science and technology activities of these voluntary associations. Nor is it clear whether instrumental and public relations activities should be considered part of free-choice learning. Yet, on health-related topics, the information provided by these organizations is often the most readily available to members of the public, and so it seems reasonable to include them as part of the infrastructure for free-choice science education.

Scientific Trade Associations

Several of the large membership organizations run by scientists have made major commitments to public communication of science and technology. In some cases, the commitment to public communication has been explicitly incorporated into the organizational charter. The American Association for the Advancement of Science, for example, is committed "to increase public understanding and appreciation of the importance and promise of the methods of science in human progress." As that statement suggests, the goal of the scientific organizations is both altruistic and self-serving—it stresses both understanding and appreciation.

Two of the most active organizations are the American Association for the Advancement of Science (AAAS) and the American Chemical Society (ACS). Both have memberships of about 130,000 to 150,000. Both have very active public information offices, which provide information about organizational activities and coordinate press coverage of the national meetings of the organizations. In addition, both organizations sponsor a variety of additional activities, often in collaboration with other groups and with funding from a variety of sources. Several other scientific societies, such as the Sigma Xi honor society, the American Geophysical Union, and the American Institute of Physics, engage in activities similar to those of AAAS and ACS but on a smaller scale.

With regard to AAAS activities, for more than 50 years the AAAS has given awards for excellence in science journalism and, more recently, in public understanding of science. Funding for these awards has come from industry and from philanthropic organizations. During the last decade, the AAAS has developed a number of specific science and technology public communication projects, ranging from television specials and community outreach programs to regular radio shows (D. Crippens, KCET, November 1993; S. Malcom, AAAS, November 1993; J. Keefe, AAAS, November 1993, personal communications). And the ACS's activities range from a National Chemistry Week (in which each of the society's nearly 200 local sections sponsors chemistry demonstrations, school visits, media tours, and other activities) through sponsorship (with corporate funds) of some weekly science pages in national newspapers (A. Messmore, ACS, personal communication, December 1993).

Science Communication Organizations

A few nongovernmental organizations (NGOs) are specifically devoted to public communication of science and technology. Most of these groups are primarily oriented toward helping journalists get information about science, but such is the nature of public communication of science and technology that related activities frequently get added on.

Science Service. The oldest of these groups is Science Service. Founded in 1921 as a joint venture of three scientific organizations, today Science Service is an independent organization. It publishes a weekly 16-page news magazine called *Science News*, which has a circulation of about 250,000. Science Service also runs a nationwide "science talent search," now in its 54th year. By encouraging students to engage in scientific activities and to present their activities at high-school-based science fairs, Science Service tries to get students interested in scientific research. The science fairs (which are also coordinated by Science Service) provide another dimension to public communication of science and technology (D. Harless, personal communication, December 1993).

Media Resource Service. The Media Resource Service (MRS), whose origins can be traced to an early 1960s activist group, today provides journalists with referrals to experts on a vast array of technical subjects. With nearly 30,000 experts in its files, the MRS can help journalists quickly find experts to comment on all sides of technical issues. Clones of the media resource service have been established in England and France, and the United Nations has supported development of similar services in Sri Lanka, the Philippines, and Indonesia (A. McGowan & F. Jerome, AAAS, personal communications, November 1993).

Council for the Advancement of Science Writing. In 1960, the National Association of Science Writers created a *wholly disowned subsidiary* to undertake activities that would "increase the quantity and quality of science writing." The new organization, the Council for the Advancement of Science Writing (CASW), continues today to support a range of activities intended to improve the quality of science journalism. The most visible activity is an annual conference at which scientists on the cutting edge of research present talks to audiences consisting entirely of journalists and public information officers. With funding from major media organizations, government agencies, and especially private foundations, these *New Horizons* meetings attract both experienced science journalists and newcomers to the field. Thus they serve as an occasion for the folklore of the profession to be passed on to younger writers, in addition to their role as a source of stories on important technical developments in the sciences (B. Patrusky, CASW, personal communication, February 1993). The CASW also sponsors fellowships for graduate students pursuing training in science writing. And, in recent years, it has sponsored study trips abroad, taking journalists to Central and South America to discover stories that U.S.-based journalists often miss.

Each of these nongovernmental organizations demonstrates the interconnectedness—a component of what constitutes "infrastructure"—of many public
communications of science and technology activities. The funding for the public
communication of science and technology activities these organizations undertake (often provided on a project-by-project basis) comes from the same government agencies, private foundations, and corporate donors that are described elsewhere in this paper. The people involved in these organizations, both at the staff
and the advisory levels, are often active in trade associations or advisory panels
in other public communication of science and technology activities as well.

Nonprofit Foundations

Like corporations, private philanthropies are major supporters of public outreach
activities in science. A wide range of foundations support science journalism
training, public television programs, community organizations involved in science, interactive science centers, and the many other activities in public communication of science and technology that are discussed here (Lewenstein, 1992).
Most of the work is subsumed under the categories discussed above. Nonetheless, because of their important funding role, foundations are important to consider in this survey. No comprehensive data have been compiled specifically
on the role of private philanthropies in public communication of science and
technology. But foundations such as the DeWitt Wallace–Reader's Digest Fund,
the Sloan Foundation, the Howard Hughes Medical Institute, the Packard family
foundations, and the Hewlett Foundation are all known to commit tens of millions of dollars annually to various activities in which free-choice learning can
take place.

CONCLUSION

The first conclusion from this attempt to describe the infrastructure for learning
and education in the United States must be that the dimensions of the field are
not yet known. The definitional problems in the federal PUNS working group's
report, the almost complete lack of information about commercial television
programs, the questions about how to count public health activities—all of these
points suggest that there is much work to be done toward defining the boundaries and structures of this field.

However, some broad generalizations about the state of public communication of science and technology in the United States are possible. The first pertains to scale: The federal government alone spends, as stated earlier, in the
hundreds of millions, perhaps billions, of dollars on public communication of
science and technology activities. When the resources of local industries, com-

mercial television, other media producers, and so on, are factored in, the American expenditure for public communication of science and technology activities is in the billions of dollars.

The second pertains to scope: Although mass media productions, including newspapers, magazines, radio, and television shows, are among the most visible public communications of science and technology activities, they are by no means the only place where the public encounters science and technology in a free-choice environment. Museums, community groups, youth groups, school-based activities tied to museums or television programs, and the activities of nongovernment organizations such as environmental groups and voluntary health organizations all create a vast public space where communication about science and technology take place.

As the discussions of free-choice learning proceed, it is this combination of size and public space that must be understood. Any debate about how free-choice learning takes place, or where resources should be invested, or how to measure effectiveness, or a host of related questions, must first acknowledge the complexity of the context. Many would dearly love to find simple answers. But the world isn't a simple place. It would be wrong to expect simple answers in that complex context.

Nonetheless, I suggest the complexity should not be mistaken for chaos. The connections among the many activities described here seem, to me, to add up to an infrastructure—though whether for "free-choice learning" more broadly, "free-choice science education" more specifically, or "public communication of science and technology" in general is a labeling question to be addressed in other research.

REFERENCES

Alexander, E. P., & Alderson, W. T. (1996). *Museums in motion: An introduction to the history and functions of museums* [Serial]. Walnut Creek, CA: AltaMira Press.

Association of Science-Technology Centers. (1993). ASTC/Cimuset Directory & Statistics. Washington, DC: ASTC.

Bader, R. G. (1990, Spring). How science news sections influence newspaper science coverage: A case study. *Journalism Quarterly, 67*(1), 88–96.

Burnham, J. (1987). *How superstition won and science lost: Popularizing science and health in the United States.* New Brunswick, NJ: Rutgers University Press.

Carson, R. (1962). *Silent Spring.* Boston: Houghton Mifflin.

Crane, V., Nicholson, H., Chen, M., & Bitgood, S. (1994). *Informal science learning: What the research says about television, science museums, and community-based projects.* Dedham, MA: Research Communications Ltd.

Goodall, R. (1980). The gene craze. *Columbia Journalism Review, 41–45.*

Goodall, R. (1986). How to kill a controversy: The case of recombinant DNA. In S.

Dunwoody, S. M. Friedman, & C. Rogers (Eds.), *Scientists and journalists* (pp. 170–181). New York: Free Press.

Hays, S. P. (1972). *Conservation and the gospel of efficiency: The progressive conservation movement, 1890–1920.* New York: Atheneum.

Hays, S. P. (1987). *Beauty, health, and permanence: Environmental politics in the United States, 1955–1985.* New York: Cambridge University Press.

Hudson, K. (1987). *Museums of influence.* New York: Cambridge University Press.

Inverness Research Associates. (1993, July). Youth science movement growing rapidly. *The Informal Science Review, 1*(1), 1–6.

Jerome, F. (Ed.). (1984, Autumn). Newspaper science sections. *SIPIscope, 12,* 1–17.

Jerome, F. (Ed.). (1986, Autumn). Newspaper science sections spreading nationwide. *SIPIscope, 14,* 1–17.

Jerome, F. (Ed.). (1992a, Fall). For newspaper science sections: Hard times. *SIPIscope, 20*(1), 2–3.

Jerome, F. (Ed.). (1992b, Fall). Hard times hit science sections. *SIPIscope, 20*(1), 1–9.

Katz, M. S. (1987). *Ban the bomb: A history of SANE, the Committee for a Safe Nuclear Policy, 1957–1985.* New York: Greenwood Press.

LaFollette, M. C. (1990). *Making science our own: Public images of science, 1910–1955.* Chicago: University of Chicago Press.

Lewenstein, B. V. (1987a). *Public understanding of science in America, 1945–1965.* Unpublished doctoral dissertation, University of Pennsylvania, Philadelphia.

Lewenstein, B. V. (1987b, Spring). Was there really a popular science 'boom'? *Science, Technology & Human Values, 12*(2), 29–41.

Lewenstein, B. V. (1988). Emergence of environmental reporters in the United States: A new breed in the 1960s. In O. Johnson (Ed.), *Proceedings of International Association for Mass Communication Research: Vol. 8* (pp. 9–23). Barcelona, Spain: International Association for Mass Communication Research.

Lewenstein, B. V. (1992). The meaning of 'public understanding of science' in the United States after World War II. *Public Understanding of Science, 1*(1), 45–68.

Lewenstein, B. V. (1994). A survey of public communication of science and technology activities in the United States. In B. Schiele (Ed.), *When science becomes culture* (pp. 119–178). Boucherville, Quebec: University of Ottawa Press.

Marchman, K. L., & Jason, J. (1992). Evaluating the 'America responds to AIDS' campaign. In B. V. Lewenstein (Ed.), *When science meets the public* (pp. 69–82). Washington, DC: American Association for the Advancement of Science.

Miller, J. D., & Heltne, P. (1992, April). *The use and impact of science and technology museums in the United States: An historical and empirical examination.* Paper presented at the Conference on Museums and the Public Understanding of Science, The Science Museum, London.

National Performance Review. (1993). *From red tape to results: Creating a government that works better and costs less.* Washington, DC: U.S. Government Printing Office.

National Science Board. (1996). *Science & engineering indicators: 1996* (appendix table 7.14). Washington, DC: U.S. Government Printing Office.

National Science Board. (1998). Science and technology: Public attitudes and public understanding. In *Science & engineering indicators: 1998* (chap. 7). Washington, DC: U.S. Government Printing Office.

National Science Foundation, Informal Science Education Program. (1992). *Future directions of informal science education: Project abstracts.* Arlington, VA: Author.

Nelkin, D. (1987). *Selling science: How the press covers science and technology.* New York: W. H. Freeman.

NPR's saddest story is its own. (1983, May 27). *New York Times,* p. A14.

Public Understanding of Science (PUNS) Working Group. (1993a, July 30). *Committee on education and human resources, implementation plan for public understanding of science, fiscal years 1995–1999.* Washington, DC: PUNS.

Public Understanding of Science (PUNS) Working Group. (1993b, July 30). *Committee on education and human resources, implementation plan for public understanding of science, fiscal years 1995–1999,* pp. 7–8. Washington, DC: PUNS.

Rasmussen, W. D. (1989). *Taking the university to the people: Seventy-five years of cooperative extension.* Ames: Iowa State University Press.

Siegfried, T. (1992). Newspapers. In B. V. Lewenstein (Ed.), *When science meets the public* (pp. 113–124). Washington, DC: American Association for the Advancement of Science.

St. John, M., & Grinell, S. (1989). *Interactive science education in science museums: Current status and future trends. A review of the 1987 ASTC survey of science museums.* Washington, DC: Association of Science-Technology Centers.

Wax, N. (1993). *A conflict of cultures: An analysis of the problems scientists and journalists have communicating with each other and disseminating science information to the public.* Unpublished master's thesis, Cornell University, Ithaca, NY.

Yarbrough, P., & Scherer, C. (1991, September 5). *How audiences use the media.* Paper prepared for USDA/University of Missouri *"Poised for the Press"* videoconference.

CHAPTER 3

Achieving Scientific Literacy: Strategies for Insuring That Free-Choice Science Education Complements National Formal Science Education Efforts

Rodger W. Bybee

At the 1998 Annual Meeting of the National Academy of Sciences (NAS), then President Bruce Alberts announced a major gift from a NAS member to build and operate a new public science center. The gift includes renovation of a building and an endowment for continuing operation. The plan is to locate the new science center on the grounds of the National Academy facilities in Washington, D.C.

My opportunity to participate in planning this center with the National Research Council (NRC) made discussions of free-choice science education very real for me. It also raised issues, such as how to design experiences based on the theme "science in service to society" and how to develop greater understanding of the nature of science through educational exhibits and experiences. I had to deeply consider what contribution this new science center could make to national efforts in science education. The following discussion presents my effort to reconcile the current divide that I perceive between school-based and free-choice science education initiatives, to reveal some important formal education trends and efforts aimed at reform and advancement, and to propose a course that bridges the current divide.

ESTABLISHING A COMMON GOAL

Most individuals associated with efforts to promote the advancement of science education believe that achieving scientific literacy is a central purpose of their work. Admirable as this goal may be, it remains a challenge. The public understanding of science is not what it could, or should, be according to some in the field (Miller, 1983). And learners' attainment falls short of these proponents' goal of general science literacy (National Center for Education Statistics, 1998). Some individuals criticize the goal (Shamos, 1995), and some argue to maintain the goal as a means for improving the educational system (Bybee, 1997a, 1997b).

Achieving Scientific Literacy

Although many view the school as the central institution for public education, I feel it is time to broaden this view to include all parts of the educational infrastructure that are responsible for achieving higher levels of science literacy. Specifically, the free-choice learning community must be included in any view of achieving scientific literacy. If different parts of the educational infrastructure work at cross-purposes, the result can be waste and conflict. I would argue that this is currently the case. It seems to me that an initial step on this road to better science education, and a way to avoid waste and conflict, is to agree on a mutual purpose, such as achieving scientific literacy. This purpose is broad, abstract, and accommodates the mission and structure of both the free-choice and formal educational sectors.

Focus on Both Formal and Free-Choice Education

American education has a long history of placing attention on schools to achieve social aspirations (Cremin, 1988), such as achieving scientific literacy. Similarly, there is a long-standing perception and reality in America that knowledge is available from many, many sources—what Cremin (1988) called the "configurations of education." An increasing number of educators interested in promoting widespread science literacy realize the advantages of formal and free-choice education institutions that work in concert rather than separately. Such efforts seem essential for accommodating the scale of change required to advance the ambitious goal of achieving scientific literacy. However, large-scale improvement of science education has been a difficult and elusive goal for both formal and free-choice institutions. In fact the goal is so difficult and so elusive that, combated separately, it has not been achieved (Elmore, 1996). By combining the efforts of the formal and free-choice education sectors, we can recognize the scale of the problem and, in that sense alone, we can view it as a constructive alliance.

Addressing the Fundamental Issue

Let me address what I see as a central issue. The free-choice science education community, which includes science centers, community outreach programs, museums, media, and other cultural institutions aimed at educating audiences outside the formal education system, has a history of independence and autonomy. This independence and autonomy contrasts with the formal educational system with its burdens of bureaucracy and authority. Any recommendations for free-choice science education must accommodate simultaneously the unique features of the formal educational community in order to help achieve the common goal of scientific literacy.

AN EXPANDED VIEW OF EDUCATION

Science learning can take place in many venues. Free-choice science learning is difficult to define, particularly when trying to determine its complementary relationship to compulsory science learning (Hofstein & Rosenfeld, 1994).

Two Frameworks for Learning

The literature identifies two frameworks for considering the relationship of compulsory and free-choice learning. The first framework draws a sharp dichotomy between the two (Wellington, 1991). This framework, however, does not take into account the varied characteristics of free-choice learning; for example, visits to science museums can be voluntary or compulsory, structured or unstructured, integrated into the school science program or occasional, and sequenced or unsequenced. The second type of framework is a hybrid, one that includes both compulsory and free-choice education (Crane & Chen, 1994). In this framework, free-choice education refers to activities that occur outside the school setting, which are not developed primarily for school use and are not developed as part of an ongoing school science curriculum. However, free-choice education experiences may be, and often are, structured to meet a stated set of objectives. Commonly, free-choice activities are used as supplements to formal education, as in school field trips; less commonly, free-choice activities are used in schools by teachers.

The Advantages of Free-Choice Education

Increasingly, there is agreement that the notions of learning that exist in school settings are too narrow to capture the kinds of experiences available to children and families going to science centers, museums, natural history parks, geological sites, zoological parks, botanical gardens, nature centers, environmental educa-tion centers, and other comparable free-choice learning settings (St. John & Perry, 1993). In contrast to the classroom experience (where learning usually involves the acquisition of predetermined concepts and abilities over extended periods of time, taught by teachers to classrooms of students), free-choice expe-riences allow the learner opportunities to stop at will, repeat at will, spend more or less time, and share the learning process with friends or family members. These free-choice learning experiences, admittedly, cannot be tested in the same manner as more structured classroom learning (Falk, 2001; Falk & Dierking, 1995). However, "no one flunks museum," as noted by Frank Oppenheimer, founder of the San Francisco Exploratorium. Instead, learners of all levels and abilities are offered experiences that can be considered complementary to school learning. Such experiences also have been known to inspire a lifelong interest in science. Millions of Americans visit the various free-choice learning venues annually, and these institutions must be viewed as an important support for this expanded form of learning experience.

Blurring Boundaries Between Formal and Free-Choice

Other free-choice learning resources also contribute to public understanding of science. These include network and cable television, electronic media, and com-mercial enterprises. As technology continues to expand, bringing what tradition-ally were school-based experiences into the home and what traditionally were home-based experiences into other free-choice settings, the lines between free-choice and compulsory learning are becoming blurred (Crane & Chen, 1994). The explosion of the "edu-tainment" industry is an outgrowth of these changes that is being taken seriously by television producers and theme parks as an opportunity to increase ratings or attendance (Falk & Dierking, 2000). It remains critical, however, that the science content conveyed through these media be informed by discussions about goals for achieving higher levels of scientific literacy. In this dialogue, educational institutions in the free-choice learning community can provide the necessary reinforcing infrastructure for learning about science.

THE *NATIONAL SCIENCE EDUCATION STANDARDS*: AN IMPORTANT LINK

If the nation is going to achieve scientific literacy, it will need to recognize the importance of a combined effort of both the formal and free-choice education communities. In the words of B. W. Honeyman (1996), "This is a time when we need to forge partnership between both formal and [free-choice] science education sectors" (p. 32). My position is that the *National Science Education Standards* (National Research Council [NRC], 1996), represents an essential connection or link between these two systems. People learn science from a variety of sources, for a variety of reasons, in a range of different ways (Wellington, 1990).

Given the important place of free-choice learning in local communities, the society as a whole, it seems imperative to build a complementary relationship between free-choice science education and formal education. This relationship would enhance learning opportunities through alignment of educational goals. In this complementary relationship, each sector brings special expertise to the collaboration. The free-choice learning community has been working for years on the challenge of communicating science to the public and, in some cases, has developed innovative community-based support and outreach programs for children, families, and teachers. The cornerstone of this collaboration should be the NRC's *National Science Education Standards* (1996). The standards represent a national effort to define content that constitutes a scientifically literate public.

NRC Standards and Free-Choice Science Education

I propose that the *National Science Education Standards* (NRC, 1996) be seriously considered in the attempt to identify ways for free-choice science education to complement school-based national science education efforts. The *National Science Education Standards* address a challenge set forth by the National Committee on Science Education Standards and Assessment to "create a vision for the scientifically literate person and standards for science education that, when established, would allow the vision to become reality." The standards, founded in exemplary educational practice and contemporary views of learning, are designed to guide the entire science education system toward its goal of a scientifically literate citizenry in productive and socially responsible ways.

I attempt here to elaborate on themes addressed earlier, which point to ways in which the standards can be used by free-choice science education institutions to educate the public on science (Hofstein, Bybee, & Legro, 1997). Using the standards would not require every organization or institution to provide opportunities for learners in all content domains. More important, using the standards would not require that the unique features of free-choice learning be abandoned. However, using the standards may prompt greater overlap among the different sources from which individuals learn science.

The Standards as Passport for Border Crossings

Although one can find support for the road I recommend, there are "border crossings" to be met that would require recognizing different educational cultures. Although I recognize this critical checkpoint, I also recognize the power of a passport, namely, the universal nature of science content that can be supported by the use of the standards.

The standards clarify what all children should know and the abilities all children should develop, and provide a means to achieve those goals. The standards' "call to action" recognizes the critical role of those who work in the diverse range of nonschool institutions that educate. The point is, the standards suggest that society, and those institutions that are responsible for educating people about science, can work toward the lifelong goal of science learning. The free-choice learning community is challenged "to use the Standards as an opportunity to collaborate in providing rich science learning experiences for learners." The standards do not elaborate on the question of how such a collaboration should occur; this remains, in part, the task of all players in the realm of communicating science, to whom I proffer and dedicate the ideas herein.

The Vision: Comprehensive Educational Improvement

The *National Science Education Standards* present a vision of a scientifically literate populace through the education of children. They outline what learners need to know, understand, and be able to do to be scientifically literate. The document includes standards aligned with grades K–4, 5–8, and 9–12. They describe an educational system in which all learners demonstrate high levels of performance, educators in formal and free-choice settings make the decisions essential for effective learning, communities are focused on learning science, school science programs are coherent and coordinated, and educational systems nurture higher levels of achievement.

A LOOK AT THE STANDARDS

Attaining this vision of science education requires a comprehensive approach to educational improvement, one that views free-choice and formal education as two components of one inclusive educational system. I feel that the standards can facilitate this larger educational improvement. The following sections briefly describe the standards.

Science Teaching Standards

The science teaching standards describe what any teacher of science should know and be able to do. They are divided into six areas and are paraphrased as follows: planning inquiry-based science programs; strategizing to guide and facilitate learning; assessing teaching and learning methods; developing environments with time, space, and resources for learning science; creating communities of science learners; and planning and developing school science programs.

Effective teaching, whether in classrooms or on museum floors, is at the heart of implementing the standards and achieving scientific literacy. Good teachers of science create environments in which they and their learners work together. Educators continually expand their theoretical and practical knowledge about science, learning, and science teaching.

Professional Development Standards

The professional development standards present a vision for the development of knowledge and skill among all those responsible for teaching science. The professional development standards are paraphrased here as learning essential science content through the perspective and methods of inquiry; integrating knowledge about science with knowledge about learning, pedagogy, and learners and applying that knowledge to science teaching; developing the understanding and ability for lifelong learning; and integrating coherent professional development programs for teachers of science.

Effective science teaching has a foundation in science content, in particular, the concepts and abilities outlined in the standards. An important aspect of professional development involves learning science through inquiry-oriented experiences.

Assessment Standards

The assessment standards provide criteria against which to judge progress toward the goal of scientific literacy. They cover five areas as follows: consistency of assessments with the decisions they are designed to inform; assessment of learners' achievement and learners' opportunity to learn science; technical quality of data collected matches the decisions and actions taken on the basis of their interpretation; fairness of assessment practices; and soundness of inferences made from assessments about student achievement and opportunity to learn.

In the contemporary view, assessment and learning are two sides of the same coin. Assessments provide an operational definition of standards in that they define in measurable terms what learners should learn. When learners engage in assessments, they should learn from those assessments. For example, the experience of completing an investigation as part of an assessment should, in itself, constitute a learning experience and provide the student and teacher with feedback about what the student has learned and, by extension, how well the teacher has taught.

Science Content Standards

The science content standards outline what learners should know, understand, and be able to do in the natural sciences over the course of K–12 education. They are divided into eight categories: unifying concepts and processes in science; science as inquiry; physical science; life science; earth and space science; science and technology; science in personal and social perspective; and history and nature of science.

Each content standard states that the content of the standard is understood or certain abilities are developed as a result of activities provided for all learners in those grade levels. The standards refer to broad areas of content, such as objects in the sky, the interdependence of organisms, or the nature of scientific knowledge. Each standard includes illustrative discussions of how learners can learn the material. Similarly, the discussion of each content standard concludes with a guide to the fundamental concepts that underlie that standard—and are designed to illustrate the standard (see Table 3.1).

Those using the standards must translate them into programs that reflect local contexts and policies. This can be done in many ways, because the standards do not dictate the order, organization, or curriculum framework for science programs.

Science Education System Standards

These standards consist of criteria for judging the performance of the overall science education system. They include the following seven areas: congruency of policies that influence science education with the teaching, professional development, assessment, content, and program standards; coordination of science education policies within and across agencies, institutions, and organizations; continuity of science education policies over time; provision of adequate and appropriate resources to support science education policies; equity embodied in

---

Table 3.1. Example of a Content Standard

As a result of activities in grades K–4, all learners should develop understanding of:

- Characteristics of organisms
- Life cycles of organisms
- Organisms and environments

science education policies; review for possible unanticipated effects of policies on science education; and responsibility of individuals to achieve the new vision of science education portrayed in the standards.

Those implementing the standards will use systems that support the premise that the formal education sector is not the sole provider of science education. The standards do not create a blueprint for the cooperation of the free-choice and formal sectors, but they do suggest that both individuals and organizations will share a common vision and implement coherent, consistent, and coordinated policies. In this scenario, there is every reason to imagine that effective science programs can be sustained by both formal and free-choice educational institutions.

What the Standards Provide. The standards present an integrated set of policies designed generally to improve science education and specifically to develop higher levels of scientific literacy. The content standards do not prescribe a curriculum; the assessment standards are not examinations; and the teaching standards are not licensure requirements.

The standards could serve many functions for different organizations and institutions, depending on the perspectives and goals of the person or group using the standards. Overall, the standards serve three main purposes.

1. National standards define what learners should know and be able to do, thus shifting the focus of educational reform from changing inputs (what influences learning?), what is put across to learners, to achieving outcomes (what is actually learned?).
2. National standards for science education describe more than content outcomes; they also underscore the means of achieving the outcomes—teaching, professional development, assessment, science programs, and systemic support.
3. National standards should be viewed as a primary policy document that can be used as a guideline for science programs in both the formal and free-choice learning setting.

Strengths and Limitations

The *National Science Education Standards* provide a powerful set of policies to guide the improvement of all science education programs. As important and challenging as the development of the standards was, they represent only one step in the progress of standards-based improvement of science education. Examining strengths and limitations of the standards as they apply to settings in which free-choice science learning occurs will help set a direction for using them most effectively.

Strengths. An important strength of the Standards is that they present a comprehensive and coordinated set of policies designed to improve science education. In this case, *to improve* is interpreted as bringing about higher levels of achievement for all learners. Seven general principles guided development of the Standards (see Table 3.2). These principles include, but are not limited to, an accurate and complete representation of contemporary science. Addressing these principles required an expansion of the domains—the fields of inquiry— that the standards would address and, in the end, provided a stronger, more usable document.

Another strength centers on content standards. The content standards were developed by a team of scientists representing many disciplines in the scientific field, school science teachers, and university science educators. They had the difficult task of identifying the most important and fundamental knowledge and abilities that characterize science (and in one instance, technology). The task was not easy. The content standards simply could not include all the topics, skills, and ideas that a learned group of science professionals could identify. Rather, the challenge was to focus on major concepts that form a core for tradi-

Table 3.2. Guiding Principles for Development and Implementation of Standards

Universal access	All learners, regardless of gender, cultural or ethnic background, physical or learning disabilities, aspirations, or interest and motivation in science, should have the opportunity to attain higher levels of scientific literacy than they do currently.
Complete learning	All learners will learn all science in the content standards.
Science knowledge within different perspectives	All learners will develop science knowledge as defined in the content standards and an understanding of science that enables them to use their knowledge as it relates to scientific, personal, social, and historical perspectives.
The process	Learning science is an active process.
Needed resources	For all learners to understand more science, less emphasis must be given to some science content and more resources, such as time, personnel, and materials, must be devoted to science education.
Intellectual tradition	School science must reflect the intellectual tradition that characterizes the practice of contemporary science.
Education reform	Improving science education is part of systemic education reform.

tional science disciplines—physical, life, and earth. In addition, the content had to incorporate ways of thinking about, working with, and investigating the natural world and the relationships of science to society. These mandates resulted in the content standards on inquiry, technology, personal and social perspectives, history and nature of science, and unifying concepts and processes.

Taken as a whole, the content standards provide a conceptual framework of knowledge and skills that learners need to continue their study of science. The content standards expand the traditional view of subject matter in ways that address fundamental goals of education:

1. Learners should know and be able to do what is central to science (standards on physical, life, and earth sciences, and inquiry).
2. Learners should use their minds well within the study of science (standards on inquiry and technology).
3. Learners should be prepared for responsible citizenship and apply knowledge and skills to a variety of personal and social problems (standards on technology, personal and social perspectives, history and nature of science).

Similarly, the standards reflect a broad consensus within the science education community. During the development process, feedback and support were continually sought from science and education professionals and the general public. The process was as thorough and comprehensive as time, budget, and personnel would permit.

Another strength is that the standards were crafted to be developmentally appropriate. By designing standards for grade levels K–4, 5–8, and 9–12, outcomes were stated that would be achievable regardless of learners' perceived abilities.

Finally, the standards leave ample flexibility to accommodate the range of differences among the institutions that might use them for guidance. The tradition of local interests and the requirements of student interests and abilities need not be sacrificed as the standards are implemented in curriculum, instruction, and assessment.

Limitations. Standards represent a primary policy instrument; this fact also points to some limitations of the standards.

It could be asked: Will widespread dissemination of national standards provide adequate guidance for the implied transformation of educational programs? That was the goal. However, those using the standards must understand the assumptions upon which they were developed (LeMahieu & Foss, 1994) and consequently not assume that dissemination of the standards alone will result in the changes proposed. By design, the standards do not prescribe educational experiences. Practitioners with the technical expertise to read, interpret, and use all dimensions of the standards will have to implement the policies as programs and innovative experiences.

Common sense and educational research (Fullan & Stiegelbauer, 1991; Hall & Loucks, 1978) support the conclusion that practitioners in both the formal and free-choice science education sectors would need to do more than adopt standards to initiate and sustain the goals outlined in the standards. There are several reasons for this conclusion, which can be perceived as limitations. For one, the standards document presents practitioners with a formidable amount of information. Although the standards are well thought out, provide clear and accurate descriptions of content, and include some examples, they do not lend themselves to direct use as teaching materials. They must be translated into educational experiences appropriate to the varied institutions that educate.

For the most part, the standards do not provide clear and compelling descriptions of processes for translating the various standards. This observation should not come as a surprise, because describing the process of implementing the standards was not the purpose of the document. Rather, the standards simply describe what learners should know and be able to do. They do not describe the processes of curriculum development (Bybee, 1995) or of implementation (Fullan & Miles, 1992; Hall & Hord, 1987; Hall & Loucks, 1978). And they do not describe what might be initiated by those in the free-choice science education community.

The changes implied by the national standards present a complex array of interdependent factors involving content, teaching, assessment, professional development, science programs, and systemic reform. Individuals and groups do not commonly review standards on the basis of the array of interdependent factors; rather, they center on the single factor most closely aligned with that individual's or group's professional interest and, on the basis of that review, infer what standards may apply. Examining and understanding the standards as an integrated set of policies is a professional obligation, but this obligation is neither intuitively obvious nor commonly practiced. It certainly should be practiced, though, by leaders of contemporary reform in both the free-choice and formal science learning sectors.

Practitioners who have to interpret and translate the standards are often bound by their current views of science education programs and practices. These views often contrast with the spirit of the standards and are sustained by peers and the historical culture of education. I believe that these views must be challenged and shown to be inadequate and new ideas—programs and practices—that are meaningful, feasible, and usable must be proposed.

The development of the standards required two paradoxical assumptions: first, that they be clear and usable to those in the educational community who would understand what the standards required; and second, that they not proscribe a national curriculum or assessment. At best, the standards provide examples of teaching and learning, but they stop short of recommendations that would be interpreted as a national curriculum or assessment. By design, this approach assumes that enlightened professionals would assume the responsibility for appropriate and adequate implementation of the standards.

A final limitation rests on the need for easy, quick, and inexpensive solutions to complex, multifaceted, and expensive educational problems. Rather than perceiving the standards as a comprehensive set of policies to be implemented, many practitioners approach the document as a technical manual from which one need only look up the answer to a particular problem—such as, What should I teach about ecology?—and don't bother to study the entire document.

To summarize, I suggest that the strengths of the standards include that basic principles guided their development; content represents fundamental and enduring knowledge and abilities of science; they reflect a broad consensus, are developmentally appropriate, and leave flexibility for the design of educational programs. The limitations include that implementation requires high-level technical expertise by practitioners; they require translation to both school and free-choice science education programs and practices; and adequate implementation requires coordinated efforts by diverse aspects of the science education community.

USING CONTENT STANDARDS IN EFFORTS

The content standards in the *National Science Education Standards* elaborate what learners should know and be able to do as a result of their educational experience (Bybee, 1997a, 1997b). In general, these standards state that as a result of inquiry-oriented activities, learners should develop an understanding of fundamental concepts and abilities. I suggest that to establish complementary goals between the formal and free-choice science education sectors, the educators use the content standards as a guide when designing free-choice science learning experiences. The following content standards may be of particular interest to free-choice educators: science as inquiry, science and technology, science in personal and social perspectives, and history and nature of science. I specifically elaborate the content standards on inquiry, as many educators in the free-choice science education community have embraced this aim.

Science as Inquiry

An essential component of scientific literacy, and subsequently of science programs, is the content and abilities of inquiry. This goal includes abilities necessary to do scientific inquiry and understandings about scientific inquiry. As a result of their science studies, learners will be able to ask questions, plan and conduct scientific investigations, think critically, construct and analyze alternative explanations, and communicate scientific arguments. The essential outcomes of science as inquiry include cognitive abilities, such as using logic and evidence in formulating and revising scientific explanations, recognizing and analyzing alternative models, and communicating and defining scientific arguments (Bybee, 1997a, 1997b). In some free-choice science settings (science centers in particular), inquiry happens every day and thus could constitute a valuable resource to complement formal science education. The Exploratorium in San Francisco is such a science center (Oppenheimer, 1975). Let us review what science as inquiry may mean.

Views of Science as Inquiry. Release of the standards has again engaged professionals in discussions of inquiry. Different perspectives that categorized inquiry include strategies for teaching science; models for learning science; and content for science education. In Table 3.3, I summarize statements that exemplify these perspectives. It seems that we educators have overemphasized the

Table 3.3. Perspectives on Inquiry

	Inquiry in free-choice education is—
Strategies for teaching science	• Using strategies that include activities • Basing experiences on student questions • Emphasizing the processes of science • Having learners actively involved • Using investigations to learn scientific ideas
Model for learning science	• Acquiring knowledge through activities • Using the processes of science • Emphasizing curiosity and desire to know as the basis of learning • Pursuing questions designed to help learners learn subject matter • Developing intellectual abilities
Content for science education	• Emphasizing how we know what we know from a scientific point of view • Presenting knowledge about what scientists do • Understanding that science is a community discourse about knowledge • Developing explanations based on empirical evidence • Understanding how science is done

teaching strategies and underemphasized the scientific basis for including inquiry in educational programs (Hackett, 1998; Hinman, 1998).

I challenge some contemporary views of inquiry and present the standards as an alternative perspective. The alternative view of inquiry is based in science and provides a definition that incorporates science content and teaching strategies.

How scientists know and explain the natural world and what they mean by knowledge and explanation are directly related to the processes, methods, and strategies by which they conduct their work. What are the basic elements that underlie science as a way of knowing and explaining the natural world? Scientific knowledge of the natural world, in its succinct form, must be based on observations and experimental data, and explanations about the way the world works must be evaluated against this empirical evidence.

Two aims of educational experiences extend from this discussion of inquiry. First, as a result of their experiences, learners should develop an understanding of the defining qualities of science as a way of knowing and explaining the natural world. A second aim complements this goal; namely, as a result of their experiences, learners should develop some cognitive abilities and manipulative skills associated with scientific inquiry.

The following quotation summarizes the vision of inquiry presented in the standards:

> Scientific inquiry refers to the diverse ways in which scientists study the natural world and propose explanations based on the evidence derived from their work. Inquiry also refers to the activities of learners in which they develop knowledge and understanding of scientific ideas, as well as an understanding of how scientists study the natural world (NRC, 1996, p. 23).

This quotation affirms inquiry as grounded in science. It also presents an educational connection; namely, inquiry has something to do with the activities of learners and, by implication, the strategies of education. The quotation points to educational experiences having something to do with developing learners' understanding of scientific ideas.

Content standards for science as inquiry indicate that, as a result of activities, all learners should develop abilities necessary to do scientific inquiry and understandings about scientific inquiry.

The standards also clarify and define what is meant by abilities and understandings. Table 3.4 includes summary statements of the abilities and understandings for science as inquiry.

Science teaching standards refer to an inquiry-based program for learners. Here, to be consistent, the referent for *inquiry-based programs* must be the

Table 3.4. Science as Inquiry

Abilities necessary to do scientific inquiry	*Important understandings for scientific inquiry*
• Identify questions that can be answered through scientific investigation.	• Different kinds of questions suggest different kinds of scientific investigations.
• Design and conduct a scientific investigation.	• Current scientific knowledge and understanding guide scientific investigations.
• Use appropriate tools and techniques to gather, analyze, and interpret data.	• Mathematics is important in all aspects of scientific inquiry.
• Develop descriptions, explanations, predictions, and models using evidence.	• Technology used to gather data enhances accuracy and allows scientists to analyze and quantify results of investigations.
• Think critically and logically to make the relationships between evidence and explanation.	• Scientific explanations emphasize evidence, have logically consistent arguments, and use scientific principles, models, and theories.
• Recognize and analyze alternative explanations and predictions.	• Science advances through legitimate skepticism.
• Communicate scientific procedure and explanations.	• Scientific investigations sometimes result in new ideas and phenomena for study, generate new methods or procedures for investigation, or develop new techniques to improve the collection of data.
• Use mathematics in all aspects of scientific inquiry.	

standards for *science as inquiry* because that, along with other science concepts, is the content or outcome of educational experiences. The teaching standards express various factors associated with that goal—that is, facilitating; learning; assessing; providing time, space, and resources; developing communities of learners; and designing science programs. Combining the content standards with the teaching standards describes the goal of inquiry in educational programs and the various means of achieving those goals.

Science and Technology

In addition to inquiry, I also believe that the content standards of science and technology, science in personal and social perspective, and history and the nature of science may be of particular interest to the free-choice learning sector.

In recent years, the integration of science with its respective technological applications has become an important component in science education. In the standards, the similarities and differences between science and technology are clarified by including the development of learners' abilities associated with technological design and the understanding of science and technology. The standards provide learners with opportunities to develop decision-making abilities relative to technology in a societal and personal context. By integrating the presentation of science with technology, free-choice education institutions could contribute significantly to learners' understanding and abilities.

Prime examples of this effort are science centers. The main achievements of these centers for science and technology have been to relate science and technology to the objects that people see and use in everyday life; far more often than occurs in schools. However, with the advent of these centers the broader public now has opportunities to view these relationships.

Science in Personal and Social Perspectives

Another contemporary vision of scientific literacy includes connections between the scientific knowledge needed for decisions that children and adults make about personal and social issues. For example, the content standards for science in personal and social perspectives for grades 9–12 include the following knowledge and understanding categories: personal and community health, population growth, natural resources, environmental quality, natural and human-induced hazards, and science and technology in relation to local, national, and global changes.

Developing greater understanding of science in personal and social perspectives will help learners fulfill their obligations as future citizens. Positive examples of the contribution free-choice settings make to this standard are museum exhibitions such as the Human Body Discovery Space (HBDS) at Boston's Museum of Science and the Hall of Life at the Denver Museum of Natural History. These exhibitions contain a variety of interactive exhibits on topics related to human biology and medicine, including exhibits on cholesterol, human growth, calcium content in food, medicinal herbs, fat content in food, amount of blood in a human body, pulse and electrocardiogram, senses, insulin and glucose control, and clinical chemistry (Boisvert & Slez, 1995). These are fairly complicated issues to be introduced in the formal setting of science education, and the contribution of free-choice settings to this topic area should not be overlooked.

History and the Nature of Science

In keeping with the personal relation to science, the content standards on the history and nature of science present science as a human endeavor. Contemporary science has developed a history of advancing knowledge through a series of established rules of conduct, such as using empirical evidence, applying logical arguments, and encouraging skeptical review. These include the limitations of science; the contribution of individuals to our current scientific knowledge; the interactions and interdependencies between science and society; and the fact that science is fundamentally a human enterprise. There is no doubt that experience in the free-choice education community can play a significant role in illuminating these aspects of science.

CONCLUSION

One educational lesson of standards-based reform, which includes the science education standards, has been to differentiate the aims, goals, and outcomes of education from the means, methods, and techniques of education. Logic suggests that one begins designing programs and recommending experiences by first identifying the educational outcomes, then implementing the means for achieving the outcomes, and finally evaluating the degree to which learners have attained the outcomes. This is a simple and obvious point, but one that seems clouded and obscure in many educational discussions.

I would suggest that the infrastructure for free-choice science learning could, and should, play an important role in reinforcing some of the goals of the *National Science Education Standards*. The standards could help free-choice science education institutions strengthen their roles and relationships with schools and teachers within their local communities and help to increase learners' achievements in science. Recently, there have been constant calls to bridge the gap between the formal and free-choice science education sectors. I suggest that the standards could provide a solid and reliable bridge with which to connect these two sectors.

REFERENCES

Boisvert, D. L., & Slez, B. J. (1995). The relationship between exhibit characteristics and learning-associated behaviors in science museum discovery space. *Science Education, 79*, 503–518.

Bybee, R. W. (Ed.). (1995). *National standards and the science curriculum: Challenges, opportunities, and recommendations.* Dubuque, IA: Kendall/Hunt.

Bybee, R. W. (1997a). *Achieving scientific literacy: From purposes to practices.* Portsmouth, NH: Heinemann.

Bybee, R. W. (1997b, May). Meeting the challenge of achieving scientific literacy. Presentation at the International Conference on Globalization of Science Education, Seoul, Korea. Unpublished.

Crane, V., & Chen, M. (1994). *Informal science learning: What the research says about television, science museums, and community-based projects.* Ephrata, PA: Science Press.

Cremin, L. (1988). *American education: The metropolitan experience.* New York: Harper and Row.

Elmore, R. F. (1996). Getting to scale with good educational practice. *Harvard Educational Review, 66*(1), 1–26.

Falk, J. (Ed.). (2001). *Free-choice science education: How we learn science outside of school.* New York: Teachers College Press.

Falk, J., & Dierking, L. (1995). *Public institution for personal learning.* Washington, DC: American Association of Museums.

Falk, J., & Dierking, L. (2000). *Learning from museums: Visitor experiences and the making of meaning.* Walnut Creek, CA: AltaMira Press.

Fullan, M. B., & Miles, M. B. (1992). Getting reform right: What works and what doesn't. *Phi Delta Kappan, 745–752.*

Fullan, M. B., & Stiegelbauer, S. (1991). *The new meaning of educational change.* New York: Teachers College Press.

Hackett, J. (1998). Inquiry: Both means and ends. Using the standards to define inquiry methods and outcomes. *The Science Teacher, 65*(6), 34–37.

Hall, G., & Hord, S. (1987). *Change in schools: Facilitating the process.* Albany: State University of New York Press.

Hall, G., & Loucks, S. (1978). Teacher concerns as a basis for facilitating and personalizing staff development. *Teachers College Record, 80*(1), 36–53.

Hinman, R. T. (1998). Content and science inquiry. *The Science Teacher, 65*(7), 25–27.

Hofstein, A., Bybee, R. W., & Legro, P. L. (1997). Linking formal and informal science education through science education standards. *Science Education International, 8*(3), 31–37.

Hofstein, A., & Rosenfeld, S. (1994). Bridging the gap between formal and informal science learning. *Studies in Science Education, 2*(8), 87–112.

Honeyman, B. W. (1996). Science centers: Building bridges with teachers. *Science Education International, 7*(3), 30–34.

LeMahieu, P., & Foss, H. (1994, May). Standards at the base of school reform. *The School Administrator, 16–22.*

Miller, J. D. (1983). Science literacy: A conceptual and empirical review. *Daedalus: Journal of the American Academy of Arts and Sciences, 112*(2), 19–48.

National Center for Education Statistics. (1998). *Pursuing excellence: A study of U.S. twelfth grade mathematics and science achievement in international context.* Washington, DC: Author.

National Research Council. (1996). *National science education standards.* Washington, DC: National Academy Press.

Oppenheimer, F. (1975). The exploratorium and other ways of teaching physics. *Physics Today, 28,* 9–13.

Shamos, M. H. (1995). *The myth of scientific literacy.* New Brunswick, NJ: Rutgers University Press.

St. John, M., & Perry, D. (1993). Rethink role, science museums urged. *ASTC Newsletter, 21*(4), 1.

Wellington, J. (1990). Formal and informal learning in science: The role of the interactive centers. *Physics Education, 25,* 247–252.

Wellington, J. (1991). Newspaper science, school science: Friends or enemies? *International Journal of Science Education, 13,* 363–372.

CHAPTER 4

The Use of Time and Space in Assessing the Potential of Free-Choice Learning

Geoffrey Godbey

Learning historically has been perceived as a formal exercise that takes place primarily inside classrooms. But more realistically, that perception is one-dimensional, as learning occurs in many situations, on many levels within daily life.

The fact is that learning in general and science learning in particular takes place every day during myriad activities sponsored by thousands of organizations nationwide spending billions of dollars from private and public sources. This supra educational community exists beyond schools and universities—indeed it is an enterprise or infrastructure of information sources from which people derive the everyday developments of science.

The extent to which people recognize the potentially critical role that is played by the educational infrastructure within their community, will, in-part, dictate whether they learn more or less from the information available. Entering into the twenty-first century the sequencing of school, paid work, housework, leisure, and travel time can all be customized to allow people more time to utilize these free-choice educational settings and engage in what is known as free-choice learning. To tap into this arena of well spent leisure time in a viable way, and to nurture the process of free-choice learning, all the players involved in science education must understand the time-use patterns of people's daily lives and indeed the values they place on time management.

INCREASING FREE TIME ACROSS THE LIFE SPAN

Peter Drucker (1989) and others argue that where business has succeeded in Western societies, it has succeeded so well that people can now consider satisfying noneconomic needs. "Half of the expansion in wealth-producing capacity was used to create leisure time by cutting the hours worked while steadily increasing pay" (p. 122).

This phenomenon is also shown to be taking place in most other modern nations (Ausubel & Grubler, 1994). Not only has there been a decline in hours of work per year in the countries discussed, but it is also suggested that, contrary to some popular opinions, the average American worker is not overworked compared with their counterparts in Germany or Japan.

In this new scenario, work is taking a smaller and smaller fraction of the hours of people's lives. Though we are not a society of leisure, we have gained free time—not only on a daily basis but as a percentage of our total lives.

The implications of an increase in free time among people of western cultures has led to the study and support of free-choice learning. This extra free time is shown to provide sufficient time in daily life for Americans to use a wide variety of community-based resources for learning science and other subjects.

Where Does This Time Come From?

Central contributing factors to the trend of declining portions of life spent working are later entry into the labor force, deferred marriage, fewer children, and earlier retirement with longer life expectancy. U.S. workers now retire or partially retire, on average, in their late 50s or early 60s. American men who reach the age of 65 now have a life expectancy of 80 years, whereas women's life expectancy is 84 years. On average, about 12 of these years after age 65 will be relatively healthy. The elderly are no longer disproportionately poor; in fact, if wealth is measured as financial assets, they are among the wealthiest age groups in society (55 to 64 is the wealthiest). This portion of the American population currently has the greatest potential (of any age group) to use the infrastructure for free-choice learning in a community.

Our current society hoards huge amounts of free time to be spent only during the last 15 to 20 years of life. The Prussian bureaucrat, who is reputed to have established 65 as the age of retirement payment, is said to have done so completely arbitrarily—probably never imagining that the institution of retirement would today consume almost one fifth of a person's life. Fewer than one out of five of the 52 million Americans age 55 and over are in the labor force—a stunning indicator of where free time has grown most quickly.

THE SHRINKING WORKWEEK AND
MALDISTRIBUTION OF FREE TIME

According to Gershuny's (1992) meta-analysis of time use in 15 countries, the portion of our lives devoted to both paid work and housework is decreasing, and it appears that such declines are predicted by rising economic standards of living. He also added that, "there is no basis, theoretical or empirical, for thinking that we are 'running out of time'" (p. 16).

In the United States the total number of hours per week devoted to paid work, the commute to work, and total family care declined 6.2 hours a week for women and 6.0 hours a week for men from 1965 to 1985, as shown by nationally representative time-diary studies. Preliminary analysis of 1995 time diaries and other data sources (Bureau of Labor Statistics [BLS] workweeks, Neilson figures) generally show that the amount of free time has held steady or has increased since 1985 (J. Robinson, personal communication, July 30, 1998).

However, the organization of work, school, and home life is such that most free time comes on weekdays in small segments, limiting its usefulness for some form of learning. For example, although it is true that free time has increased since 1965 by about 6 hours per week to 40 hours of free time a week, this free time has increased across the workweek, not the weekend. Free time increases from 5 hours a day on weekdays, to 6 hours on Saturdays, to 7.5 hours on Sundays. Across the week, then, 25 of the 40 weekly hours of free time occur on weekdays. Unfortunately, free time during the week may have more limited value in terms of its possibility for leisure. In other words, with a whole day of free time, a broader range of activities is possible, such as taking a trip, sailing a boat, or perusing books at a local library. These activities would be very difficult to squeeze into the 45-minutes-per-day gains on workdays.

This distribution may be a problem, because free time in larger segments has expanded potential for leisure purposes. For instance, the nature of free time differs dramatically on vacation. Even though the 7.4 hours of free time on vacation days are barely more than a typical Sunday, there is a dramatic decline in television viewing to under 20 minutes a day (Hill, 1985). In its place, reading time more than doubles and communication time almost doubles (although visiting time is cut in half). The biggest increase is in sports, walking, and other outdoor activity—nearly 2 hours. The increases in sleep and mealtime and the decrease in grooming time also suggest a more leisurely pace.

As work has seeped into the weekend and free time has seeped into weekdays, unsatisfying changes appear to be taking place in people's use of free time. One reason for this may be that the many short segments of free time do not provide a psychological escape from necessity. People do not feel the transition from a rushed work pace to relaxed and tranquil leisure.

Thought must be given to reorganize free time in ways that produce longer segments of time away from work and, if possible, beyond the reach of work. Readily available advanced technologies, such as laptop computers and cellular phones, have made it more difficult for some to feel that they can ever escape work. People need time to participate in activities that are intrinsically motivated rather than completing tasks required of them to fulfill someone else's expectations, and ways must be found for them to do so.

Survey respondents generally report they would rather have their increases in free time in the form of 3-day weekends or larger blocks of time. In spite of this, the chores of weekdays appear to be expanding into the weekend, even as free time expands during weekdays. The expansion of free time on the weekday may help explain the greater amount of time devoted to television viewing during the last two decades of the twentieth century (Robinson & Godbey, 1997).

TELEVISION'S EFFECT ON LEISURE TIME

To a great extent, modern leisure has been organized around television. Preliminary analysis of 1995 time-diary data show an increase in time devoted to TV since 1985. Of the 40 hours of free time per week that Americans average, only 2.2 are devoted to participating in art, music, drama, hobbies, crafts, games, active sports, and outdoor recreation. Social or entertainment activities such as attending sports events, going to the movies, parties, bars, and lounges, and social visiting account for 6.7 hours per week. Religion and cultural events each take less than an hour per week. By far the largest time consumer is television watching, with 15 hours per week and another 5 hours per week as a secondary activity—while engaged in doing something else.

In fact, it is estimated that almost all the gains in free time since 1965 have been used for more television viewing! Television has become the pivotal use of free time, and most of its content is based around both escapism and consumption. Such TV viewing, about 40 percent of all free time, overwhelms all other uses of free time. The growing recognition of this and the controversy surrounding how appropriate television is as a principal use of leisure may cause systematic efforts to minimize TV's influence and its use.

FEEDING THE TIME FAMINE

If Americans have more free time than ever, they don't feel as if they do. Many Americans believe they are in the midst of an unprecedented "time famine," a phenomenon that the Swedish economist Staffan Linder (1969) identified as an emerging trend in 1970. Linder argued that various cultures can be put on a scale from those who have a time surplus, such as India, to those in the middle, such as Sweden, to those who have time famines. The United States and Japan have become the ultimate time-famine cultures.

In time-famine cultures, the balance between accomplishment in work and leisure has been destroyed as worker productivity has accelerated, increasing the yield on an hour of work. As work time became more economically valuable, it was regarded as more scarce, as any commodity whose value had increased relative to others would be.

Although the effects of increased productivity during hours of work are complex, in terms of our psychological perception of time, this perceived scarcity of time may be seen to culminate in a negative effect. For example, rushing and the increasingly frantic pace of life may reduce the potential of the abundant free time for many Americans. Also lost have been the patience, tranquility, and long attention spans that historically have been necessary for much of the understanding of science.

It is seen that as the "yield" on time devoted to work has increased, people have also tried to increase the "yield" on time devoted to leisure, striving to get more out of leisure to balance the increasing productivity at work. In time-famine cultures, people's leisure is transformed into a frantic race to get as much as possible out of every minute spent in leisure activities. To do this, use of goods is combined with use of activities in a variety of ways to increase the yield on use of time, much as technology increased the yield on use of time at work. Examples of such strategies include the following:

1. *Simultaneous consumption*, such as bringing food, drink, and a miniature TV to a football game.
2. *Faster consumption*, such as having a "birthday party" in which All the gifts are opened and the refreshments served in an hour instead of three or four.
3. *Extensive consumption*, such as buying the accoutrements of an expensive wedding that involves high-end equipment and products for sit-down dinners, expensive gifts, and limos rather than a stand-up wedding in a church with a cake and punch in the back room.

Linder (1969) speculated that activities in which the yield can't be increased by combining them with money or material goods (such as contemplation, singing, writing poetry, or dancing) are valued less highly and tend to have less time devoted to them. Time devoted to activities that can be successfully combined with material goods—such as playing golf using better equipment, or a golf cart, or by playing two balls, or watching TV on bigger sets equipped with cable and VCRs or with stereo sound—will increase. This tendency has led to a "commodification" of leisure activity in which leisure is conceived primarily as a time to interact with material goods.

Although people want to keep increasing the yield on their time in various activities by combining them with the use of more and more goods, the additional usefulness (marginal utility) of adding increasingly more goods declines. These techniques can lead to a mentality in which time always is insufficient to do what a person envisions he or she would like to accomplish. And more and more goods are consumed. Thus Linder described an emerging world in which exponentially increasing productivity and consumption produced a time famine begging to be fed.

TIME DEEPENING: TAKING MULTITASKING TO NEW HEIGHTS

As time famine increases, people develop "time deepening" skills. Time deepening means that some people develop increasingly higher rates of "doing" than others; rather than thinking of time as an either–or proposition—I can either read the newspaper or watch television or eat dinner—people develop the ability to do all three simultaneously through time-deepening techniques. Time, in effect, becomes transformed from a fixed commodity to one that can be stretched almost infinitely. What used to be either–or time-use decisions are now often "more–more" decisions. People who work longer hours, for instance, also engage in more forms of active recreation than those who work shorter hours.

More–More Behavior

In the past, some might have argued that if people spend more time on activity A, they must by necessity spend less time on activity B or C to make up for it. Not so. Instead, using time-use or the more-more theory, busy people remain more active in several areas. Of particular interest are the counterintuitive results in relation to the zero-sum property of time. Rather than discovering that people felt temporal or activity constraints on their behavior, Robinson and Godbey (1997) found several instances of the more–more phenomenon among the public—more arts participation or organizational participation by people with longer work hours, more survey participation by people with less free time, greater gains in free time by those already having more free time, more participation in outdoor recreation by those working longer hours, more reading among those who spend more time with microcomputers and higher outputs from those with fewer related time inputs. The main exceptions to the more–more syndrome came from two activities that were very time-consuming and less active, namely, TV viewing and sleep. In order to fit in all their daily outside activities, more active people sleep less and watch less TV.

Consequently, those most likely to use community-based organizations for learning purposes are not those with the most free time. Indeed, these individuals are likely to have slightly less than average amounts of free time. They are likely to be well-educated and have relatively large incomes; they are unlikely to use only one community-based resource but rather a variety of them. These time-use, and economic, factors are seen to affect free-choice learning environments. Almost all the organizations providing free-choice learning opportunities, from municipal recreation and park departments to private nonprofits such as botanical gardens and planetariums, are increasingly dependent upon fund-raising, fees and charges, and marketing approaches to support them. Organizations, such as museums or libraries, that used to receive most of their operating budget from tax dollars must now raise funds from wealthy donors and use fees and charges as a more critical part of their revenue. These conditions may lead to a strategy of minimizing service to the "have-nots" as a primary responsibility.

As leisure time is increasingly treated as if it were money, time deepening in American society is seen to take at least four forms of time management and multitasking. First, we try to shorten the amount of time we devote to some activity. Thus a secretary who used to average 30,000 keystrokes per hour was expected to average 80,000 by 1987 (Rifkin, 1987). Second, we replace more time-consuming activities with less time-consuming substitutes. The drive-through zoo and drive-through fast-food restaurant are examples. Third, we try to be more precise with regard to time used in our activities—perhaps planning our schedules with only 5-minute tolerances. Fourth, we combine activities so we are doing more than one thing at the same time. In multinational time-diary studies, for example, Americans were more likely than respondents from other nations to record multiple activities in their diaries (Szalai, Converse, Feldheim, Scheuch, & Stone, 1972).

Time saving thus becomes a component of all behavioral decisions, particularly for individuals who feel most rushed. In terms of child-rearing, for example, a new term has crept into our vocabulary—*quality time*. Quality time with a child first and foremost takes for granted that less time will be spent. In effect, being with the child, which is viewed as a means to an end, can be made more efficient so that more positive things can be accomplished. Of course, the amount of time spent doing them is reduced.

Other Causes of the Time Famine and Time Deepening

Certainly, this almost scientific management of time and use of technological advances are not solely responsible for the galloping pace of life. We must also look to shifts in our values as the economy, society, and technology change. One place to start is with changes in assumptions about life made by the baby-boom generation, born between 1946 and 1964. These people were most affected by the era of optimism following World War II, which gradually brought about the idea that progress was infinite, as were increases in the material standard of living. As America rose to the position of the world's greatest economic power after the war, people began to believe in infinitely expanding economic opportunity. Consumption of goods came to be thought of in open-ended terms, that is, with no ceiling on what could be purchased and owned. Mobility was infinitely upward. A "psychology of entitlement" emerged in which such increasing levels of consumption came to be thought of as more or less automatic—owed to the individual by the system. The concept of "enough" disappeared.

Slowly, this mentality shifted to the consumption of experiences. Just as things could be consumed in infinitely increasing progression, so could experiences. Paralleling our insatiable desire to have was our desire to do. Open-ended consumption of experiences brought into question the very notion of leisure activity as voluntary. "Voluntary" historically implies a choice among many alternatives. Such a choice meant, in effect, that a person willingly gave up several other alternatives in order to undertake the most satisfying one. In short, pleasure involved sacrifice. Although voluntary is often thought of as a dichotomously scaled variable—to do or not to do—experiencialism made such decisions into intervally scaled variables—not a choice of doing or not doing but rather of how to maximize the activities done in a given unit of time.

Today, through time deepening, many people seem to be more nearly able to avoid the sacrifice of one activity for another, seeking instead to do it all and see it all, and to do it now and see it now. Time, in effect, has become a commodity, and time viewed as a commodity appears to have made our lives seem shorter and less tranquil. Little wonder, then, that our experience of life is catalogued in terms of "been there, done that."

Parallel with this turning of experiences into commodities was a shift in how individuals define who they are. Many Americans have become virtual walking resumes, defining themselves only by what they do. We depend less on our ascribed statuses (those conditions we were born with and did nothing to achieve, such as gender, ethnic heritage, or religion) to convey who we are and instead use achieved statuses to define ourselves (those that represent our accomplishments, such as director of marketing at XYZ Corp., black belt in karate, or connoisseur of wine drinking). The existential belief that we are born without a fixed nature and literally create who we are through authenticating acts is increasingly common. From such a perspective, the line between free time and work is largely irrelevant—to do nothing is to be nothing, and both work and free time activity are important in defining who we are. Little wonder that the preparation of resumes has become a science and that such resumes now often include information about our free-time activities as well as our work.

The accelerated pace of life also has been shaped by increases in technology that have resulted in the rise of efficiency as the most important value in our society (Rifkin, 1987). Efficiency—doing or producing more in less time with less expenditure of resources and personnel—is an open-ended concept. One can always become more efficient. Technology can always find ways to do things quicker and cheaper.

If our scientific time management reshaped our notions of time, so did the computer. An estimated one half of the U.S. labor force now uses electronic computer terminal equipment. The development of the computer represented the complete abstraction of time and its separation not only from the rhythm of nature but also from human experience. Although we may think that computers have become "user friendly," what really has happened is that people have had to become "computer friendly," using them whether they wish to or not. The use of this swift technology has even made us less patient in our conversation and other everyday behaviors. Now people who are slow, late, or like to dwell at length on a single issue in their conversation are avoided.

Thus our computer culture influences our everyday life, especially our leisure. "Efficiency" has never been a friend of leisure. Historically, leisure has meant behavior undertaken without reference to time. In the ancient Greek notion of leisure, contemplation was an ideal. Later, leisure was thought of as pastimes, but one cannot "pass" the time if efficiency is the primary goal; one can only "spend," "invest," and "save" it, or one will surely "lose" it. Whereas leisure activity traditionally has been slow-paced, luxuriating in time, the cult of efficiency has reshaped our free time in fundamental ways. In this post-Modern era, all human acts are becoming the means to some other end: instrumental behavior. We walk for fitness, play golf for contacts, and read to improve our minds. Passing the time in activities that are pleasurable in and of themselves is an almost foreign notion. Efficiency rules our work and our leisure.

Not only has the pace of life accelerated owing to our adjustment to technological change, it has also become faster owing to simple demographic reality. It happens that almost one third of the U.S. population, the baby-boom generation, is between the ages of 36 and 55, which is the most harried period of life with marriage, careers, and families dominating.

The unprecedented bulge in the population pipeline contributes mightily to the frantic pace of life. However, as this group ages, the pace of life will likely decrease. Imagine that a mere 20 years from now almost one third of the population will be between the ages of 49 and 67. Life should be slower.

But for the time being, how are we to judge the impact of this massive acceleration of life? In one sense, it means we can experience more than any generation in history. The repertoire of experiences for people of means can be enhanced almost indefinitely. However, the benefits are beginning to be outweighed by the costs. The stress that accompanies such accelerated life styles is a major cause of early death. For example, Levine (1990) has shown that the faster the pace of life in a city, the higher the rate of coronary heart disease.

Rushing and Feeling Rushed

There is widespread evidence that Americans perceive they are running out of time because the pace of life is speeding up. For example, in a 1992 national survey of 1,300 households (Godbey & Graefe, 1993), 38 percent of the American public always felt rushed compared with 22 percent who responded this way in 1971 and 32 percent in 1985. Those who were most likely to always feel rushed were working mothers, 64 percent of whom always felt rushed. Because working mothers are the key players in household management, this condition is likely to change what is done and how it is done within the household. In other surveys concerning people's leisure behavior, lack of time is mentioned more than any other factor (including lack of money) as inhibiting participation in desired leisure activities.

Similar findings were reported by Robinson (1991), who developed a time-crunch scale to measure the extent to which Americans felt rushed. Women generally feel more time crunched than men, and single working mothers have the highest time-crunch scores of any demographic group. The peak ages for feeling the time crunch were between 30 and 49, and these people did not associate rushing only with work. Twenty-six percent blamed their leisure activity for making them feel rushed, 38 percent blamed both work and leisure; only 36 percent blamed it only on their work. What seems to have changed is that the temporal conditions under which daily activities take place are rather different. Speed and brevity are more widely admired, whether in the time it takes to serve a meal, read a magazine article, or have a conversation. Many market analysts believe time was to the 1990s what money was to the 1980s. That is, time replaced money as the most valued resource—the one for which demand has increased the most relative to supply.

If Linder's (1969) assumption that the marginal utility of adding more and more goods to activities to increase the yield on them will exponentially decline, we would expect not only a more rushed culture but also an increasingly dysfunctional attitude toward time on the part of the public (Robinson & Godbey, 1997). That is, the strategy of increasing the yield on time by adding more goods is making us more rushed, failing to make us happier, producing mindless consumerism and, in the process, shorter attention spans and more stress. The effect of all this whirlwind of consumption with its emphasis on speed and efficiency cannot but have an impact on free-choice learning activities.

Time Spent Traveling

The amount of time left over, after working and completing other requisite tasks, poses a limiting factor in terms of the use of the educational infrastructure within a community, particularly the free-choice learning sector. Arguably, one of the reasons that learning about science and other topics has been largely assigned to public schools is that children's travel time is limited and is often only to school. Adults are also affected by proximity to free-choice learning sites. Thus access to automobiles, parking, and cost of parking become important variables in terms of what educational sites people will visit within a community.

There is a remarkable consistency in terms of the amount of time spent traveling and the duration and number of trips taken in daily life, and the number of minutes left over for exploring. Although there are a few exceptions, such as Californians, who spend 109 minutes per day traveling, most of the world spends about one hour in daily life going from point A to point B (Zahavi, 1981). Research by Hupkes (1988) found that on average, people make three to four trips per day, whether they are rich or poor; one of these trips is a major one lasting on average 40 to 50 minutes.

While people average three or four local trips per day, they also average three or four trips per year outside their territory. These longer trips may be ones where the potential for use of the infrastructure for free-choice science education is greatest, even though it is often other parts of a city that are prime tourist destinations. Vacations constitute a larger block of time, television is viewed much less, and many side visits from the original destination take place, often of an educational nature (Robinson & Godbey, 1997). However, in everyday life, for community-based institutions where voluntary learning takes place, such as museums, historic sites, planetariums, arboretums, and recreation and park departments, the competition is not each other but television.

It should be further noted that about 4 out of every 5 miles traveled in the United States are by automobile (Robinson & Godbey, 1997). Americans walk an average of only 1 kilometer a day, which is about 12 minutes worth of walking (Ausubel, Marchetti, & Meyer, 1998). These statistics show how limited the potential is, on average, for people to walk to educational resources within their community.

LEARNING AND THE MASS CUSTOMIZATION OF TIME

To facilitate free-choice learning, the most critical issue in temporal terms is the mass customization of time. This is already happening in regard to the production of goods and services to a remarkable extent. As a young woman in a California restaurant informed her friend, after telling the server exactly what she wanted for lunch, "Oh, I never order off the menu any more." Technology allows this customization to happen—only attitudes prevent it. The standardization of time use occurred during a period in which industrialization ruled. People were told what to do and when, and the routine of daily life was scheduled for them. As the customization of time continues, the free-choice learning community can benefit by helping individuals follow their learning interests at a time and place convenient and efficient for them.

The mass customization of time will make individuals more "agile." Many businesses and government agencies have already become more agile, able to respond to accelerating and discontinuous change, because the persons with whom they interact are no longer likely to be "customers." That is, people are less likely to follow "customs." As the education level of people in modern societies has increased dramatically, such individuals have become more likely to experiment, compose a life, and otherwise evolve in ways that "customers" did not in mass culture with mass production. Such changes signal the end of the mass scheduling of time.

The mass customization of time will mean profound change—schools open when they are needed, with different attendance configurations for each student. Why should public schools offer common time periods for students whose life situations are extremely different—some who may reside with one parent who works long hours during weekdays, some with two parents who both work full time but on different daily schedules, or some with two parents, one of whom works outside the home in the evenings?

Retirement, rather than being a period of life, will be a bank of hours on which individuals can draw as needed throughout their life. Whether a holiday exists will depend on who one is and where one comes from. Circadian rhythms will be considered for reasons of economic efficiency. Those who like to awaken early and retire early will be able to adjust their travel, work, and leisure to their individual sense of time.

The mass customization of time will allow people to use free time in different ways. No longer will nonwork hours be bits and pieces to be filled with TV, unless an individual wants them to be. Longer periods of time away from obligation will be possible. Attention spans may increase, and free time may be used more often for activities that involve skill. And free-choice learning opportunities may be just the thing to fill this ever increasing bank of time.

However, perhaps the most important issue facing free-choice learning in America is the growing schism between the "haves" and "have-nots." In the emerging have–have-not society, it is doubtful that a single strategy will increase free-choice learning participation for residents of a given community or area. The haves are likely to be more mobile, travel more quickly through time and space, feel more rushed, be more likely to do two things at once, request more information, and be less deterred by fees and charges. They may also place a higher value on services such as museums, publications, and libraries. The have-nots will possess more free time, be less mobile, have less money to spend on fees and charges, and quite possibly possess less intellectual curiosity.

They will also likely be less certain that free-choice institutions and resources are appropriate for them. Although the logistics of time, and for some money, are important variables for shaping the future of free-choice learning, also important will be the development and encouragement of intellectual curiosity and the marketing of free-choice learning as an important, appropriate, and accessible resource for all citizens.

REFERENCES

Ausubel, J., & Grubler, A. (1994). *Working less and living longer: Long-term trends in working time and time budgets* (Working Paper, pp. 94–99). Laxenburg, Austria: International Institute for Applied Systems Analysis.

Ausubel, J., Marchetti, C., & Meyer, P. (1998). Toward green mobility: The evolution of transport. *European Review, 6*(2), 137–156.

Drucker, P. (1989). *Post-capitalist society.* New York: Harper Business.

Godbey, G., & Graefe, A. (1993, April). Increase in Rushin' Americans. *American Demographics,* 26–28.

Gershuny, J. (1992). Are we running out of time? *Futures, 1,* 1–18.

Hill, M. (1985). Patterns of time. In F. J. Juster & F. P. Stafford (Eds.), *Time, goods and well being* (pp. 133–176). Ann Arbor: University of Michigan, Institute for Social Research.

Hupkes, G. (1988). The law of constant travel time and trip rates. *Futures, 1*(14), 38–46.

Levine, R. (1990, September–October). The pace of life. *American Scientist, 93*(3), 449–460.

Linder, S. (1969). *The harried leisure class.* New York: Columbia University Press.

Rifkin, J. (1987). *Time war: The primary conflict in human history.* New York: Henry Holt and Sons.

Robinson, J. (1991, November). Your money or your time? *American Demographics,* 22–24.

Robinson, J., & Godbey, G. (1997). *Time for life: The surprising ways Americans use their time.* University Park: Penn State Press.

Szalai, A., Converse, P. E., Feldheim, P., Scheuch, E. K., & Stone, P. J. (1972). *The use of time.* The Hague, The Netherlands: Mouton.

Zahavi, Y. (1981). *Travel Characteristics in Cities of Developing and Developed Countries* (World Bank Staff Working Paper no. 230). Washington, DC: World Bank.

PART II

Research Case Studies

CHAPTER 5

The Effects of Early Childhood TV-viewing on Learning

John C. Wright, Daniel R. Anderson, Aletha C. Huston, Patricia A. Collins, Kelly L. Schmitt, and Deborah L. Linebarger

During the twentieth century, the emergence of the mass media—and television in particular—profoundly advanced the public dissemination of educational information. As young and old consumed a smorgasbord of informational fare, the mass media became a rich source of readily available public information.

But just how much or how deeply does educational TV programming count as a true source of free-choice learning? Although 1995 statistics from the National Science Board estimate Americans consume more than 400 hours of TV news and 80 hours of TV science annually (Lewenstein, 1987), the learning curve from such a choice media diet is difficult to assess (Lewenstein, 1987; National Science Foundation, 1992).

Although systematic data on the effects of TV-watching on education were collected more than a decade ago (Lewenstein, 1987; National Science Foundation, 1992), the extensive availability of cable-TV that now exists had not yet appeared at the time the research was conducted. Now analysts predict that in the near future, 500-channel viewing systems—some involving interactive capabilities—will be available to the public. Yet studies on the educational impact of television viewing remain rare.

Perhaps what is most important is that very little attention has been paid to the question of just how much educational value children actually extract from their experiences with educational television-viewing.

THE ADVENT OF CHILDREN'S TELEVISION

Television-viewing today has become a dominant activity in the lives of American children as more of their time is spent watching television than in any other waking activity. In fact, television now occupies more of children's time over the course of a year than school does.

Criticizing TV-viewing

As often happens with the popular media, critics have been quick to point to risks involved in children's television-viewing, and as early as 32 years ago, teachers and communications researchers began to tabulate all of the charges against the medium at large. That chorus of opprobrium has continued more or less unabated ever since FCC Chairman Newton B. Minnow described television programming in America as a "vast wasteland." Advocates for family values and child welfare have been among the most vociferous, while larger organizations such as the National Parent Teacher Association and the American Medical Association have identified violence and aggressiveness on television as the most potentially harmful kinds of content for children.

Understanding TV-viewing

Defenders of television viewing point to the planned, positive, and informative qualities that have become the hallmark of public, commercial, and cable educational-TV programming for children today. Indeed, some children's educational programs recently have been the subject of credible research that shows television programs for children, which have certain key ingredients, have measurable, positive effects on children's verbal and language development, on social adjustment during transition from preschool to day school, and on formal records of academic achievement in school over time.

However, what is clearly missing from the existing literature are studies addressing the long-term effects of TV-viewing. As there had not been a long-term study conducted relating the long-term effects of early childhood TV-viewing to later academic achievement, we undertook such a study, based on a review of both the negative and positive literature on the effects of TV-viewing. That long-term research is now called the Recontact Study. The launching point for the study was prior research demonstrating both negative and positive effects on children from children's TV-viewing in general.

THE ROOTS OF CHILDREN'S EDUCATIONAL TV

In addition to commercial networks and cable-TV, the Public Broadcasting System (PBS), coordinated by a government-sponsored agency, is a major broadcaster of popular science programming in the United States. Funding is provided by a mix of federal and state dollars and individual viewership. In addition, individual programs or program series are underwritten by private philanthropic foundations or corporate donors.

Pioneers in Children's Programming

PBS developed the flagship children's program, *Mister Rogers' Neighborhood*, which was designed to entertain children while teaching a preacademic curriculum. Several philanthropic foundations along with federal agencies not affiliated with PBS funded the development of the Children's Television Workshop's production, *Sesame Street*. These programs provide serious competition to the growing mass of commercial entertainment programming that commands the bulk of the TV-viewing child audience.

The programs quickly became popular with children as well as parents and soon were joined by other educational programs such as *Electric Company*, which focuses on early reading skills, and *3-2-1 Contact*, which focuses on science.

At least two generations of American children now have experienced their earliest learning through innovative, educational TV programming.

Clearly, in addition to animated and action programming, children are attracted to programs that were and are designed to teach academic and social skills.

Educational Content. *Sesame Street* in particular became highly successful. Not only is the program still produced and broadcast on American television, but *Sesame Street* or its coproductions are broadcast in dozens of countries worldwide. The show made full use of professional writers and producers as well as sophisticated television production techniques.

Educators and child development specialists advised on the development of curriculum goals, and formative research was used to devise the most effective ways of achieving those goals. Experimental segments were written and produced and then tried out on children at a convenient preschool or day-care center. Data were collected on moment-to-moment visual attention to the TV screen, on children's interest, investment of mental effort to understand, judgments of the comprehensibility of the segment to themselves, and recall of key intended educational messages after viewing, both immediately after viewing and several days or weeks after viewing.

QUESTIONING THE EFFECTS OF TV-VIEWING

There have been a number of theories put forth in recent years in an attempt to explain the influence of educational TV programming on young children. Although there is no clear consensus among these theories, there is much concern about the effects of TV-viewing in general. Some of this concern has taken the form of skepticism about the medium of television as a whole. Some saw in children's TV-viewing an "addiction" to a medium that posed a threat to basic literacy, the development of intellectual and aesthetic independence, or imagination and creativity. Indeed, television as a whole was excoriated by authors who saw, in its great appeal to children and youth, signs of the decay of civilization.

Moderate scholars have reminded us that each new medium of mass communication has suffered the same sweeping charges in turn, including basic literacy itself. Radio, telecommunications, motion pictures, comic books, and paperback publishing all have had their turn being blamed for the imagined faults of the generations of youths who first made them popular. Video and computer games, virtual-reality play environments, and Internet involvement are now under fire. Although not all of these media are blameless, the more plentiful and varied their content has become, the less credible has seemed the monolithic derogation of the medium as a whole, and the more useful has become selective analysis of the programs, software, and content of what is presented rather than sweeping evaluations of the medium, itself.

LEADING THE WAY TO THE EARLY LEARNING MODEL

In the early 1990s, the faculty and students of the Center for Research on the Influences of Television on Children (CRITC) at the University of Kansas conducted a longitudinal study of about 300 children living in low-income, urban neighborhoods. There were two cohorts:

1. Children who were 2 years old at the start of the study and 5 when it ended.
2. Children who were 4 years old at the start and 7 at the finish.

Measuring School Readiness

Four annual assessments were conducted. Each assessment included a 2-hour visit to the child's home to complete the Home Observational Measure of the Environment (Caldwell & Bradley, 1984). Each assessment also included a family visit to CRITC's labs, where mothers were interviewed at length; children were given a battery of school readiness tests; and mother and child engaged in structured play and TV-viewing sessions that were videotaped and coded.

In the 1-year intervals between these assessments, children's time use was measured periodically by telephone. The caller asked the parent or care giver to account for every waking minute of the child's previous day. When television-viewing was mentioned either as a child's focal activity or as a background activity, the name of the program viewed was recorded. The 700 TV programs mentioned in the diaries were coded as Child-Informative, Child Entertainment (mostly cartoons), or General Audience programs by various genres.

The school readiness measures included the Woodcock-Johnson tests of letter–word recognition, reading, and applied problems (math skills). Also included were the Peabody Picture Vocabulary Test, the Bracken School Readiness Test, and a rating of school adjustment and readiness to learn completed by the teachers of those children in kindergarten or grade school. The school readiness measures were then tested as possible consequences of television-viewing diets 1 to 3 years earlier. Strong statistical controls were needed to level the playing field and rule out "third variables" that might have caused both educational TV-viewing earlier and good school readiness later. We controlled for the child's initial vocabulary score (a strong correlate of later IQ), family income–needs ratio, parents' years of education, and whether English was the primary language in the home.

Readiness Tests Results. The results showed that children who watched a lot of educational programming also spent more time with books (reading or being read to) and in other educational activities, and also watched fewer cartoons and other entertainment programming, as compared with those who watched little educational programming. By contrast, those who watched mostly entertainment programming early on spent less time with books and later spent more time with video games like *Nintendo* or *Sega*.

The results also demonstrated that children who watched a lot of educational programming had a small but significant advantage in school readiness test scores and in teachers' ratings of readiness to learn when they got to school (Wright & Huston, 1995). A corresponding disadvantage was found on the same measures for those who had watched mostly entertainment programming 1 to 3 years earlier. In the same sample of children the positive effects of educational TV-viewing were the rough equivalent of about five points on an IQ test for the first half hour of educational programming in an average weekday. The negative effect of commercial entertainment viewing was of about the same magnitude on the same children. The stronger effects were in the younger cohort, between the ages of 2 and 5. At that time, about 80 percent of the younger cohort's time spent in viewing educational children's programs was devoted to watching *Sesame Street*.

Support for the Early Learning Model

The school readiness study made us optimistic that the long-term effects of early viewing might result from a straightforward early learning model, one that predicts positive effects of educational programming on school achievement and negative effects of commercial entertainment programming. As a consequence of early experiences with educational television, a child would be led to enjoy learning from television, to view the medium as a means of learning, and to expect its content to be worth remembering. Such a model would not predict that early-learned content would be directly useful in later schooling but would predict that attitudes and learning skills resulting from that early experience reinforce learning and would continue to motivate and energize intellectual development in a school context.

OTHER MODELS FOR THE EFFECTS OF TV-VIEWING

Language Deficit Model

Much of the general concern over early TV-viewing is aimed at the medium of TV as a whole. For instance, writers such as Winn (1977) and Healy (1990) have claimed that the picture-dominated medium of TV is a threat to verbal thinking. In effect, they suggest that TV's visual appeal detracts from young viewers' verbal and linguistic processing, discouraging vocabulary development and interfering with learning to read. However, other research suggests that watching educational TV programs as early as age 2 is associated positively with vocabulary size and pre-reading skills 3 years later (Wright & Huston, 1995).

The Attention Span Model

It has also been suggested that educational TV programs such as *Sesame Street* are too fast paced with their magazinelike segments, which are difficult for children to process actively, thoughtfully, or carefully. These programs, it has been argued, shorten children's attention span and teach them to be passive viewers and ineffective processors of information by the time they get to school (Singer & Singer, 1983). Recent research, however, has documented evidence for children's active rather than passive processing of educational TV content (Anderson, 1998; Anderson & Collins, 1988; Huston & Wright, 1997, 1998).

The Entertainment Model

We consider next more specific criticism of educational programming made for children. The first is directed at the fact that successful educational children's programs are designed to be entertaining. That fact has been seen by some as sugar coating of the educational pill, and dire predictions have been made for the child who is led to expect all learning to be as entertaining as professionally produced television. Once again, *Sesame Street* is the prime target, but the attack puts the entire medium on the defensive.

Critics saw the charm and humor of the gentle characters in the *Sesame Street* program as a part of show business and thus fundamentally incompatible with serious educational aims. Children, or so the argument goes, will come to expect all education to be imbedded in having fun and will thus be unable to adjust to the serious demands of schooling. Ironically, within the industry the same kind of narrow thinking has led to the popular perception that any programming that makes a serious effort to teach the viewer will be inherently boring to large audiences, who are only in search of circuses. For many years, *Captain Kangaroo* was the only successful educational program for children on commercial television.

Despite these major blocks of opposition, programs like those in the PBS *Ready-to-Learn* series for young children have had remarkable success in following the *Sesame Street* model of blending deliberate instruction with charming whimsy for young audiences. Among the current and recent offerings that meet this criterion are the PBS preschool lineup: *Story Time, Puzzle Place, Magic School Bus, Shining Time Station, Lambchop's Play Along, Barney and Friends, Wishbone*, as well as *Sesame Street* and *Mr. Rogers*.

For school-age children, a similar burgeoning of deliberately entertaining educational programs has occurred in recent years. After *Electric Company* and *3-2-1 Contact* came *Square One*, a math program, *Ghost Writer*, a literacy-focused series, *Bill Nye, The Science Guy*, and a variety of prosocial programs, not all on PBS, such as *DeGrassi Junior High, My So-called Life, Hot Hero Sandwich, Pee Wee's Playhouse*, and *Freestyle*.

Although such programs often were praised and won numerous awards, they typically did not survive in the ratings-driven world of commercial broadcasting. Cable-TV has also brought positive programming for children on the Nickelodeon channel, where they are somewhat more protected from the demand for large audiences, and three of their programs meet the criterion of planned educational goals combined with an entertaining format: *Alegra's Window, Blue's Clues*, and *Gulla Gulla Island*. Thus it seems clear that deliberate educational programming can be appropriately combined with entertaining stories in a variety of formats.

The Parental Disengagement Model

Another implicit model found in the analyses of kinds of harm that early television-viewing can lead to is based on the idea that when young children view mostly an adult-selected diet of general-audience programs, that fact marks a family in which parental disengagement from concerns over the child's early learning environment may put the child at risk for some sort of general television addiction.

The Time Displacement Model

Another popular theory posits that TV-viewing takes up time that would otherwise be devoted to more educationally relevant pursuits. If children were not watching so much TV, they would be reading more and engaging in other activities that would later support educational achievement. The literature does not give any encouragement to this theory and in fact many studies suggest that TV-viewing merely displaces other media use such as radio, telephone, and other nonprint media.

The Violence–Aggression Model

A more promising model of effects of early viewing is contained in the work of Huesmann and Eron (1986) and Huesmann, Eron, and Yarmel (1987). Their longitudinal work having established the long-term effects of early violence viewing on aggressive behavior some 20 years later, they then hypothesized that a secondary effect of that early violence viewing would be poor academic achievement in school. They hypothesized that aggressive children and youths would do poorly in school because of a negative cycle of unfortunate outcomes: Their aggressive behavior would disrupt classroom learning, lead to disciplinary problems, make them unpopular with peers, and give them a negative attitude toward school. Consequently they would acquire a negative reputation among present and future teachers and a negative self-image, both of which would lead to low grades and test scores.

Lack of Supporting Research. Despite the fact that overall viewing of entertainment television is often found to be somewhat negatively correlated with school grades, most of the models of negative effects have received little research support. For one thing, the critics usually have not clearly distinguished between the impact of entertainment programs as compared with educational programs. Many of the entertainment programs are violent, and research indicates that the effects are quite different from those of educational programs (see Huston & Wright, 1997, for an extensive review). Moreover, evaluation studies have found that children usually acquire the intended lessons from educational TV programs, and children who watch educational television are better prepared for school (for reviews see Bryant, Alexander, & Brown, 1983; Huston & Wright, 1997, 1998; Wright & Huston, 1995).

There is also little evidence that television induces mental passivity in children or retards language development (for reviews see Anderson, 1998; Anderson & Collins, 1988; Huston & Wright, 1997, 1998). Nevertheless, there have been no long-term studies relating early television-viewing to later achievement. To fill that gap, we undertook the Recontact Study.

THE RECONTACT STUDY

In the early 1980s, we had intensively studied the TV-viewing of 655 preschool children in both Topeka, Kansas, and Springfield, Massachusetts (Anderson, Field, Collins, Lorch, & Nathan, 1985; Huston, Wright, Rice, Kerkman & St. Peters, 1990). We collected detailed TV-viewing diaries, maintained by parents, when the children were 5 years old. We also recorded time-lapse videotapes of the TV-viewing room in 99 of the children's homes during one of the 10-day periods in which the parents maintained the viewing diaries. After the Readiness Assessment study had given us indication that there may be a straightforward Early Learning Model, we realized that by recontacting and further studying these children, who were by then in high school, we could examine the long-term impact of early TV-viewing on high school achievement.

Sample

We located 92 percent of the children, now teenagers, from our original study. Of the 655 children in the original investigations, we were able to interview 570, or 87%. In addition to the interview, we obtained official transcripts of high school grades. The interview focused on a variety of issues, including media use, aggression, cigarette smoking and alcohol use, satisfaction with one's own body and appearance, and other possible correlates of early viewing. In this paper, however, we describe our results for high school grades and book reading only. Our other findings are described in a monograph in preparation.

From the original studies we had accumulated detailed TV-viewing diaries, maintained by parents, when the children were 5 years old. In the original study by Anderson et al. (1985), time-lapse videotapes of the TV-viewing room in 99 of the children's homes were recorded during one of the 10-day periods in which the parents maintained the viewing diaries. Analysis of those videotapes showed that the diaries were reasonably accurate in reporting the children's TV-viewing. We are therefore confident that we have detailed and accurate records of the children's early television-viewing. The Kansas and Massachusetts early viewing studies had used identical diary forms and instructions to recording parents.

Methods

Our recontact interview of the children, now teenagers, was conducted by telephone. We asked the children a variety of questions related to academic achievement in high school. When we compared the teens' reports of their own grades to the official high school records that we obtained for 86% of them, we found that the teens had slightly overstated their own achievement. We appropriately adjusted the reported grades for the remaining 14% of the children for whom we did not have official school records.

Our primary analyses focused on the relationship between TV-viewing patterns of 5-year-old children and their high school grades 10 years later. We were particularly interested in whether the best predictions of children's later academic achievement would come from the total time the children spent with TV at 5 years of age or from the details of their early TV-viewing *diet*.

Consider the analogy to nutrition. Although the total amount that a person eats has some value in predicting health status, it is far more useful to know *what* the person eats. Similarly, we felt that which programs a child watched on TV was probably more important in predicting academic achievement than how much TV the child watched.

In order to characterize viewing diet, we placed each TV program recorded in the viewing diaries in one of four categories. *Child Informative* programs were those programs such as *Sesame Street* whose primary purpose was educating or informing children. *Child Entertainment* programs had entertainment as their primary intent but did not include a substantial amount of violence or exciting action. *Action-Violent* programs were entertainment programs for children or adults that included a substantial amount of violence or action. *Other* programs included any TV programs experienced by the children that did not readily fit into any of the previous three categories.

Children's family experiences can influence both their early television-viewing and their academic achievement. To account for differences in families, our statistical analyses considered parents' education level and the birth order of the children. We took these particular variables into account because TV-viewing patterns differed according to whether the child had well-educated parents and whether the child had older siblings. For example, children of highly educated parents were more likely to watch *Sesame Street* and children who had older siblings were less likely to watch *Sesame Street*. We also included these variables as statistical controls because they were likely to be associated with high school grades.

Findings

Our findings indicated that young children's TV-viewing *diet* was a better predictor of academic achievement than the total number of TV-viewing hours. In other words, the kinds of programs that children watched were more important for academic achievement than how much TV they watched. The most significant category was Child Informative programs. The more Child Informative programs 5-year-old children watched, the *better* were their high school grades 10 years later. Not only were overall high school grades better, but grades were better in each of the core areas of English, mathematics, and science.

Gender and TV-viewing. Two interesting findings emerged from this study relative to gender and the impact of TV-viewing on academic achievement. First, the positive relationship between Child Informative TV-viewing at 5 years of age and high school grades was substantially larger for boys than for girls.

For instance, when we analyzed *Sesame Street* viewing separately, we found that teenaged boys who had watched 5 hours of *Sesame Street* each week when they were 5 years old demonstrated a 0.35 increase in their high school grade point average 10 years later. For teenaged girls the increase in high school grades was only 0.10 for 5 hours of *Sesame Street* viewed each week at 5 years of age. Second, teenaged girls who had watched Child Entertainment programs when they were 5 years old had lower high school grades than girls who had not watched such programs at 5 years of age.

Reading and TV-viewing. Finally, although there have been some claims that early TV-viewing reduces interest in reading, we found that children who watched more Child Informative TV programs when they were 5 years old spent more of their leisure time reading books as teens.

Preliminary Conclusions

It is clear that our results contradict the view that television necessarily harms educational achievement. If educational television for young children has long-term positive effects, the question arises as to how this happens. It is apparent that watching programs like *Sesame Street* cannot directly improve high school grades. After all, high school examinations do not test students on number and letter identification or the appropriateness of sharing one's toys. Rather, we believe that children who have watched educational TV programs enter school not only with better preacademic skills (Wright & Huston, 1995) but also with a more positive attitude toward learning. These skills and attitudes may provide children with a better early school experience. Early school success, in turn, fosters a greater enthusiasm about school and ultimately produces a cascading set of positive consequences.

Support for the Early Learning Model

Our initial hypothesis, called the *Early Learning Model*, is the most strongly and completely supported of the models we sought to evaluate. All the results were in the direction predicted by this model, though it did not predict the interaction with gender of child.

Implications for the Other Models

The Language Deficit Model was not supported by the findings. Educational programming had positive links to vocabulary size in early childhood and high school English grades 10 years later.

   The Attention Span Model also failed to receive support. The effects of early viewing of fast-paced *Sesame Street* and slow-paced *Mr. Rogers' Neighborhood* were both positive, counter to the predictions of that model.

   The Entertainment Model received some small support, but not over the 10 years of the recontact interval. Entertainment viewing was stable over the interval, but support comes from contemporaneous teenage data: The more they watched entertainment programming as teenagers, the poorer were the indicators of academic success.

   The Parental Disengagement Model received no support from our findings. Watching mostly adult programming as a preschooler had no effects on later achievement.

   The Time Displacement Model similarly failed to gain support from the recontact findings. Watching television as a preschooler was not related to time spent reading. Nor was total TV-viewing as a teenager related to teenage leisure-time reading.

   The Violence–Aggression Model received some encouragement from our results. Early viewing of cartoons and action-adventure shows, the most violent genres coded, was stable and continued in the teen years. Early violence viewing bore no relationship to aggressiveness reported by parents in the preschool study but was positively related to violent behavior in teenage self-reports for boys. Early violence viewing was directly and negatively related to high school grades, which in turn were negatively related to self-reported teenage aggressiveness. Aggressiveness was also negatively related to some other indicators of academic success in high school.

Summary and Discussion

In sum, the Early Learning Model was strongly supported; portions of the Entertainment Model and the Violence–Aggression Model received some support; and the rest of the models received no support from the results of the study.

The question remains as to why the positive effect of educational television is greater for boys. We do not yet have a good explanation for this unexpected finding. We do not think that boys liked and watched educational programs more than girls did in the early 1980s. Our research with programs such as *Sesame Street* indicated that attention and comprehension were the same for both sexes. Boys are generally less mature than girls, and American boys' early socialization experiences may be less supportive for later success in school. As a consequence, boys may benefit more from the kinds of instruction provided by programs such as *Sesame Street* and *Mister Roger's Neighborhood*. Girls who watch programs with a lot of action and violence may be more disruptive in school and thereby have early negative experiences in the school setting, while the same acting-out behavior in boys would be more general and, accordingly, more generally tolerated.

CONCLUSION

In sum, we speculate that early TV-viewing may have for each sex a kind of "against the stream" effect: In those who are already on a track that will be educationally successful, early viewing of entertainment television can cause increased risk, but early viewing of educational television cannot further enhance an advantage that is already present. For boys however, the situation is reversed. A general focus on less educationally relevant concerns means for them that early viewing of educational programming has a special opportunity to counter the stereotypical focus on action and adventure. Conversely an early TV diet full of action and adventure cannot further amplify the risk factors that are already present. We stress again that this interpretive reasoning is so far speculative and we intend to follow up with further investigation.

On the basis of the Recontact Study and other research, we believe that there is good news and bad news about the impact of early TV-viewing on children's learning in later years. There appears to be television content that is good for children, that helps them to develop language and social skills, and that has a positive impact on academic achievement in later years. However, it is also possible that there is TV content that is bad for children and may produce long-term negative outcomes. This study indicates that Marshall McLuhan's famous dictum may need to be reversed for children's early TV-viewing patterns: Perhaps it is the message and not the medium that is most important.

REFERENCES

Anderson, D. R. (1998). Educational television is not an oxymoron. *Annals of the American Academy of Political and Social Science, 557,* 24–38.

Anderson, D. R., & Collins, P. A. (1988). *The impact on children's education: Television's influence on cognitive development.* Washington, DC: U.S. Department of Education.

Anderson, D. R., Field, D. E., Collins, P. A., Lorch, E. P., & Nathan, J. (1985). Estimates of young children's time with television: A methodological comparison of parent reports with time-lapse video home observation. *Child Development, 56,* 1345–1357.

Bryant, J., Alexander, A., & Brown, D. (1983). Learning from educational television programs. In M. J. Howe (Ed.), *Learning from television: Psychological and educational research* (pp. 1–30). London: Academic Press.

Caldwell, B. M., & Bradley, R. H. (1984). *Home observation for the measurement of the environment.* Little Rock: University of Arkansas.

Healy, J. (1990). *Endangered minds: Why our children don't think.* New York: Simon and Schuster.

Huesman, L. R., & Eron, L. D. (1986). The development of aggression in American children as a consequence of television violence viewing. In L. R. Huesmann & L. D. Eron (Eds.), *Television and the aggressive child: A cross-national comparison* (pp. 45–80). Hillsdale, NJ: Lawrence Erlbaum.

Huesmann, L. R., Eron, L. D., & Yarmel, P. W. (1987). Intellectual functioning and aggression. *Journal of Personal and Social Psychology, 52,* 232–240.

Huston, A. C., & Wright, J. C. (1997). Mass media and children's development. In W. Damon, I. E. Sigel, & K. A. Renninger (Eds.), *Handbook of child psychology: Vol. 4. Psychology in practice* (pp. 999–1058). New York: Wiley.

Huston, A. C., & Wright, J. C. (1998). Television and the informational and educational needs of children. *Annals of the American Academy of Political and Social Science, 557,* 9–23.

Huston, A. C., Wright, J. C., Rice, M. L., Kerkman, D., & St. Peters, M. (1990). The development of television viewing patterns in early childhood: A longitudinal investigation. *Developmental Psychology, 26,* 409–420.

Lewenstein, B. V. (1987). *Public understanding of science in America, 1945–1965.* Unpublished doctoral dissertation, University of Pennsylvania, Philadelphia.

National Science Foundation, Informal Science Education Program. (1992). *Future Directions of Informal Science Education: Project Abstracts.* Arlington, VA: National Science Foundation.

Singer, J. L., & Singer, D. G. (1983). Implications of childhood television viewing for cognition, imagination, and emotion. In J. Bryant & D. R. Anderson (Eds.), *Children's understanding of TV: Research on Attention & Comprehension* (pp. 265–295). New York: Academic Press.

Winn, M. (1977). *The plug-in drug.* New York: Viking Press.

Wright, J. C., & Huston, A. C. (1995). *Effects of educational TV viewing of lower income preschoolers on academic skills, school readiness, and school adjustment one to three years later.* Lawrence: University of Kansas, Center for Research on the Influences of Television on Children.

CHAPTER 6

The Acquisition and Retention of Scientific Information by American Adults

Jon D. Miller

There is broad agreement that the impact of science and technology on our society and our daily lives grew substantially during the last half of the twentieth century. In a democratic political system, it is assumed that most citizens will be able to understand, discuss, and reach a conclusion about the major public policy issues of the times (Almond & Verba, 1963, 1980). In the early years of the American republic, most local decisions were made in annual town meetings and most often concerned the building and repair of roads and bridges, fencing laws for farm animals, and similar issues that would be readily understood by virtually all farmers, even if they could not read or write (Miller, 1983a, 1983b, 1992, 1995). It could even be argued that the major public policy controversies during the first half of the twentieth century concerned the issue of collective bargaining, and that most workers and business owners understood the issues on the basis of their own personal experiences.

Scientific and technical issues arising during the second half of the twentieth century, however, often involve ideas and constructs such as radiation, DNA, molecules, viruses, global warming, and ozone depletion that require levels of understanding beyond everyday experience. Despite Popkin's (1994) generally persuasive argument about the ability of citizens to cope with issue complexity by using extrapolations from everyday experience, the evidence suggests that many are unable to understand and follow issues that involve science and technology. I (Miller 1982, 1983a, 1983b, 1995) and others (Almond, 1950; Rosenau, 1974) have suggested that modern political life is sufficiently complex that an increasing level of political and issue specialization is required, generally resulting in smaller attentive publics that follow specific sets or clusters of issues.

Some citizens may focus their political attention on economic or agricultural issues, whereas others may focus on foreign policy or environmental issues. Given the scope and complexity of most issue areas, it is a rare citizen who can follow more than three or four major areas at one time. But in a series of national and cross-national studies, I and others found that substantial portions of the public who pay attention to scientific and technical issues have relatively inadequate levels of understanding of the major scientific constructs involved in those issues (Miller, Pardo, & Niwa, 1997).

THE SCIENCE EDUCATION POLICY ISSUE

There is broad agreement that the pace of scientific and technological change will continue to increase in the decades ahead and that a higher level of scientific understanding—or literacy—will be required for effective participation in the economy and in our democratic political system. The issue is to identify the approach or approaches that will produce this result.

Two major responses have addressed this situation. Some observers have stressed the importance of improving science education in the precollegiate years (Rutherford & Ahlgren, 1989; Stevenson & Stigler, 1992), and the recent emergence of national standards in mathematics and science reflects a pervasive sense that too many high school graduates have insufficient competence in these subjects to meet their responsibilities as citizens or to participate in an increasingly technology-driven global economy (National Council of Teachers of Mathematics, 1989; National Research Council, 1989, 1996; Schmidt, McKnight, & Raizen, 1997). Other observers have argued that the growing array of free-choice science resources and programs in the United States can provide a short-term bridge to compensate for inadequate formal schooling and perhaps a longer-term source of scientific and technical understanding for citizens and consumers (Crane, Nicholson, Chen, & Bitgood, 1994).

This chapter argues that neither approach is sufficient by itself, but that effective formal schooling is an essential prerequisite for the utilization of free-choice science learning by adults. Building on a national study of American understanding of and attitudes toward science and technology, conducted in 1997 for use in preparing the National Science Board's *Science and Engineering Indicators* report (1998), this analysis seeks to develop empirical measures of adult understanding and models of information acquisition and retention that may inform the judgments of science policy leaders.

TWO MEASURES OF THE UNDERSTANDING OF SCIENTIFIC CONSTRUCTS

In several previous analyses, I (Miller 1983b, 1987, 1995, 1998) constructed a general measure of civic scientific literacy for the United States and for other countries and developed models to predict the relative influence of formal schooling and other factors on the level of public understanding of science. This measure of civic scientific literacy requires an understanding of (a) a vocabulary of scientific constructs and (b) the nature of scientific inquiry (Miller, 1998). In this measure of civic scientific literacy, the vocabulary measure includes a wide array of constructs, ranging from molecules to plate tectonics to the solar system. Although this measure of civic scientific literacy has been broadly accepted, it is reasonable to ask whether some individuals might have a higher level of understanding of clusters of these scientific constructs. And if some individuals have a stronger interest than others in some aspects of science, it is reasonable to hypothesize that they might have differential levels of understanding and, further, that they might obtain current information on these different domains from different sources.

Separate Scales

To explore the questions of whether there are marked differences in the public understanding of science by substantive area and whether differences in interest may involve differential information-acquisition strategies, separate scales were developed to measure the level of understanding of biomedical constructs and of space science constructs. Fortunately, the 1997 study included a sufficiently broad and diverse set of knowledge items that it was possible to construct two separate scales, with only one overlapping item.

Item Response Theory. Using the standard test construction technique called Item Response Theory (IRT), each set of questions was scaled in terms of item difficulty and efficiency (Bock & Zimowski, 1997; Zimowski, Muraki, Mislevy, & Bock, 1996). The IRT technique is used in constructing the Graduate Record Examination and other high-stakes tests in the United States and in other nations. In broad terms, the process is similar to that in scoring of an Olympic diving competition. In diving, each dive has a difficulty score and each performance of that dive is given a quality rating, which is multiplied by the difficulty score. In IRT testing, each item has a difficulty coefficient and an efficiency coefficient, and the difficulty coefficient is weighted by the efficiency coefficient. In IRT testing, a guessing parameter can also be entered into the scoring, and a guessing coefficient was used in both of these scales because of the relatively small number of items and the extensive use of true–false type questions.

The concept underlying the IRT approach is that the responses to any knowledge item will form an item response curve. Assuming that all respondents taking any given test can be arrayed in an order reflecting their knowledge of the domain being tested, the *x*-axis of the item response curve is an estimate of knowledge or ability. The *y*-axis is simply the probability that a respondent will answer the question correctly, given his or her level of knowledge or ability.

Biomedical Construct Understanding Scale. Substantively, the Biomedical Construct Understanding Scale includes eight items, ranging from an open-ended definition of DNA to recognition that the oxygen we breathe comes from plants (see Table 6.1). The items vary over a wide range of difficulty. Only 11 percent of American adults were able to provide an acceptable open-ended definition of a molecule, but 84 percent recognized plants as a source of oxygen.

The items are listed in Table 6.1 in the order of their IRT difficulty coefficient to provide the reader with some sense of the relative importance of each item. Ideally, every item would have an efficiency coefficient of 1.0 or higher, but when scales are constructed from limited sets of previously asked items, it is often necessary to include less efficient items to provide adequate size and scope for the test items. This simple test is a good indicator of adult understanding of basic biomedical constructs and is useful for our purposes.

Space Sciences Construct Understanding Scale. The Space Sciences Construct Understanding Scale includes 10 items, ranging from an open-ended definition of radiation to recognition that the center of the Earth is very hot (see Table 6.2). The items also covered a wide range of difficulty. Only 11 percent of American adults could provide a correct open-ended definition of radiation, but 82 percent knew that the core of Earth is very hot. The items are listed in Table 6.2 in the order of their IRT difficulty coefficient. In contrast to the Biomedical Construct Understanding Scale, all but three of these items have an efficiency coefficient of 1.0 or higher, indicating that this scale contains less measurement noise than the biomedical scale. For the purpose of rating the level of public understanding of selected space science concepts, this is a useful scale.

The results of IRT scaling are usually expressed as standardized scores, with a mean of zero and a standard deviation of 1.0. In practice, this means that half of the respondents have a negative score, which is often confusing when applied to knowledge scales. To provide a more comprehensible metric, the

Table 6.1. Items Included in the Biomedical Construct Understanding Scale, 1997

		Item Response Theory scaling	
	Percent Correct	*Difficulty threshold*	*Slope or efficiency*
Agreement that "human beings, as we know them today, developed from earlier species of animals"	43.7	1.51	.92
Open-ended definition of a molecule	11.3	1.33	1.73
Open-ended definition of DNA	21.7	.92	1.39
Open-ended explanation of an experiment	38.6	.65	1.16
Disagreement that "antibiotics kill viruses as well as bacteria"	43.0	.58	.70
A four-part question on the meaning of one in four applied to an inherited trait	53.4	-.29	.62
Agreement that "it is the father's gene which decides whether the baby will be a boy or a girl"	62.1	-.80	.47
Agreement that "the oxygen we breathe comes from plants"	84.2	-2.78	.39

Mean scale score = 50.0; standard error = .45; median score = 48.2.

mean of each scale was set to 50, with a standard deviation of 20. The resulting scores range essentially from zero to 100.

FORMAL SCHOOLING AND SCIENCE EDUCATION

Using these two scales of construct understanding, it is reasonable to begin by examining the relationship between each individual's level of understanding and his or her formal schooling. Although a number of critics have questioned the

Table 6.2. Items Included in the Space Sciences Construct Understanding
Scale, 1997

	Percent correct	Item Response Theory scaling	
		Difficulty threshold	Slope or efficiency
Open-ended definition of a molecule	11.3	1.54	1.50
Open-ended definition of radiation	10.7	1.47	2.32
Recognition that astrology is "not at all scientific"	59.1	.93	1.14
Agreement that "the universe began with a huge explosion"	31.7	.71	.35
Agreement that "electrons are smaller than atoms"	43.5	.69	1.19
Disagreement that "lasers work by focusing sound waves"	38.8	.57	1.56
Recognition through a pair of questions that the Earth goes around the Sun once each year	48.2	.40	1.23
Recognition that light travels faster than sound	74.9	-.10	1.39
Agreement that "the center of the earth is very hot"	81.6	-.78	.85
Agreement that "the continents on which we live have been moving their location for millions of years and will continue to move in the future"	77.9	-1.48	.61

Mean scale score = 50.0; standard error = .45; median score = 48.3.

efficacy of formal schooling, most individuals still acquire a substantial part of their store of knowledge from their formal educational experiences. In this analysis, the relative influence of formal education and free-choice learning are examined empirically.

The analysis employs two measures of formal education. First, a five-category measure of the highest level of formal education completed is used (see Table 6.3). Approximately 20 percent of American adults have a baccalaureate degree. Second, a three-category measure of the number of college-level science courses is used, categorizing respondents as having taken no college-level science courses, one to three such courses (or essentially 1 year), and four or more. For the levels of knowledge measured, any effort to differentiate between high numbers of college-level science courses would not be productive.

Table 6.3. Mean Construct Vocabulary Scores by Level of Education and Number of College-level Science Courses, 1997

	Number of college-level science courses		
	None	*1-3 courses*	*4 or more courses*
Mean score on the Biomedical Construct Understanding Scale			
Less than high school	35.1	—	—
High school graduate	46.1	55.8	69.1
Associate degree	46.0	53.1	64.6
Baccalaureate	52.3	61.2	70.8
Graduate or professional degree	—	65.3	70.7
Mean score on the Space Sciences Construct Understanding Scale			
Less than high school	38.8	—	—
High school graduate	45.0	54.7	71.9
Associate degree	44.2	52.0	61.6
Baccalaureate	51.7	57.6	69.5
Graduate or professional degree	—	61.6	72.5
Number of respondents			
Less than high school	420	0	0
High school graduate	761	193	69
Associate degree	60	57	49
Baccalaureate	38	88	131
Graduate or professional degree	13	38	85

— Indicates means are not reported for cells with fewer than 20 respondents.

Understanding and Higher Education Levels

To examine the influence of formal education and science-course-taking on the understanding of biomedical and space science constructs, the mean score for each index was computed for each level of college science course taken within levels of formal education (see Table 6.3). The results show that the mean scores on both scales tend to increase for each level of educational attainment, and that within each level of educational attainment, the mean score increased by the number of college-level science courses completed. This result shows that (a) education and college-level science courses are positively associated with the level of understanding of biomedical and space science constructs and (b) they tend to act jointly, that is, at the same time and in the same general direction. We cannot tell the relative influence of each factor from this kind of descriptive table. In order to estimate the relative influence of formal educational experiences and free-choice learning experiences, we need to construct multivariate models.

THE USE OF FREE-CHOICE SCIENCE EDUCATION RESOURCES

In addition to examining the role of formal schooling, assessing the role and impact of free-choice science education resources on adult understanding of basic constructs in the biomedical and space sciences is important. The last half of the twentieth century has witnessed a substantial growth in the availability and utilization of a wide array of free-choice science education resources, including expanded newspaper coverage of science and technology; new science and health magazines; a variety of science television shows; increased numbers of science museums, natural history museums, and specialized science or technology centers; the growth of science programming on radio; and the emergence of the Web and other electronic media.

By 1997, statistics showed that nearly 50 percent of American adults read a daily newspaper, 15 percent read one or more science magazines each month, and 53 percent watched one or more science television show each month. Approximately 60 percent of adults visited a science or natural history museum at least once a year, and 31 percent reported that they had purchased one or more science book during the preceding year (National Science Board, 1998).

An examination of the patterns of use for these free-choice science learning resources indicates a high degree of overlap. Some individuals are relatively high science-information consumers, actively seeking timely information from newspapers, magazines, books, television shows, museums, and on-line resources. On the other hand, many adults do not use any of these resources. If there is an information-acquisition behavior underlying these separate kinds of utilization reports, all of the major forms of free-choice science learning should load on a common dimension in a factor analysis.

Testing for Free-Choice Learning Resource Usage

To test this proposition, the free-choice science learning data from the 1997 *Science and Engineering Indicators* study were examined with a confirmatory factor analysis (see Table 6.4). The results demonstrated that all of these separate activities load on a single factor, meaning that a summary measure of free-choice science-learning resource utilization can be constructed that will be an accurate reflection of an underlying science-information acquisition behavior.

Table 6.4. Factor Pattern for Free-Choice Science Education Resources, 1997

Measures of annual use	Free-choice science education factor	Proportion of variance explained
Number of public library visits	.65	.42
Number of science museum visits	.62	.39
Number of science television shows watched	.61	.37
Number of hours of home computer use	.57	.32
Number of news magazines read	.55	.30
Number of science magazines read	.53	.28
Number of newspapers read	.50	.25

$\chi^2 = 15.5/8$ degrees of freedom; Root Mean Square Error of Approximation (RMSEA) = .02; upper limit of the 90 percent confidence interval = .038.

In practice, the factor scores were converted into a zero-to-100 index, with zero reflecting no use of any free-choice learning resource and 100 indicating high-level use of virtually every kind of free-choice learning resource.

The mean score on this Index of Free-Choice Science Education Resource Use was 33 for all adults aged 18 and over (see Table 6.5). Americans with higher levels of formal education and with more college-level science courses had higher scores on the index than did less well-educated citizens. Adults with children under the age of 18 living in their households reported a higher level of free-choice science-education resource use than did adults without minor children. Individuals employed in science-related jobs were also more likely to use free-choice science education resources than were adults employed in other sectors or outside the work force. And men recorded slightly higher free-choice science-education resource use than did women.

Implications for Free-Choice Science Education. Although these simple tabulations are interesting, they do not provide enough information about the relative influence of age, gender, education, child in the home, employment in a science-related job, or other variables on the use of free-choice science education resources. It is possible, however, to construct a multivariate analysis of free-choice science-education resource use that will provide estimates of the simultaneous influence of each of several variables. Often referred to as structural equation modeling, this technique combines a standardized path analysis with a measurement model that allows the specification of the reliability or accuracy of each of the variables in the model. The general form of the model is shown in Figure 6.1.

Table 6.5. Mean Scores on the Free-Choice Science Education Use Index,
1997

	Mean score	Number of respondents
All adults aged 18 and over	33	2,000
Age 18–24	36	289
Age 25–34	34	452
Age 35–44	37	411
Age 45–54	35	314
Age 55–64	32	187
Age 65 and over	22	333
Women	31	1,070
Men	34	930
Less than high school	22	420
High school graduate	32	1,023
Associate degree	40	165
Baccalaureate	44	257
Graduate or professional degree	47	135
No college-level science courses	28	1,292
1–3 college-level science courses	39	375
4 or more college-level science courses	45	333
Have children under age 18 at home	36	707
Do not have children under age 18 at home	31	1,293
Work in science-related job	38	190
Do not work in science-related job	32	1,810

Structural Equation Models

Although a full discussion of structural equation models is beyond the scope of
this chapter, it may be useful to discuss briefly the general form of the analysis.
In the model included in Figure 6.1, it is assumed that the variables on the left
side of the model are the oldest or the most basic, logically or chronologically.
In this case, everyone has a birth date and a gender from birth, and these variables do not change. In general, variables to the right are thought to be influenced, or caused, by variables to the left. In this model, it is reasonable to expect
that older adults had fewer opportunities for higher education than did younger
respondents, or that men were more likely than women to attain higher levels
of education in earlier generations. Influence is indicated by an arrow, usually
called a path.

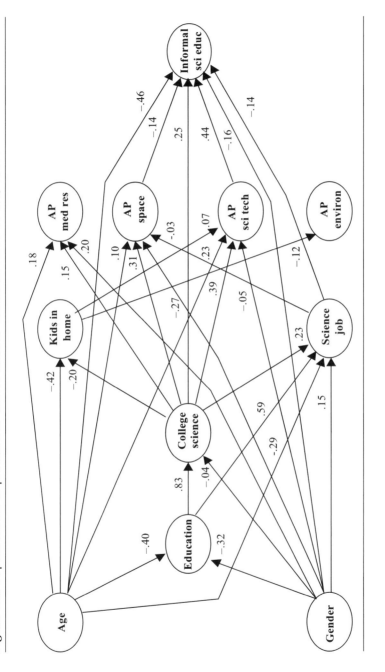

Figure 6.1. A path model to predict free-choice science-education resource use, 1997.

The strength of a relationship, or path, is shown in Figure 6.1 by a coefficient placed over or near the path. This path coefficient is a standardized beta coefficient and reflects the relative strength of the relationship, holding constant all of the other variables parallel with or to the left of the predictor variable (the source of the path).

In Figure 6.1, for example, the path from respondent education to the number of college science courses has a path coefficient of .83. This is a strong relationship and means that each increment (one standard deviation) in the level of educational attainment will produce an increase of .83 units (standard deviations) in the number of college-level science courses taken, holding constant differences in age and gender. The total influence, or impact, of any variable in the model can be computed by multiplying the path coefficients in all possible paths from any given variable to the outcome, or predicted, variable. Although the individual path coefficients are interesting, it is the total effect of each variable that is of primary analytic interest.

Independent Variables

To understand the structure of factors that account for each individual's level of free-choice science education resource use, a basic model was constructed that includes demographic, educational, occupational, family, and issue-attentiveness variables. Before turning to a discussion of the total effect of each of these variables on free-choice science-education resources use, it may be helpful to discuss briefly each of the independent, or predictor, variables included in the model.

Education. As noted above, education is expected to provide a solid foundation of science and mathematics understanding that will continue to serve individuals throughout their adult years. For this analysis, the highest level of education completed was entered as one variable, and a separate variable was constructed to reflect the number of college-level science courses taken. These two variables allow an examination of the relative role of formal education in the use of free-choice science education resources during adulthood.

Number of Dependent Children. The number of children under the age of 18 living in the household was included in the model to test the widely held idea that adult use of museums, science television, and other free-choice science education resources is influenced, at least in part, by the presence of minor children in the home.

Occupational Interest. Employment in a science-related job is also included in the model to test the proposition that some portion of adult interest in science and technology and adult use of free-choice science-education resources reflects occupational interests.

Issue Attentiveness. In addition, four separate measures of issue attentiveness are included in the model. To be classified as attentive to an issue, an individual must report a high level of interest in the issue and classify him or herself as very well informed about it. Prior research has shown that individuals who are attentive to an issue are more likely to follow it in the news and attempt to stay informed about relevant new developments. In this analysis, separate measures of attentiveness to new medical discoveries, space exploration, environmental issues, and science and technology policy are included in the model. The inclusion of these variables allows an examination of the role of issue attentiveness as a filter or catalyst for adult utilization of free-choice science-education resources.

Effects of Variables. Looking at the total effects of each of these variables, the analysis found that age, gender, education, and attentiveness to science and technology policy were the major factors influencing the level of adult use of free-choice science-education resources (see Figure 6.2). Holding constant other factors, younger Americans are substantially more likely to use free-choice science-education resources than are older adults.

Holding age, education, and other factors constant, men were more likely than women to use free-choice science-education resources. (The negative value was due to the fact that females were given a value of zero.)

The total effect of the level of educational attainment was .21, and the total effect of the number of college-level science courses taken was .35 (see Figure 6.2). The combination of these two effects indicates that education is strongly and positively associated with the use of free-choice science-education resources, and better educated Americans with some college-level science courses are significantly more likely than other Americans to use these resources. This strong positive relationship between education and free-choice science-education resource use suggests that free-choice experiences are being used to update and enrich an individual's understanding of science. This result contradicts the idea that free-choice science education replaces deficient or nonexistent formal schooling in science and mathematics.

There is a very small, but statistically significant, positive effect associated with having children under the age of 18 living at home. The total effect of .03 means only that parents with minor children in the household are very slightly more likely to use free-choice science-education resources.

Individuals working in a science-related job were less likely than others to use free-choice science-education resources, suggesting that workers in such jobs may already know more about science and are less likely to find a science

Figure 6.2. Total effects of selected variables on free-choice science-education resource use.

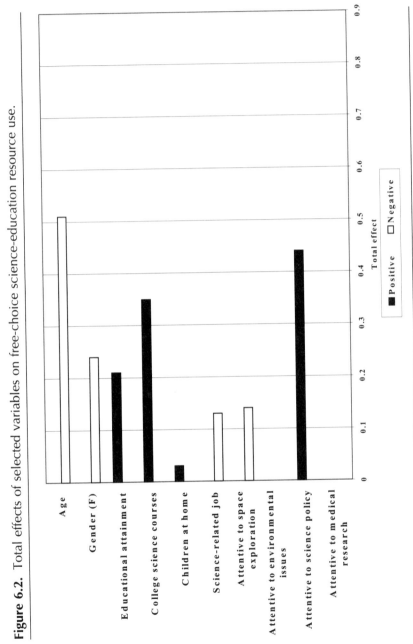

magazine, television show, or radio show interesting than are persons employed in other sectors or out of the work force.

Citizens who are attentive to science and technology policy issues were significantly more likely to use free-choice science-education resources than were individuals not concerned about those issues, with a total effect of .44 (see Figure 6.2). This result suggests that policy interest—rather than personal educational gain—is one of the factors associated with the level of free-choice science-education resource use.

Citizens who are attentive to space exploration, however, are relatively less likely than others to use free-choice science-education resources, holding constant the other variables in the model, with a total effect of −.14. It is important to recognize that this relationship is a relative assessment. Given the structure of the model, the effect of attentiveness to space exploration is measured with attentiveness to science and technology policy, to environmental issues, to medical research, and all of the background and educational variables held constant.

Neither attentiveness to medical research nor attentiveness to environmental issues was significantly related to the level of free-choice science-education resource use. Because attentiveness to medical research is strongly associated with age and personal health concerns, the absence of a relationship is not surprising. The absence of a relationship between attentiveness to environmental issues and free-choice science-education resource use is surprising. It appears that virtually all of the information-acquisition patterns associated with individuals concerned about environmental issues were fully accounted for by their age, education, and other variables, leaving no residual effect from attentiveness to environmental issues per se.

The combination of all of the variables in this model account for, or explain, 49 percent of the total variance in the use of free-choice science-education resources by American adults. All of the other fit parameters indicate that this model fits the data closely, significantly reducing the possibility that the relationships noted above result from chance correlations.

THE MARGINAL INFLUENCE OF FREE-CHOICE SCIENCE RESOURCE USE

By extending the previous model, it is possible to examine the marginal influence of free-choice science resource use on the level of understanding of biomedical and space science constructs. The addition of the two construct-understanding measures discussed above to the right side of the model allows us to estimate the relative effects of age, gender, education, other variables, and use of free-choice science-education resources on the level of understanding of each of these areas of knowledge (see Figures 6.3 and 6.4).

Figure 6.3. A path model to predict biomedical construct understanding, 1997.

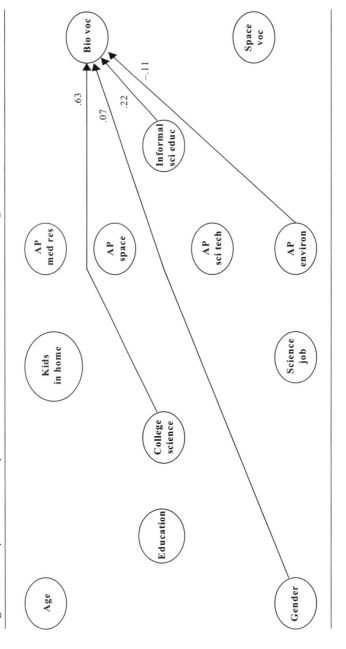

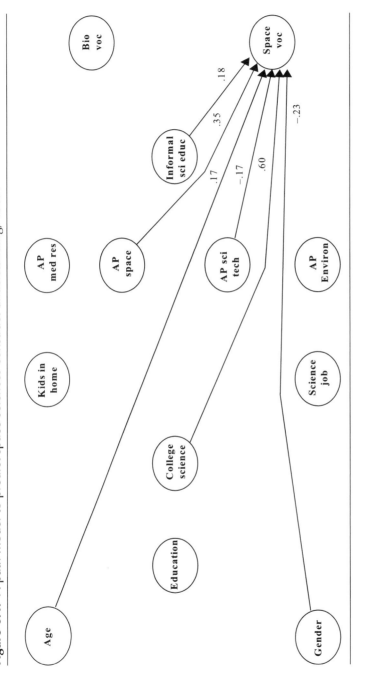

Figure 6.4. A path model to predict space sciences construct understanding, 1997.

Indications

The results indicate that education is the primary predictor of the understanding of biomedical and space science constructs (see Table 6.6). The total effect of educational attainment on biomedical construct understanding is .61 and that of college science courses .73. Similarly, the total effect of educational attainment on space science construct understanding is .59 and that of college science courses .70.

Comparatively, the total effect of free-choice science-education resource use on biomedical construct understanding is .23 and on space science construct understanding .18. Thus the use of free-choice science-education resources has a significant influence on the level of biomedical and space science construct understanding, but the magnitude of its impact is significantly lower than that of formal education.

Because several previous analyses of the impact of components of free-choice science education—science museums, science television, and science magazines—found little or no effect on the level of civic scientific literacy, this result suggests the importance of examining a broader range of free-choice science resources, recognizing that free-choice science education is not a curriculum but a smorgasbord of resources from which individuals may pick and choose according to their interests and needs.

Table 6.6. Total Effects of Selected Variables on Biomedical and Space Science Constructs

Independent variables	*Understanding of biomedical science constructs*	*Understanding of space science constructs*
Age	-0.41	-0.32
Gender (F)	-0.17	-0.56
Educational attainment	0.61	0.59
College science courses	0.73	0.70
Children at home	0.03	0.09
Science-related job	-0.04	-0.03
Attentive to space exploration	-0.04	0.32
Attentive to environmental issues	-0.12	0.00
Attentive to science policy	0.10	0.00
Attentive to medical research	0.00	0.00
Use of informal science-education resources	0.23	0.18

The model also demonstrates how demographic differences in interest can produce significant differences in retained knowledge about selected areas. Although younger respondents displayed a higher level of understanding of both biomedical and space science constructs, the age skew was strongest for biomedical construct understanding. This pattern appears to reflect the strong genetic biology component of the Biomedical Construct Understanding Scale and the fact that Sputnik occurred 40 years ago. Men displayed a significantly higher score than did women on space science construct understanding and a slightly higher score on biomedical construct understanding.

The model is also informative about the role of policy interests in the use of free-choice science-education resources. Individuals attentive to space exploration displayed a significantly higher level of space science construct understanding than did those inattentive to these issues, but these same individuals displayed a slightly below average level of understanding of biomedical constructs, illustrating a pattern of information specialization. Attentiveness to medical research was not related to the level of understanding of either biomedical or space science constructs. Attentiveness to environmental issues was negatively related to the level of biomedical construct understanding and unrelated to the level of space science construct understanding. Individuals attentive to science and technology policy broadly scored slightly higher than average on biomedical construct understanding, but attentiveness to science and technology policy issues was unrelated to the level of space science construct understanding.

These patterns indicate that policy interest in selected areas, such as space exploration, can result in differentiated levels of both free-choice science-education resource use and construct understanding, but that policy interest does not automatically produce this kind of differentiation.

The model suggests that the presence of minor children in a household is associated with slightly higher levels of construct understanding, but the magnitude of the impact is very small. The presence of minor children in the home was slightly more closely associated with space science construct understanding than with biomedical construct understanding.

Finally, the model indicates that employment in a science-related job does not necessarily mean that the individuals so employed have a substantially higher level of construct understanding than do others. It is important to recognize that the construct knowledge scales were designed to measure understanding of basic concepts with a lesser emphasis on applied knowledge. A person employed as a nurse or a computer programmer, for example, may have a large store of applied technical knowledge relevant to his or her daily job but a lesser understanding of basic constructs like DNA or molecules. Although these workers may not need an understanding of these basic constructs for their day-to-day work, they may need such understanding to read and absorb a newspaper report on gene therapy for Parkinson's disease or the effect of carbon fuel use on global warming.

The combination of these variables accounted for 55 percent of the total variance in biomedical construct understanding and 73 percent of that in space science construct understanding. The model met all of the criteria for goodness of fit.

CONCLUSION

The preceding analysis suggests four conclusions with important implications for educational policy in the United States.

First, to examine levels of scientific construct understanding in specific, specialized areas is useful. Although measuring public understanding of science broadly is also useful for many purposes, individual interests and needs tend to be somewhat narrower. This analysis of the level of public understanding of both biomedical and space science constructs provides an interesting contrast in retained knowledge and in information acquisition but emphasizes the substantial contribution of formal schooling.

Second, this analysis demonstrates that free-choice science-education resource use—free-choice learning—is positively related to the level of construct understanding among adults, holding constant differences in age, gender, formal schooling, family, and issue interest. Although longitudinal studies of information acquisition and retention among adults are critical to understanding the dynamics of the process, this finding of a significant level of free-choice science-education influence within the context of an extensive model reflecting demographic differences, educational differences, and occupational differences is persuasive evidence of the net contribution of free-choice learning to public understanding of science.

Third, constructing a measure of free-choice science-education resource use indicates the value and necessity of viewing free-choice learning broadly rather than examining its components singly. The literature illustrates that single free-choice science education activities—museum visits, science television viewing, science magazine reading—have few significant effects. But recognizing that individuals select from these resources as if they were a smorgasbord and tailor their menus to their own interests and needs provides an important analytic and programmatic insight into free-choice science education.

Fourth, this analysis reaffirms the central role of formal education and schooling in developing adult understanding of scientific constructs. By delineating the relative roles of educational attainment and college-level science courses, it is possible to understand better the educational contribution to adult acquisition and retention of basic scientific constructs. The full model identifies the maintenance and enrichment role of free-choice science education, suggesting more of a partnership than a competition.

REFERENCES

Almond, G. A. (1950). *The American people and foreign policy.* New York: Harcourt, Brace.

Almond, G. A., & Verba, S. (1963). *The civic culture.* Princeton, NJ: Princeton University Press.

Almond, G. A., & Verba, S. (Eds). (1980). *The civic culture revisited.* Boston: Little Brown.

Bock, R. D., & Zimowski, M. F. (1997). Multiple-group IRT. In W. J. van der Linden & R. K. Hambleton (Eds.), *Handbook of modern Item Response Theory* (pp. 433–448). New York: Springer-Verlag.

Crane, V., Nicholson, H., Chen, M., & Bitgood, S. (1994). *Informal science learning.* Dedham, MA: Research Communications Ltd.

Miller, J. D. (1982). A conceptual framework for understanding public attitudes toward conservation and energy issues. In D. Conn (Ed.), *Energy and material resources.* Boulder, CO: Westview Press.

Miller, J. D. (1983a). *The American people and science policy: The role of public attitudes in the policy process.* New York: Pergamon Press.

Miller, J. D. (1983b). Scientific literacy: A conceptual and empirical review. *Daedalus, 112*(2), 29–48.

Miller, J. D. (1987). Scientific literacy in the United States. In D. Evered & M. O'Connor (Eds.), *Communicating science to the public* (pp. 19–40). London: Wiley.

Miller, J. D. (1992). From town meeting to nuclear power: The changing nature of citizenship and democracy in the United States. In A. E. D. Howard (Ed.), *The United States constitution: Roots, rights, and responsibilities.* Washington, DC: Smithsonian Institution Press.

Miller, J. D. (1995). Scientific literacy for effective citizenship. In R. E. Yager (Ed.), *Science/technology/society as reform in science education* (pp. 185–204). Albany: State University of New York Press.

Miller, J. D. (1998). The measurement of civic scientific literacy. *Public Understanding of Science, 7,* 1–21.

Miller, J. D., Pardo, R., & Niwa, F. (1997). *Public perceptions of science and technology: A comparative study of the European union, the United States, Japan, and Canada.* Madrid, Spain: BBV Foundation.

National Council of Teachers of Mathematics. (1989). *Curriculum and evaluation standards for school mathematics.* Reston, VA: Author.

National Research Council. (1989). *Everyone counts: A report to the nation on the future of mathematics education.* Washington, DC: National Academy Press.

National Research Council. (1996). *The national science education standards.* Washington, DC: National Academy Press.

National Science Board. (1998). *Science and engineering indicators: 1998.* Washington, DC: U.S. Government Printing Office.

Popkin, S. L. (1994). *The reasoning voter.* Chicago: University of Chicago Press.

Rosenau, J. A. (1974). *Citizenship Between Elections.* New York: Free Press.

Rutherford, F. J., & Ahlgren, A. (1989). *Science for all Americans.* Washington, DC: American Association for the Advancement of Science.

Schmidt, W. H., McKnight, C. C., & Raizen, S. A. (1997). *A splintered vision: An investigation of U.S. science and mathematics education.* Norwel, MA: Kluwer Academic.

Stevenson, H. W., & Stigler, J. W. (1992). *The learning gap: Why our schools are failing and what we can learn from Japanese and Chinese education.* New York: Summit Books.

Zimowski, M. F., Muraki, E., Mislevy, R. J., & Bock, R. D. (1996). *BILOG-MG: Multiple-group IRT analysis and test maintenance for binary items.* Chicago: Scientific Software International.

CHAPTER 7

Investigating the Role of Free-Choice Learning on Public Understanding of Science: The California Science Center L.A.S.E.R. Project

John H. Falk, Pauline Brooks, and Rinoti Amin

What contribution to public understanding of science do free-choice learning settings such as museums, science centers, zoos, and aquariums make? How successfully do science centers and other comparable institutions accomplish their educational missions? Do science centers and similar institutions actually facilitate long-term science learning and, if so, what is the nature of this learning? Unfortunately, definitive answers to these questions currently are not available.

A handful of studies show some kind of learning takes place in museumlike settings (Crane, Nicholson, Chen, & Bitgood, 1994; Falk & Dierking, 1995, 2000; Hein & Alexander, 1998), but the data are too limited to make a completely convincing case. With these issues in mind, the Institute for Learning Innovation, in collaboration with the California Science Center (California Museum of Science and Industry, prior to February 1998), initiated a 10-year longitudinal research study in 1996 named the Los Angeles Science Education Research (L.A.S.E.R.) Project. An initial overview of the project and early baseline results are reported here. But, more important, the L.A.S.E.R. Project is a case study of how one might go about conceptually and practically tackling the major questions of assessing the influence of free-choice education on public understanding of science.

The goal of the L.A.S.E.R. Project is to assess comprehensively the effect of the Science Center on the science and technology understanding, attitudes, and behaviors of the general public in greater Los Angeles. It is intended to help elucidate the fundamental relationship between a free-choice learning facility and the public whom it serves. The L.A.S.E.R. Project has been several years in the planning and requires many more years to implement. In conceptualizing this complex research and evaluation study, we had to consider a number of fundamental issues, including the role of any given educational institution within a community, how people learn science, the interrelationship between leisure and education in our society, and the parameters of this research enterprise itself. Most important, we had to be realistic about the limitations for a study of this kind in order to scale the study to what we could reasonably expect to accomplish, given the time and resources available. Accordingly, the large, multiyear investigation is predicated on a series of fundamental assumptions.

First and foremost, we assume that the Science Center is but one part of a larger educational infrastructure, which includes schools, colleges and universities, libraries, books, television, radio, the Internet, newspapers, periodicals, community organizations, and a myriad of other sources of science information. Although an important part of this infrastructure, the Science Center is unlikely, in and of itself, to be totally responsible for a significant percentage of any individual's science and technology understanding, attitudes, and behaviors.

Second, we assume that any study of the knowledge, attitudes, and behaviors of a population as large and diverse as that of Los Angeles will be liable to considerable sampling bias. We appreciate that it is a moving target and the best we can hope for is a series of snapshots, a time-series investigation that captures critical junctures in what is an ever-changing and dynamic system.

Third, we assume that the Science Center currently and historically has had an influence on its community, as it has been an important and ongoing part of the greater Los Angeles science education community for over a generation. However, we also assume that this influence will increase measurably over the next decade as a number of major expansions and new initiatives come on-line at the museum (e.g., the opening of a new 245,000-square-foot facility (February 1998), initiation of a regional science education resource center (2000), opening of a new museum school (2003)—all of which are designed to increase and enhance the institution's educational impact.

Fourth, we assume that this research investigation will answer fundamental questions vital to the economic and educational well-being of greater Los Angeles (and, by example, the nation) as well as directly enhance the effectiveness of the Science Center at accomplishing its short- and long-term educational mission.

Finally, we assume that assessing something as complex as the public's science and technology understanding, attitudes, and behaviors is an extremely difficult task, one that requires a long-term commitment of time and resources. Given our current understanding of the problem, the questions posed cannot be researched completely; however, the information collected is intended to partially answer the questions posed as well as significantly advance our ability to reframe the questions and methods to insure better and more complete answers in the future.

CONCEPTUAL STRUCTURE OF RESEARCH

The research is structured as a series of nested investigations that begin with a macroscopic view of science learning and iteratively focus down on smaller and smaller components of the institution and its influence on the public. Thus the study begins at the level of the community, narrows to the level of the institution, then to the level of major programs, features, and exhibitions of the institution, all the way down to smaller programs and individual exhibits embedded within the institution.

At each level of investigation, the design attempts to create connections and common data sets allowing direct comparison across different levels of institutional influence. The investigation uses a mixture of quantitative and qualitative measures. These measures have been employed using two basic approaches to track influence—what we have termed *outside-in* and *inside-out* approaches. The outside-in approach (Figure 7.1) queries a randomized sample of people from the various communities that are influenced by the science center; this approach literally goes outside the institution to assess whether or not the institution is having a detectable effect. Through large-scale random telephone surveys and face-to-face interviews, the institution's effect on the science awareness, attitudes, and understanding of the community of greater Los Angeles is assessed and monitored.

By contrast, the inside-out approach (Figure 7.2) involves focused investigations of specific exhibitions and programs. Many investigations are designed as longitudinal case studies. All are designed to identify current users of the institution and to assess the short- and long-term effects of the various projects, activities, and exhibitions of the institution. Inside-out studies focus on everything from casual visitors with only a several-hour exposure to the museum to intensive programs such as Youth ALIVE!/Curator Kids and the Manual Arts High School Internship Program where participants are involved in an intensive relationship with the institution for a period of several months.

Baseline outside-in data were collected in 1997 and are summarized here; comparison data will be collected in 2000. Inside-out data collection has only just begun and will be reported upon in subsequent publications.

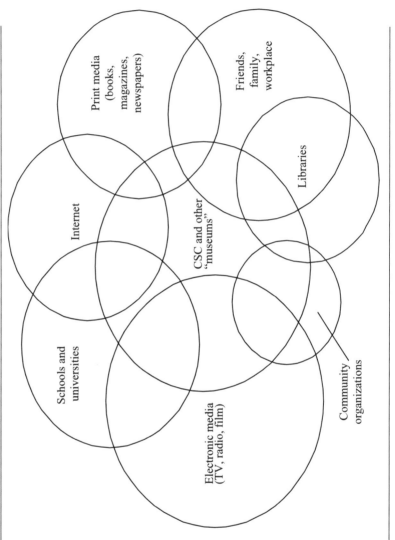

Figure 7.1. Outside-in.

Figure 7.2. Inside-out.

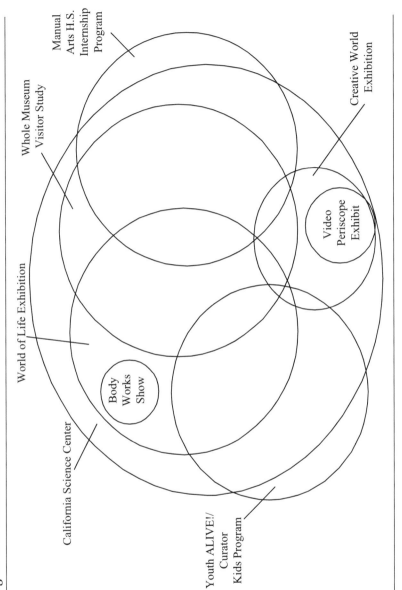

Outside-In Methods

A major first step in this research effort was to establish a baseline understanding of the public's utilization of science education resources in general and their relationship to the Science Center in particular. Although major science centers currently exist within most major cities in the United States, no two institutions or cities are totally comparable. In fundamental ways both the Science Center and Los Angeles are unique, making it impossible to determine a valid *control*. We decided to focus on measuring the change in the Science Center's influence within greater Los Angeles rather than that between the Science Center and some other institution in some other city. Timing of this baseline data collection was also critical. As mentioned, although the Science Center has existed for many years, it was assumed that its historic influence, if not minimal, would at least be less than its future influence, given the major changes being implemented. Thus, in late 1996, we set out to establish a sound baseline of information from which to measure future influence.

As a first step toward implementing the outside-in phase of the project, a series of random, open-ended, face-to-face interviews were conducted in shopping malls, libraries, and parks throughout greater Los Angeles. The goal of these interviews was to generate sufficient data to enable us to construct a valid instrument for use in a random telephone survey. The purpose of this survey was to discover more about the informational sources the public utilizes to learn about science; to determine the science information role played by free-choice learning institutions such as museums, science centers, zoos, and aquariums; and to specifically determine what, if any, role the Science Center might have played in facilitating public understanding of science. Face-to-face interviewing was carried out in an iterative fashion over a 9-month period, each iteration representing a refinement in questioning over the previous period. In all, approximately 200 interviews were conducted. The results from these interviews were used to develop a 29-item telephone survey instrument.

Telephone Survey. Interviewers collected 1,007 telephone surveys from five racially, ethnically, and socio-economically different communities. These five, all in the county of Los Angeles, were Canoga Park, El Monte, Santa Monica, Torrance, and South Central Los Angeles.

Respondents were limited to persons who attested to being at least 18 years old and who were otherwise identified as "the person in the household who could best answer questions about how household members spend their free time and what activities they may choose."

Phone interviews took an average of 20 minutes, were conducted throughout the late morning through evening hours, usually between 10:30 a.m. and 9:30 p.m. Pacific time, 7 days a week. The most productive times were weekends and evenings. Thirty interviewers conducted the surveys over a 5-week period from October 15, 1997, to November 19, 1997. The survey instrument for the most part asked closed-ended questions, although a few open-ended questions were included. Subsections of closed-ended items were recorded verbatim in lists, phrases, and short sentences. The order of questions asked during telephone interviews was changed at random to avoid set patterns in responses. Questions, which included open-ended ones, were also randomly monitored to protect against interviewer bias.

All results were entered into SPSS, a comprehensive data analysis program, and summary statistics were done. As warranted, and as time has permitted, additional statistical analyses have been done. Reports on a few of these analyses are now available and described below.

Sample Demographics. Ten percent of the telephone survey respondents were interviewed in Spanish, the other 90 percent in English. Females slightly outnumbered males, 55 percent to 45 percent. Self-reported yearly *household* income ranged from less than $10,000 to more than $100,000. Overall, 18 percent of respondents reported a yearly income under $20,000 (6 percent of the overall sample indicating a household income under $10,000), 9 percent reported an income of $90,000 or more, and 13 percent refused to indicate whether their household made more or less than $50,000.

Thirteen percent of respondents reported that they had not completed high school; at the upper educational end, another 13 percent reported some graduate school or an advanced degree. Twenty-four percent completed high school, 25 percent had some college experience, and 21 percent had completed college. Nearly half of the respondents were married and half were not (18 percent formerly married but not currently, and 32 percent never married) at the time of the telephone interview. Forty percent of all respondents had children, and 63 percent of those with children indicated that their children had been to the California Museum of Science and Industry (Science Center).

Fifty-five percent of the sample were ethnically/culturally "other than White": 26 percent Hispanic/Latino, 15 percent African American/Black; 9 percent Asian, and 5 percent Other. This diversity was also reflected in the language statistics, 43 percent of respondents reporting that languages other than English were spoken in their homes. Spanish only accounted for 6 percent; English and Spanish, 22 percent; and English and other, 15 percent. Dozens of languages other than English were spoken within the homes surveyed.

Outside-In Results

People were asked to rate their interest in science and technology. On a scale from 1 to 10 (1 indicating very low and 10 very high interest), the median response was 7.0 (mode = 10, $SD = 2.6$); nearly half indicated a scale score of 8 or higher. Respondents consistently expressed high interest in science and technology, regardless of their education, income, race, ethnicity, or gender.

Similarly, on a 5-point scale, people were asked to rate their knowledge of science as compared with that of "the average person." Respondents overwhelmingly rated their knowledge of science and technology to be the same as, or higher than, that of the average person. Thus most respondents in this survey declared themselves to have a very high *interest* in science and technology and a *knowledge* level about science and technology equivalent to or slightly "higher than the average person's."

Sources of Science/Technology Knowledge. In an effort to explore the variety of sources of science and technology information that the public uses, telephone interviewers asked people what sources they relied upon for science and technology knowledge. After posing the interest and knowledge question, the interviewers followed up by saying, "Everybody knows something about science and technology. This knowledge comes from many different sources. Which of the following sources have you relied upon when you learned about science and/or technology?" Respondents confirmed that they relied upon multiple sources of information for their science and technology knowledge. The rank ordering of these sources of information from "most relied upon" (1) to "least relied upon" (8) is shown in Table 7.1.

Notice that in the three rankings shown in Table 7.1, museums fell near the middle of each ranking. Museums, zoos, and science centers were ranked fifth for the combined category "some or a lot"; sixth for being relied upon "a lot"; and fifth for the category "not at all."

When respondents were asked how many visits they had made in the last 12 months to any combination of zoos, aquariums, observatories, planetariums, science centers, or botanical gardens, 26 percent said none, 16 percent said one, 14 percent said two, and 43 percent reported three or more visits.

Exposure to and Experience With the Science Center. The telephone survey posed a number of questions related to public awareness and utilization of the Science Center. The following represents a *preliminary* exploration of some of these questions covered on the survey. As shown in Table 7.2, 707 respondents (70 percent) said that they had heard of the California Museum of Science and Industry. More than half (63 percent) of those 707 respondents had also visited the Science Center. Thus 44 percent of the overall sample of 1,007 self-reported having been to Science Center at some time and 56 percent said they had never been there. Of the 441 respondents who reported having been to the Science Center, more than one fourth had been there within the past year, 38 percent had been there within the past 1 to 5 years, and 34 percent had

Table 7.1. Ranking of Sources Relied Upon "A Lot," "Some or A Lot," or "Not At All" for Learning About Science and Technology ($n = 1,007$)

Rank order	Relied upon "a lot"		Relied upon "some or a lot"		Relied upon "not at all"	
	%	Category/source	%	Category/source	%	Category/source
1st	46	School, courses	76	Books, magazines, *not* for school	37	Radio, audiotapes
	46	Books, magazines, *not* for school				
2nd	42	Life experiences	74	Life experiences	23	On the job
			74	TV, cable		
3rd	39	TV, cable	68	School, courses	18	Family/friends
4th	36	On the job	65	Museums, zoos	15	School, courses
5th	30	Museum, zoos	57	On the job	13	Museums, zoos
6th	24	Family/friends	55	Family/friends	10	TV, cable
7th	11	Radio, audiotapes	31	Radio, audiotapes	8	Books, magazines, *not* for school
8th					8	Life experiences

Note: There are three pairs of tied rankings; the middle category is a sum of two categories "A Lot" and "Some."

Table 7.2. Self-Reported Familiarity with CSC (n = 1007)

	Yes	No	
Have you heard of CSC?	70%	30%	
If you have heard of CSC, have you ever been to CSC?	63%	37%	

	Within the past 12 months	Within the past 1–5 years	More than 5 years ago
If you have been to CSC, how recently have you been to CSC?	28%	38%	34%

visited the Science Center more than 5 years ago. Within the context of the overall sample of 1,007, these figures indicate that 12 percent of the entire sample visited the Science Center within the past 12 months, 17 percent visited within the past 1 to 5 years, and 15 percent visited more than 5 years ago.

Characteristics of Science Center-goers and Nongoers. For analysis, we broke the sample into two populations: those who had both heard of the Science Center and visited the institution at some point in their lives (SC-goers) and those who may have heard of the Science Center but had never visited (nongoers). A comparison of general free-time activities between these two populations revealed significant differences (Table 7.3). Although SC-goers and nongoers engaged in the same activities, SC-goers did so more frequently. In particular, SC-goers were significantly more likely than nongoers to "do hobbies," "use computers," "do activities with organized clubs, church, or religious groups," "watch educational specials on TV or educational cable-TV channels," "go to libraries," "go to museums, science centers or zoos," and "go on family trips or outings."

Although SC-goers and nongoers showed no significant differences overall in prevalence of book, magazine, and newspaper reading, television watching, and radio listening, differences in the content of their reading, viewing, and listening were marked. Specifically, SC-goers were significantly more likely than nongoers to read, watch, and listen to science- and technology-related material (Tables 7.4 and 7.5).

Childhood experiences of SC-goers also differed from those of nongoers. As children, SC-goers engaged in significantly more of the following: (a) reading books, magazines, or newspapers ($t = 1.95$, $p < .05$); (b) going to museums, zoos, or science centers ($t = 3.97$, $p < .000$); (c) participating in scouts, clubs, or other organized groups ($t = 3.57$, $p < .000$); and (d) going on family trips or outings ($t = 4.24$, $p < .000$).

Table 7.3. General Free-Time Activities: Means and Significance for CSC-goers and Nongoers

General free-time activities	Been to CSC (n = 441)	Not been to CSC (n = 261)	Significance
"During my free time I ____"			
• read books, magazines and/or newspapers.	5.65	5.51	NS
• do hobbies.	4.64	4.38	0.033
• use computers.	4.61	4.03	0.001
• take classes.	2.89	2.77	NS
• do activities with organized clubs, church or religious group.	3.29	2.98	0.030
• watch educational specials on TV, cable TV channels.	4.63	4.25	0.001
• listen to educational radio programs or audio tapes.	3.33	3.04	NS
• go to libraries.	3.38	3.06	0.007
• go to museums, science centers, or zoos.	2.83	2.39	0.000
• go on family trips or outings.	3.54	3.24	0.002

Note: The scale was 6 = daily; 5 = weekly (several times a week); 4 = monthly (several times a month); 3 = several times a year; 2 = once a year (or less often); 1 = never (virtually never). NS = no significance

Confirming the self-selected nature of visitation to free-choice learning institutions such as the California Science Center was the finding that even among individuals with higher income (annual family income greater than $50,000), only those with greater interest in science, and greater self-reported knowledge of science were significantly more likely to be SC-goers (Table 7.6).

A series of analyses, culminating in a logistic regression model, were conducted to determine the characteristics of persons most likely to have visited the Science Center. The analysis included the 40 variables, which significantly correlated with respondents having visited/not visited the Science Center based on initial chi-square tests of association ($p < 0.05$). The model then sought to calculate a series of adjusted odds ratios (ORs), with an OR of greater than 1 meaning that a variable was predictive of a person's having ever visited the science center. Out of the 40 variables tested, only four resulted in ORs greater than 1 (Table 7.7).

Table 7.4. Reading Topics and Habits: Means and Significance for CSC-goers and Nongoers

General reading practices/habits	Been to CSC (n = 441)	Not been to CSC (n = 261)	Significance
"During my free time I read about ___"			
• news or current events.	5.48	5.01	0.000
• science or nature topics.	4.21	3.64	0.000
• religious topics.	3.63	3.38	NS
• computer or technology topics.	3.73	3.22	0.001
• science fiction or futuristic topics.	3.06	2.77	0.035

Note: The scale was 6 = daily; 5 = weekly (several times a week); 4 = monthly (several times a month); 3 = several times a year; 2 = once a year (or less often); 1 = never (virtually never). NS = no significance

Respondents who often read books, magazines, and/or newspapers during their free time were nearly 4 times more likely than those who did not to have visited the Science Center. Respondents who had heard of the small Pacific Coast Cabrillo Beach Marine Aquarium were 2 times more likely to have been Science Center visitors than were individuals who had not. Respondents who had visited any museum, zoo, aquarium, science center, observatory, or botanical garden within the last 12 months because they had been there before and desired to go back were 1.3 times more likely to have visited the Science Center than were those who had not. Finally, respondents who had lived in the greater Los Angeles area for more than 18 years were nearly 2.5 times more likely to have ever visited the Science Center than were individuals who had only more recently become residents of Los Angeles.

Although significantly correlated with science-center visitation, neither income, education, race/ethnicity, language spoken at home, self-defined interest in science, or knowledge of science ended up being predictive of people's visiting the science center in this regression model.

Influence of a Science Center Visit. Finally, those individuals who reported having visited the Science Center were questioned as to the effect of that experience. Specifically, they were asked to respond to the following four statements: "I learned one or more things that I never knew before"; "My understanding of things I already knew was strengthened or extended"; "I came away with a stronger interest in some area of science or technology"; and "It changed my attitudes or behaviors to be more positive toward science or technology."

Table 7.5. Watching and Listening Topics and Habits: Means and Significance for CSC-goers and Nongoers

General watching and listening habits	Been to CSC (n = 441)	Not been to CSC (n = 261)	Significance
"During my free time I watch ____"			
• news or current events.	5.43	5.42	NS
• science or nature topics.	4.51	4.26	0.022
• religious topics.	2.64	2.85	NS
• computer or technology topics.	2.98	2.78	NS
• science fiction or futuristic topics.	3.48	3.44	NS
"During my free time I listen to____"			
• news or current events.	5.16	4.69	0.008
• science or nature topics.	2.63	2.45	NS
• religious topics.	2.82	2.84	NS
• computer or technology topics.	2.44	1.99	0.005
• science fiction or futuristic topics.	2.22	1.87	0.021

Note: The scale was 6 = daily; 5 = weekly (several times a week); 4 = monthly (several times a month); 3 = several times a year; 2 = once a year (or less often); 1 = never (virtually never). NS = no significance

Table 7.6. Differences Between CSC Visitors and Nonvisitors (*n* = 707)

Characteristics	Chi-square value	Degrees of freedom	Probability
Income	14.06	1	<.000
Interest in science & technology	11.54	2	<.003
Self-reported knowledge of science & technology	25.73	4	<.000

Table 7.7. Logistic Regression Results of Visiting the CSC (*n* = 707)

Variable	Coefficient	Adjusted odds ratio
Reads a lot during general free time	1.3657	3.96
Heard of Cabrillo Beach Marine Aquarium	0.7685	2.16
Had visited a museum, zoo, aquarium, etc., and wanted to go back	0.2873	1.33
Has lived in L.A. more than 18 years	0.6481	2.36

Results are summarized in Table 7.8. Overwhelmingly, visitors reported that a visit to the Science Center resulted in increased learning and consolidation of prior learning; slightly less strongly, they indicated that a visit resulted in increased interest and changes in interest or behavior. Virtually no previous visitor felt that the visit had no effect on his or her science knowledge, interest, or behavior.

A similar set of questions were asked of respondents who indicated that their children had visited the Science Center. Parents were asked whether the visit to the Science Center had "increased their [child's] understanding of some area of science or technology"; "increased their [child's] interest in some area of science or technology"; or "changed in a positive way their [child's] behavior toward science or technology." Once again, there was an overwhelming indica-

Table 7.8. Impact of CSC Visit on Adults (*n* = 441)

	Strongly agree	Somewhat agree	Neither agree nor disagree	Somewhat agree	Strongly disagree
Learned one or more new things	65%	31%	2%	2%	0%
Understanding strengthened/ extended	60%	35%	1%	1%	1%
Stronger interest	44%	38%	6%	11%	1%
Changed attitudes or behaviors	31%	35%	13%	13%	8%

tion that the experience had been positive, particularly in terms of learning but slightly less so in terms of interest and much less so in terms of change of behavior (Table 7.9).

OUTSIDE-IN DISCUSSION AND CONCLUSION

First, it is important to appreciate that this data set was designed as a baseline study, a vantage point from which to compare future impact. Although the old California Museum of Science and Industry was assumed to have had some impact, it was hoped that the new California Science Center would be more popular and, overall, more successful in enhancing the public's understanding, attitudes, and behaviors toward science. If so, the effects of those improvements and changes could be expected to work their way through the population and be captured by subsequent surveys (currently planned for 2000, 2002, and 2004). In the meantime, though, the present analysis revealed a number of interesting findings, including confirmation of the measurable impact achieved by the old California Museum of Science and Industry.

How reliable were these telephone survey data? The findings presented here are but one of two major sets of baseline data collected during this initial outside-in phase of the project. Although the face-to-face interview data set was intended as a pilot for the telephone survey, the fact that similar questions were asked of a random but different subset of people in the greater Los Angeles area means that the two data sets can be compared to determine the reliability of the responses. The two sets, collected independently using very different methodologies, proved to be very highly correlated (Falk, Brooks, & Amin, 1998). This strong correlation coupled with the demographic comparability of the telephone survey sample with recent U.S. Census Bureau data (U.S. Census Bureau, 1992) suggests that this random telephone sample likely was a representative and generalizable sampling of the free-choice science education opinions and experiences of adults living in the greater Los Angeles area.

Table 7.9. Impact of CSC Visit on Children ($n = 252$)

	A lot	Some	Very little	Not at all	Don't know
Increased understanding	57%	30%	2%	3%	8%
Increased interest	52%	34%	3%	3%	8%
Changed behavior	38%	33%	10%	9%	10%

A large majority of respondents, across all socioeconomic and racial/ethnic groups, showed moderate to high interest and self-reported moderate to high knowledge in science. Individuals also indicated that they regularly accessed free-choice media to remain informed about science; on average, they watched educational specials on television weekly (science and nature programs slightly less frequently but still more than monthly), went to libraries monthly, and visited museum-like settings several times per year. High interest in science was also reflected in the wide diversity of science resources individuals sought out to become knowledgeable in science and to remain so. School and reading outside of school were viewed as equally important resources; so too were life experiences. Roughly a third of individuals claimed to regularly, or frequently, rely upon television and museums as important sources of science information; comparable numbers also relied upon on-the-job sources of information.

Roughly half of the sample had visited the California Museum of Science and Industry at some point in their lives. These individuals differed significantly from those comprising the other half of the sample. On the whole, the 44 percent of individuals who were SC-goers were more affluent, had resided in Los Angeles longer, were more likely to be White than Hispanic/Latino, were more interested in science and technology, and were (self-reportedly) more knowledgeable in science. These individuals were not only different because they had visited the Science Center; as a group, they were also more likely to utilize other free-choice learning opportunities for the purpose of learning about science and technology. They were significantly more likely to seek out science information through reading books, magazines, and newspapers; through viewing television; and through listening to radio. In addition, as children they were significantly more likely to have read, gone to museums, participated in organized groups, and gone on family outings.

One way to view these data is as a case study for the utilization of free-choice science education resources in the community. Such a view makes it clear that a large segment of the public utilizes free-choice science education resources and that many people do so on a regular basis. In the case of the Science Center, nearly half the public have used the facility at some point in their lives. As with any resource, interest and awareness were important factors contributing to use. A large majority (70 percent) of the public claimed to be aware of the science center, but only a minority (29 percent) had visited within the past 5 years, fewer than half this number (12 percent) within the previous 12 months.

The disparity between awareness and utilization was not surprising, given that it is well known in the leisure field (cf. Pollock, Finn, Garfield, Snyder, & Pfenning, 1983; Robinson & Godbey, 1997) that in-home resources such as television, newspapers, magazines, books, and friends are more frequently used than are resources that require a special trip—for example, to libraries and mu-seums, science centers, and zoos. What was surprising was the level of reported use. It will be interesting to see whether these numbers increase in subsequent years now that the new California Science Center has opened. Attendance at the new facility is projected to be 2 to 3 times that at the old facility. To date 3.5 million people have visited the new science center.

Equally interesting, but not surprising, was the strong self-selection in the utilization of this resource. Results from this study confirmed expectations that the public is not using educational resources equally, whether formal or free-choice. Perhaps more surprising was the high level of use by such a diverse public. Although the better educated and more affluent used the Science Center (and other free-choice science education resources) more, what is notable is the widespread use across all socioeconomic groups. Ultimately, affluence and education were not predictive of attendance at the science center. Instead, a predisposition to reading, prior experience with and interest in comparable edu-cational resources, and awareness (as measured by an awareness of a small aquarium—Cabrillo Beach—and length of residence in the community—longer than 18 years) were the most significant variables affecting visitation. Collec-tively, these findings confirm the model recently proposed by Falk (1998a, 1998b) for explaining museum-going and suggest strategies for more effectively attracting free-choice learning users.

Although self-report data are notoriously unreliable, it can be concluded that visitors to the Science Center believed that the experience affected them positively. Better than 9 out of 10 visitors felt that the visit increased their own understanding of some aspect of science and/or technology; roughly three quar-ters felt that their Science Center experience had increased their interest in some aspect of science and/or technology; and nearly three quarters felt that the expe-rience resulted in a change in their interest level or even behavior. Parents be-lieved that the experience similarly benefited their children as well. These re-sults again testify to the significant influence that free-choice settings almost certainly have on the public, although the real extent of these effects await further, more reliable testing. Efforts are currently being initiated as part of the inside-out phase of the L.A.S.E.R. Project to do just that—more reliably assess personal learning.

In conclusion, these baseline data provide a wealth of initial information about the utilization of science education resources generally and of the Califor-nia Science Center in particular. Results from this research are being used by the California Science Center to assist in gauging its progress toward attainment of its stated mission to facilitate public understanding and interest in science and technology. Additionally, this research is helping to elucidate the fundamental relationship between free-choice learning facilities and their public. Research such as this holds out the promise of establishing, once and for all, the range and extent of benefits the public receives from interactions with free-choice learning settings.

REFERENCES

Crane, V., Nicholson, H., Chen, M., & Bitgood, S. (1994). *Informal science learning.* Dedham, MA: Research Communications Ltd.

Falk, J. H. (1998a). A framework for diversifying museum audiences: Putting heart and head in the right place. *Museum News, 77*(5), 36–39.

Falk, J. H. (1998b). *Visitors: Who does, who doesn't, and why. Museum News, 77*(2), 38–43.

Falk, J. H., Brooks, P., & Amin, R. (1998, March 27). *California Science Center L.A.-S.E.R. project quarterly report.* Annapolis, MD: Institute for Learning Innovation.

Falk, J. H., & Dierking, L. D. (Eds.). (1995). *Public institutions for personal learning: Establishing a research agenda.* Washington, DC: American Association of Museums.

Falk, J. H., & Dierking, L. D. (2000). *Learning from museums: Visitors experiences and the making of meaning.* Walnut Creek: AltaMira Press.

Hein, G., & Alexander, M. (1998). *Museums: Places of learning.* Washington, DC: American Association of Museums.

Pollock, J. C., Finn, P., Garfield, E. A., Snyder, A., & Pfenning, A. G. (1983). *Where does the time go?* New York: The United Media Enterprise Report on Leisure in America.

Robinson, J., & Godbey, G. (1997). *Time for life: The amazing way Americans use their time.* University Park: Penn State Press.

U.S. Bureau of the Census. (1992). *Census of the United States 1990.* Washington, DC: U.S. Government Printing Office.

CHAPTER 8

Supporting and Documenting Choice in Free-Choice Science Learning Environments

Robert B. Lebeau, Phyllis Gyamfi, Karen Wizevich, and Emlyn H. Koster

For the past 15 years, schools have actively engaged in reform efforts directed toward the improvement of science teaching and learning. Waning are the beliefs that the memorization of science facts or the repetition of experiments whose outcomes are widely known will lead to graduates with the science savvy required for the twenty-first century. The change from science experiences of old—textbooks, filmstrip projectors, and lectures—to new experiences with hands-on materials, networked technologies, and student-developed investigations is under way.

In an effort to accelerate the adoption and implementation of these reform efforts, local, state, and federal stakeholders have encouraged schools to form partnerships with corporations, universities, and cultural organizations that share a common interest in improving science literacy. Science centers and other free-choice learning environments seem perfectly placed to play an integral role in these educational reform efforts. Most free-choice science learning environments are hallmarks of experiential learning, exploration, and discovery.

Exhibitions and programs that characterize these institutions derive from constructivist, learner-centered pedagogies. Frequently a ready source of a variety of learning resources, science centers often provide in-depth learning opportunities for both students and teachers. Those students and teachers who have visited through time report favorably about the impact of the experience. Science centers justly proclaim the singularity of their interactive environment and its ability to excite, motivate, and inspire learners of all ages and backgrounds.

Traditionally, the distinction between the characteristics of formal and free-choice science education has served as a barrier to effective collaboration and problem solving between schools and science centers. For the past 6 years, in Jersey City, New Jersey, at Liberty Science Center (LSC), educators have been working with teachers and students to design programs and activities that make the science center more than just an isolated field-trip destination. In developing programs for the school audience that have an ongoing impact and support science reform, LSC has identified five elements that lead to success: (a) alignment with accepted science curriculum standards and benchmarks; (b) extension of all contacts through pre- and postactivity connections; (c) integration with other subjects and disciplines; (d) connection of classroom experience to science center experience; and (e) insistence on student production through problem solving, construction, collaboration, and use of creativity.

This unique set of principles serves as the connective tissue that forges the links between formal and free-choice sources of science education. But how will free-choice learning institutions export their strength and uniqueness to develop a sustained, embedded impact once students and teachers return to the classroom after an experience in a free-choice learning environment? In what ways and through what means do science centers and other free-choice learning institutions become a meaningful part of a school's reformed educational curriculum?

A more purposeful and regular connection between schools and free-choice learning institutions requires greater understanding of how members of school groups exercise free choice and how those choices can be supported so that learning is likely to follow. Free-choice learning behavior is a critical characteristic of settings such as science centers, where students typically encounter a greater degree of choice over how to distribute their time and structure their activity than the ordinary school day allows. Many factors, however, influence those choices. Students' choices in science centers unfold in what is often a novel social context when compared to that of structured schoolwork: Students must negotiate their choices with others in their group and find the extent and nature of their learning activity influenced by the presence and behavior patterns of other visitors. Student choices are also strongly influenced by the design and substance of learning environments that promote or hinder sustained attention. In addition, the exercise of free choice and subsequent learning will vary in relation to students' motivations and interests, and their prior knowledge of relevant subject matter and the free-choice learning institution itself.

This chapter describes two pilot research efforts that sought to effect free-choice learning by influencing the explicit attention members of school groups pay to their own plans, interests, expectations, efforts, and learning outcomes as part of a visit to LSC. We hypothesize that the more students and teachers attend to the nature, direction, and outcomes of their free choices, the greater the chance those experiences will coalesce as part of sustained and integrated science learning. Of the two studies reported, the first examines a means for supporting informed goal-setting before a science center visit. The second explores an observation strategy for documenting how members of school groups allocate their time and link their experiences during visits to a science center.

Both studies revolve around concrete representations of the free choices learners make, or intend to make, in free-choice learning environments. In the former, students and teachers are provided with information to help plan and reflect upon their visit; in the latter, they utilize a strategy for capturing the evolution of plans, interests, and activities during a visit. Such a focus addresses possible interventions on the "demand" side of science center visits, arming visitors with tools and strategies to structure their own visits and to build stronger links to past and future learning. Such focus also reflects on the "supply" side, considering possible strategies to change the nature and type of experiences offered to visitors.

OVERVIEW

Research on formal academic study reveals that successful learners engage in a variety of behaviors by which they regulate their own learning (e.g., Zimmerman, 1998). This does not mean that self-regulated learners control all aspects of their own learning. Instead it means that successful students set goals, develop plans, implement strategies, monitor outcomes, and evaluate themselves with respect to educational topics, standards, and tasks. These goals and activities can be outlined by others, in conjunction with others, and/or by students themselves (e.g., Zimmerman, 1994). If planning, self-monitoring, and self-evaluating are critical to learning in highly structured learning environments, how much more so might such processes help students capitalize on the whirlwind of activity available in the typical science center?

We have begun to test multiple methods of observation and support for visitors that will help us and them document the planning, self-monitoring, and reflection in which they engage as part of visits by school groups to LSC. We seek both to understand the importance of these self-regulated learning processes and their intersection with the social and physical context of free-choice learning environments (Falk & Dierking, 1992) and to examine the impact of tools supporting more deliberate personal self-direction in learning within these environments.

In the first study, we examine the process of goal-setting in free-choice learning contexts by experimentally manipulating student use of a map prior to visiting the science center. The three-page map is specially designed as a simple aid for planning and reflection through its representation of areas in the science center by large, thematic graphic images. Brief descriptions of activities (e.g., "Examine amazing insects, spiders, and snakes") and space for note-taking and other writings accompany each image. The activities listed are not comprehensive and do not include some of the most popular attractions likely to be familiar to students. Our goal is to compare cognitive, affective, and motivational outcomes among students who are given the map only and those who are given the map plus suggested activities for utilizing the map to set selective goals for their upcoming visit. The results reported below provide evidence that these forms of previsit planning influence students' reported help-seeking behaviors while at the science center. Seeking help while learning is one example of enhanced self-regulation of learning experiences (Zimmerman, 1998).

Our observation strategy focuses on three elements of overt group regulation of learning during a science center visit: Where the group goes, Transitions made from one activity area to the next, and Connections to other sources of experience made by group members as a means of interpreting the activity (a framework we call WTC—where, transition, connections). This is a measure of the planning-in-action characteristic of many school groups' experiences in science centers. These observations are designed to extend knowledge of the manner in which members of school groups exercise free choice in science centers. In addition, the WTC framework provides one measure of group behavior that can be used to compare the influence of different interventions designed to promote science center exploration that is better integrated with personal interests of visitors and their subsequent learning in formal and free-choice environments.

These two research projects are linked theoretically and practically, although for the time being the projects are functionally independent of one another. The common theoretical bases for these investigations include research on metacognition (the knowledge one has of, and the regulation one exercises over, one's own cognition, e.g., Brown, 1987); self-regulated learning (the metacognitive, motivational, and behavioral components of an individual's effort, persistence, and activity choices, e.g., Schunk & Zimmerman, 1998; Winne, 1997); and distributed cognition (cognition understood as jointly undertaken by individuals interacting with each other and with surrounding physical, social, and intellectual resources, e.g., Salomon, 1993). The metacognitive components of these projects include the learning connections documented in the WTC framework. The self-regulated learning components include the goal-setting and help-seeking associated with map use and the monitoring of progress and interest level captured through the WTC. The map itself, and its potential transformation into a networked planning tool, represents elements of distributed cognition.

Finally, the social mediation of learning in museums (Falk & Dierking, 1992) can also be understood in terms of distributed cognition.

The practical connection between our study of goal-setting and our observational strategy is that both provide concrete representations of the choices free-choice learners make, or intend to make, in free-choice learning environments. These representations can help learners in their achievement of self-instructional goals, teachers in their documentation of student learning and interests, and can also serve as a measure of the nature and quality of learner engagement with science center resources. They can also help learners build upon their initial experiences in a given free-choice environment and plan for their next related encounters in formal and other free-choice settings. As such, they provide support for the self-direction, social mediation, and freedom characteristic of free-choice learning experiences (Gelman, Massey, & McManus, 1991; Schauble & Glaser, 1996).

STUDY 1: SUPPORTING INFORMED GOAL-SETTING

Setting goals is a critical element in self-regulated learning, for it is with goals that activities are chosen and sustained. A visitor's perception of possible activities in a complex and novel environment guides the visitor's selection of an activity and the pace at which he or she pursues it. Thus the information provided to or obtained by visitors, and the subsequent perceptions generated by visitors, form the initial building blocks for regulating learning during the visit. Research on free-choice learning environments suggests that providing information about the setting prior to a visit reduces novelty and enhances learning (Falk & Dierking, 1992). We investigate here how coupling a novelty-reducing activity, such as allowing visitors to first study the layout at a science center, with a goal-setting activity can serve to influence subsequent exploration and reflection as part of a science center visit. The science center offers more directed and content-based previsit and postvisit activities. This effort explores a simple strategy for reaching those organized visitors who do not elect to use these planning aids.

Method

Experimental Framework and Materials. The first step we took was to transform the one-page comprehensive map ordinarily given to visitors to the science center into a simpler document oriented toward children of middle-school age and above (grades 5 and up; ages 11 and up). Beginning around these grades, children are more capable of engaging in metacognitive and self-regulatory skills but nonetheless require opportunities to develop and practice these skills to use them productively and independently (Wigfield, Eccles, & Pintrich, 1996). The new map is composed of three pages, one page per floor of the science center, and removes almost all detail but for two or three thematic areas per floor. Each area is represented by a large graphic indicating the theme. Alongside each graphic are a title and three simple statements of what one can do in each area, for example, produce power with wind and water, simulate an earthquake, and so on.

The basic experimental framework is to randomly assign students, within a given school group, into three groups: (a) map only (Group 1); (b) map plus a worksheet on which students indicate three areas they would most like to see, two areas they are not interested in seeing, and one area in which they would like to spend the most time (Group 2); and (c) map, plus the worksheet, plus a directive to write down a question to which the student hopes to find an answer while at the science center (Group 3). As described below, the latter two conditions are known as the map + activity group.

All students completed a two-page previsit survey through which we obtained basic demographic information, identified those students who were first-time visitors to the science center (about 50 percent), and asked students to indicate whether they disagreed, agreed, or were unsure of their response to 11 statements meant to reflect attitudes toward science study and toward "out-of-school" learning, including museums.

We used two postvisit measures. One is a homework assignment (a *natural* example of student work) split into two parts: (a) *About My Trip*—questions to which students respond by recalling everything they did and by indicating what they liked best, what else they would like to have done, and what they are curious about; and (b) *My Advice to New Visitors*—questions to which students indicate why one might want to go to the science center, what to do there, and where to go for specific science-topic learning. The second postvisit measure included a reprise of some of the questions from the previsit survey, a set of rating scales for attitudes toward the trip itself, a stimulated-recall exercise in which students use the map to describe what they did and learned, and, finally, ratings of their own actual or likely help-seeking behavior.

Participants. The pilot study took place in the summer of 1998. The participants were 27 children, ages 11 to 14 (entering sixth, seventh, and eighth grade), enrolled in remedial summer school programming in a New York City school. Forty-four students were present for the previsit activity and the initial groupings were divided on this basis (an additional 25 students were absent on the first day of the study). The final number of 27 participants reflects those students who were present for the pre- and post-visit activities and who went on the trip [$n = 11$ map only; $n = 16$ map + activity (combination of Groups 2 and 3 because only 4 students out of the original 15 in Group 3 attended both the trip and were present on the day of the postvisit exercise)].

Procedure. On the day prior to the school's scheduled visit, two representatives of the science center (the first and second authors) joined students in their classrooms for the previsit survey and map distribution. We told the students of the excitement on the part of those in the science center that they were coming and that we wanted to let them know more about some of the many things to see and do at the center. We also indicated that we sought to learn their thoughts and reactions regarding their visit through a pre- and postvisit survey. To thank them for their participation, we explained that all participants would receive a small gift from the science center gift shop. We then split the students into three groups according to a random assignment completed earlier but left students with the impression that the grouping was organizational only.

All students completed the previsit survey and then received a copy of the map. The map + activity group used the map to answer the questions described above. The map only group spent an equivalent amount of time examining the map on their own and then writing a paragraph on their favorite field trip. All groups completed their activity in about the same amount of time.

On the day of the trip, the students' own teachers split them into groups of five to eight for exploring the center. No attempt was made to restrict group membership to the experimental groupings. The school spent 4 hours at the science center. Owing to an unplanned schedule change, the school spent only 45 minutes in open-ended exploration, a finding with significance in itself. The rest of the time they spent seeing two theater presentations, eating lunch, and visiting the gift shop. As students boarded the buses for the ride home, they received the homework assignment described above. The experimental procedure ended on the first school day following the trip (a Monday) with the postvisit survey described above, the distribution of the gifts, and an opportunity for students to ask any further questions of the center representatives.

Preliminary Results

The preliminary results of the pilot study contain evidence for both outcomes and processes related to planning, monitoring, and reflecting upon learning as part of a science center visit. Although limited by the small number of participating students and the limited amount of free exploration time, these results point to a number of promising directions: (a) the influence of goal-setting on help-seeking behavior; (b) the influence of a science center visit on students' perceptions of learning science; and (c) the processes initiated by the successful representation of student recollection, evaluations, and interests as a foundation for future learning. Qualitative aspects of the latter direction currently are a focus as we expand this framework.

Help-seeking. As part of the postvisit survey, as shown in Table 8.1, students indicated their agreement with responses to the following question: "If I didn't understand something at the science center, I would _____." The options to be evaluated independently of each other are listed in the table along with mean scores drawn from a Likert scale numbered 1 (*strongly disagree*) to 5 (*strongly agree*). It is interesting to note that students in the map + activity group indicated a trend toward greater readiness to interact with staff members than did those in the map only group [$M = 3.9$ (map only); $M = 4.6$ (map + activity); $F(1, 25) = 3.05$, $p < .1$]. Both groups experienced the same amount of interaction with center staff members during the previsit activity. A moderate negative correlation was found between asking a staff member and asking a classmate ($r = -.45$, $p < .05$).

Perceptions of Science Learning as Influenced by the Visit. One of the statements students evaluated pre- and postvisit was drawn from the 1996 National Assessment of Educational Progress (NAEP) survey (Allen, Swinton, Isham, & Zelenak, 1997). It read, "Learning science is mostly about memorizing,"

Table 8.1. Supporting Informed Goal-setting: *Preliminary Results*

Postvisit self-assessment of help-seeking
"If I didn't understand something at the science center, I would ____ "

MEAN SCORES FOR STUDENT EVALUATIONS OF POTENTIAL SOURCES OF HELP BY GROUP

Source of help	Map Only			Map + Activity*		
	M	SD	n	M	SD	n
Ask a teacher	3.5	1.2	11	3.6	1.0	16
Ask a center staff member	3.9ₐ	1.1	11	4.6ₐ	0.8	16
Ask another adult	2.3	1.2	11	2.6	1.1	15**
Ask a classmate	2.9	1.4	11	2.3	1.1	15**
Read a sign	3.6	1.4	11	4.1	.77	16
Stay/look longer	2.8	1.5	11	2.8	1.5	16

Note: $N = 27$; means with the same subscript differ at $p < .1$.
* Students in the "map + activity" group show a trend toward greater readiness to interact with staff members than do those in the "map only" group.
** Missing response; means drawn from Likert scale evaluations [1 (*strongly disagree*)–5 (*strongly agree*)].

and students indicated whether they agreed, disagreed, or were not sure if they agreed or disagreed with the statement. Before going to the science center, 8 students agreed with this statement, 4 were unsure, and 15 disagreed. After visiting the center, 2 students agreed, 1 was unsure, and 24 disagreed. This shift was statistically significant (Wilcoxon's matched-pairs signed-rank test; $p < .05$).

Student Recollections, Evaluations, and Interests as a Foundation for Future Learning. Student recollections, self-evaluations, and questions may provide evidence for the manner in which information and trip-planning support influence students' experiences. The initial statements and thoughts that we have obtained thus far from students are encouraging.

It often is difficult for students to reflect upon visits to science centers. Students appeared to find the consistent format of the map as part of both pre- and postvisit planning to be a good foundation for drawing together their past experiences and interests, and considering how to connect them to subsequent activity.

Discussion

Help-seeking. The possibly greater readiness to interact with staff members on the part of those in the map + activity group suggests a relationship between goal-setting and help-seeking behavior that is worth further exploration. This relationship could be negative if these students are expressing a reliance on external support at the expense of personal initiative. Asking a staff member a question may represent an easier option than persisting in individual or group activity. A more positive interpretation, however, is that support for goal-setting contributes to a readiness on the part of students to take fuller advantage of available resources as they engage in free exploration and encounter inevitable difficulties.

One limitation on help-seeking in formal academic study is the potential social embarrassment of revealing one does not understand or of appearing too interested in social settings where peer pressure mitigates academic involvement. Similar social pressures may exist in science centers where asking questions or taking a long time with an exhibit may indicate that one does not understand what to do. Such a public admission is not easy to make, but doing so is fundamental to full engagement in the complexity and challenge of many exhibits. Goal-setting and other planning activities may help ease some of this pressure by increasing visitor motivation to persist or to seek help.

The difference between both groups of students' evaluation of fellow classmates as a source of help was not significant. However, the moderate negative correlation between considering a classmate as a source of help and a staff member as a source of help is interesting. Our intervention was deliberately targeted to individuals and their own planning. Perhaps group goal-setting and other joint previsit planning will influence this relationship.

Perceptions of Science Learning The marked shift away from agreement in students' response to the statement "Learning science is mostly about memorizing" is a direction that probably is desirable—students appear to have experienced an opportunity that revealed other forms of science learning besides text-based memorization. However, this result needs to be interpreted with caution. The statement itself is likely understood as a negative portrayal of an aspect of scientific training that is useful in its own right (B. J. Zimmerman, personal communication, August 14, 1998).

Further investigation is warranted to examine any relationships that may exist between science center learning and student persistence and effort in formal science learning settings. Having a science center representative ask the question twice may have led students to give what they perceived as the desired response rather than an expression of their own feeling. If so, the results could indicate that science learning in science centers is fundamentally separate from science learning in the classroom. This finding might then hinder rather than help integration of the formal and free-choice learning sectors. The impact of simply responding twice, pre- and postvisit, to the statement regarding science learning needs to be investigated.

Nonetheless, NAEP analysts found a broad pattern among the 6,376 students assessed in the 1996 NAEP administration: Higher performance on science items was associated with disagreement with the statement regarding memorization (O'Sullivan & Weiss, 1999, p. 214). This finding is, of course, not evidence for a causal relationship, but it does indicate one potential source of evidence for the widely held belief expressed by educators that the motivational benefits of a science center or museum trip may influence critical attitudes toward learning science.

STUDY 2: OBSERVING PLANNING-IN-ACTION

At the same time that we have sought to investigate the use of tools for supporting informed choices, we have also sought to develop different observational strategies for documenting the choices members of school groups make. Our primary strategy has been for observers to travel with small groups as they engage in free exploration of the science center. These observers prioritized their observations within the aforementioned WTC framework: Where the group went, Transitions the group made from one activity to the next, and Connections group members made to other sources of experience as they interpreted the activity. The examples given demonstrate representative information uncovered using the WTC format. These preliminary observations are not meant to be a comprehensive report.

Our observers joined randomly selected groups ranging from third grade to high school. Teachers gave their consent to observers' presence either in advance of their trip or as they arrived. The explanation given to teachers, and then to the children as well, was that the center hoped to find out what seems of interest to them and what does not, as part of an ongoing effort to enhance visitors' experiences. The danger in such an observational strategy is that in the course of studying how visitors plan and evaluate, researchers may induce such activity where it might not otherwise have occurred. Although we cannot rule this out, we believe that the presence of the observers did not stimulate students and teachers to plan, monitor, or evaluate more. Our preliminary observations did not reflect high levels of any of these behaviors, and, in general, we did not find that groups behaved in any ways that could be interpreted as attempts to please the observer or otherwise make the participants look good.

Where

Observations of where the small groups went as they explored confirmed a widely reported finding in museum research: Visitors spend remarkably little time, on average, at individual exhibits (Falk & Dierking, 1992). Within given school groups, however, the smaller subgroups into which the larger group split demonstrated wide variations in this pattern. For example, in a high school group, which had been split in two, the group led by the science teacher who organized the trip exhibited an entirely different pattern from that of the group led by a teacher who volunteered that morning to accompany the students. The science teacher's group at one point spent 63 minutes in just two areas (both containing live animals and ecological exhibits). The other teacher's group spent 65 minutes during which, as the students described it, they "saw the whole place." They had indeed traversed the entire science center.

This difference in where the students went likely is a result of teacher influence, in this instance connections the science teacher made to the students' own ongoing biological study. In one sense, the groups are not comparable because of the different resources the students had available to them in the person of the teacher. However, as an example of how overt behavior patterns are captured in the focus on where groups go, these observations are instructive. When the primary teacher examined these results, she indicated that she would prepare a list of classroom connections for chaperones and other teachers in the future.

Transitions

In groups that exhibited little advance planning, two distinct transition patterns emerged. One pattern was characteristic of teacher and chaperone statements and the other of student statements. Teacher transitions from area to area were managerial and organizational. Typical statements included, "Let's move on"; "Let's walk over here"; "Want to try something else?" Less typical, but distinctly present, were comments such as "O.K., let's find something else"; "Come on, we can't spend too much time on one thing if we want to see a lot."

Typical student transitions were of a different character. Student exclamations included, "Check this out, it's really cool"; "Oh, look at this over here"; and "Let's go see animals [or some other specific exhibit area] and stuff." Students who had been to the science center before made significantly more statements of the latter sort. In many groups, these experienced students held high status, at least for the day, among their peers and functioned as de facto group leaders. Several teachers related how some of these experienced students surprised them with how engaged and forthcoming they were in comparison to their more reserved classroom participation style.

Finally, just as some teachers exerted transitional pressure on students to move on so they could *see everything* (as above), some students exerted social pressure on others not to spend too much time in any one place. Some of this pressure simply expressed the speaker's desire to use what someone else was using or to do what someone else was doing. Other comments, however, contained evaluative judgments of students' performances. For example, one group of three students was spending a significant amount of time manipulating a crane and some magnetic blocks. Other students passed by and said, "Look, the morons are still at it." The targeted students persisted, but comments such as these can lead students to desist and move on to another activity.

Connections

An observational focus on connections targets those statements and questions visitors ask that link their current experience with other sources of experience. Examples include overlapping links made to (a) personal experience, (b) school-based study, and (c) related exhibits in the science center. These connections are often not the most important ones students make as part of interaction with an exhibit—their specific questions, such as "How does it work?"; "Is that true?"; and "Why did that happen?"; and subsequent investigative activity likely make a more fundamental contribution to their basic conceptual learning. However, consistent with our focus on the regulation of learning, documenting connections made serves systematically to identify the kinds of prior and related experiences that form connections for students. Deeper understanding of these natural links allows the design of techniques that prompt students to make them and enhance their benefits for those who would not spontaneously have made them. This in turn can provide, through students' self-generated links, connections in support of sustained activity stretching across formal and free-choice sectors.

Personal sources of experience predominated in the observed student-made connections. In exhibits on health and the human body, students frequently described their own health history. Live animal exhibits prompted accounts of students' own pets and travel experiences. Students viewing exhibits on structures and related human-designed systems commented on similarities in construction and physical environment they themselves had seen. Students also connected new experiences to personal expectations by saying, "It was [or was not] like I thought it would be," and "It did [or did not] feel like they say it does." Connections between science and everyday life often were made by teachers' prompting students (e.g., "These are germs in your body").

Teacher connections, though surprisingly infrequent, were often made to the classroom: "Remember when I was teaching this in class?" Another typical connection teachers made to formal school-based study was to globally characterize an exhibit as "Oh, that's physics," "That's chemistry," and so on. These connections were often made in response to student queries in the form "What's that?" These global responses and references to formal, disciplinary knowledge appeared to constitute a satisfactory explanation to teachers and perhaps achieved the desired effect of limiting questions about topics the teachers felt unprepared to address. References to related experiences in the science center were made by both teachers and students. Most often these were statements such as "This (activity) is my favorite" and "This is like my favorite."

CONCLUSION

The pilot research described here reflects part of our current efforts to understand and enhance the free choice visitors exercise in science centers. We seek to know where to target support, how to target support, and how to measure any changes in visitor behavior and learning associated with those forms of support. The WTC framework provides information regarding where to target support. The pilot study of map use and goal-setting provides a test of how to target support. Both the WTC framework and the map yield concrete representations of activities that can serve as instructional and assessment tools of use to teachers, students, and center staff.

The WTC framework is a measure for recording group planning-in-action and reflection as an indicator of emerging plans, prior experience, and links to other sources of experience. This record serves several purposes. The information in the record provides cues for action based upon how visitors exercise free choice. An example of such a cue is the observed managerial and organizational focus of many teacher transitions. Such transitions could be targeted and trans-formed into inquiry- or activity-based suggestions that would not interfere with students' free choice but instead capitalize on teachers' unique knowledge of where their students stand in relation to exhibit options.

In addition, observations in the WTC framework can provide a record of change following an intervention. The overt patterns of exhibit exploration, the expressed rationales for moving from exhibit to exhibit, and the connections made in conversation provide a concrete representation, for students, teachers, and staff, of a science center visit as experienced by the visitors. Evaluations of the quality of what one experienced and learned can be related to this record, and groups can compare how their experience might be related to the manner in which they explored.

The WTC observations shed light on the role experienced group members play in group exploration. Those with greater experience and, therefore, more well-grounded preferences exerted great influence on the overall path taken by those in their group. This too is a cue for action. It suggests that information and planning aids that provide visitors an opportunity to learn what is in the center and thus to selectively pursue their interests can help first-time visitors to explore with some of the efficiency of more experienced visitors.

The pilot study of a specially designed map supportive of goal-setting is one such planning aid. The trend identified in help-seeking behavior in which students who engage in informed goal-setting appear oriented toward capitaliz-ing on staff as a source of help is significant. It is representative of a means of support for students' free-choice learning that helps students to regulate their own learning better through enhanced planning, monitoring, and evaluation of their learning in context.

The low levels of planning, monitoring, and reflecting that are typical are not surprising given the sometimes overwhelming array of options, people, and even simply noise students encounter during visits. Students can be helped to slow down, to think, and to inquire. One source of such "speed bumps" is the student's own personal constellation of expectations and interests. Encouraging students' hopes and curiosities and helping them to think about connections to their personal experiences and interests before their visit could make a differ-ence. We are continuing to explore whether the continuity provided by a single, consistent tool for planning and reflecting, such as using the map provided in this study, can also contribute to planning and reflecting behaviors conducive to learning.

Our focus on supporting and documenting visitors' choices is part of a comprehensive approach necessary to building tools, strategies, and design ele-ments that can enhance the learning-conducive behaviors of visitors. One obsta-cle to overcome is the several ways in which exhibit design itself—the "supply side"—can inhibit learning: design marked by a focus on isolated phenomena, divorced from any larger meaningful context; organization of exhibition content around curatorially driven principles only; and a reliance on overly structured information. These elements of exhibit design not only contrast sharply with the way our real world is experienced; they also present barriers to learning in free-choice environments. There is some indication that visitors are more engaged by and learn more from exhibitions designed in the manner of the Victorian clutter of early exhibitions (Gurian, 1991). This proposition brings with it both promise and peril, however, for the clutter that proves engaging can also prove distracting. The clutter can conceal support for personal exploration embedded in the exhibit itself.

The strategies we are exploring are designed to aid in developing self-directed visit structures that benefit from personal, social, and exhibit-based support. This initial exploration has identified sources for supporting and documenting the difficult freedom intrinsic to free-choice learning.

REFERENCES

Allen, N. L., Swinton, S. S., Isham, S. P., & Zelenak, C. A. (1997). *Technical report of the NAEP 1996 state assessment program in science.* Washington, DC: U.S. Department of Education, Office of Education Research and Improvement, National Center for Education Statistics.

Brown, A. L. (1987). Metacognition, executive control, self-regulation, and other more mysterious mechanisms. In F. Weinert & R. Kluwe (Eds.), *Metacognition, motivation and understanding* (pp. 65–116). Hillsdale, NJ: Lawrence Erlbaum.

Falk, J. H., & Dierking, L. D. (1992). *The museum experience.* Washington, DC: Whalesback Books.

Gelman, R., Massey, C. M., & McManus, M. (1991). Characterizing supporting environments for cognitive development: Lessons from children in a museum. In L. B. Resnick, J. M. Levine, & S. D. Teasley (Eds.), *Perspectives on socially shared cognition* (pp. 226–256). Washington, DC: American Psychological Association.

Gurian, E. H. (1991). Noodling around with exhibition opportunities. In I. Karp & S. D. Lavine (Eds.), *Exhibiting cultures: The poetics and politics of museum display* (pp.176–190). Washington, DC: Smithsonian Institution Press.

O'Sullivan, C. Y., & Weiss, A. R. (1999). *Student work and teacher practices in science* (NCES 455). Washington, DC: U.S. Department of Education, Office of Education Research and Improvement, National Center for Education Statistics.

Salomon, G. (1993). *Distributed cognitions: Psychological and educational considerations.* New York: Cambridge University Press.

Schauble, L., & Glaser, R. (1996). *Innovations in learning: New environments for education.* Mahwah, NJ: Lawrence Erlbaum.

Schunk, D. H., & Zimmerman, B. J. (Eds.). (1998). *Self-regulated learning: From teaching to self-regulated practice.* New York: Guilford.

Wigfield, A., Eccles, J. S., & Pintrich, P. R. (1996). Development between the ages of

11 and 25. In D. C. Berliner & R. C. Calfee (Eds.), *Handbook of educational psychology* (pp. 148–185). New York: Simon & Schuster Macmillan.

Winne, P. H. (1997). Experimenting to bootstrap self-regulated learning. *Journal of Educational Psychology, 89,* 397–410.

Zimmerman, B. J. (1994). Dimensions of academic self-regulation: A conceptual framework for education. In D. H. Schunk & B. J. Zimmerman (Eds.), *Self-regulation of learning and performance: Issues and educational applications* (pp. 73–86). Hillsdale, NJ: Lawrence Erlbaum.

Zimmerman, B. J. (1998). Academic studying and the development of personal skill: A self-regulatory perspective. *Educational Psychologist, 33,* 73–86.

PART III

Looking to the Future

CHAPTER 9

The First Free-Choice Science Learning Conference: From Issues to Future Directions

Jessica J. Luke, Betty Dunckel Camp,
Lynn D. Dierking, and Ursula J. Pearce

Free-Choice Learning: Assessing the Informal Science Education Infrastructure, a national conference held in Los Angeles in November 1998, was convened to facilitate a dialogue around two broad themes:

1. Defining the multidimensional nature of the science learning infrastructure.
2. Developing strategies for building and consolidating the infrastructure to better facilitate free-choice learning.

Throughout the 2-day meeting, participants heard and discussed papers presented by their colleagues, engaged in spirited dialogue during small and large group discussions, and exchanged information and ideas about free-choice science learning. The conference papers have been revised and edited, and are included as the first two sections of this book. This chapter provides in-depth insight into the nature of the conference dialogue, summarizing the issues and ideas that emerged from group discussions.

For instance, what is an infrastructure for free-choice science learning and does one already exist? What is the scope of that infrastructure and, more important, the benefits? What are the common terms and mental models for the infrastructure? What strategies can be used to encourage coalition building and collaboration across the infrastructure? And, finally, what are the overall goals of the infrastructure and who is the audience? Participants' thoughts on these issues are explored throughout the chapter, with a view toward both current realities and future directions for creating a stronger infrastructure to facilitate research, policy-making, and practice related to free-choice learning.

SETTING THE STAGE

The 65 conference participants represented three key groups in the free-choice science learning community: (a) researchers concerned with assessing the structure and function of the infrastructure; (b) leaders from free-choice science learning institutions and resources (e.g., museums, zoos, aquariums, science centers, broadcast and print media, the Internet, and community-based organizations such as the Humane Society); and (c) policymakers concerned with supporting and implementing community-based science learning. (A complete list of conference participants is included in the Appendix.) Although these three groups share a common interest in promoting public awareness and understanding of science, historically they have not been connected and have been only vaguely aware of each other's efforts and impacts. By providing forums for conversation, the conference encouraged significant interactions among leading researchers, practitioners, and policymakers.

The opening remarks by conference host John H. Falk, director of the Institute for Learning Innovation in Annapolis, Maryland, offered a framework for the meeting. Falk stressed that individuals learn science from a wide range of sources in the infrastructure, including the formal education system as well as free-choice sources such as libraries, museums, television, film and video, newspapers, radio, books, magazines, the Internet, organizations and clubs, and family members and friends. Although there is a growing recognition of the importance of the infrastructure for free-choice learning in facilitating public awareness and understanding of science, relatively little is known about how effective the institutions are individually and collectively; how and why the public utilizes some parts of the infrastructure and not others; how the various pieces interact to reinforce or contradict each other; or what strategies would best maximize the potential of the infrastructure.

The Work of the Conference

With the above framework in mind, participants spent 2 days discussing and strategizing ways to better define and build an infrastructure for facilitating free-choice learning. In particular, two break-out sessions during the conference encouraged idea-generating and information-sharing among participants.

In the first session, participants were divided into five small groups. Each group included a facilitator and a diverse mix of approximately 12 conference participants representing divergent orientations and perspectives—researchers, practitioners, and policymakers from museums, universities, and professional organizations as well as from broadcast and print media. The small groups were charged with the task of beginning to construct a framework for describing the multidimensional nature of the infrastructure for free-choice science learning.

In the second group-discussion session, participants turned their attention to strategies for building, strengthening, and consolidating the infrastructure. Emlyn Koster, director of the Liberty Science Center in New Jersey, suggested an agenda for this large group discussion: (a) Vocabulary—Establishing common terms and mental models within the infrastructure; (b) Strategies—Building consensus and collaborations within the infrastructure; and (c) Goals—Creating a common agenda within the infrastructure.

Terms. Before getting into the heart of the issues and ideas raised in the conference discussions, it is important to clarify the terms being discussed throughout this chapter. For the purposes of this book, an "infrastructure" has been defined as an interwoven network of educational, social, and cultural resources that work synergistically to facilitate free-choice learning more generally and science learning more broadly (cf. Chapter 1). The concept of "free-choice learning" refers to the type of learning that occurs typically outside of school, in particular, the type of learning facilitated by museums, science centers, a wide range of community-based organizations, and print and electronic media including the Internet (cf. Chapter 1).

Issues and Ideas
What is an infrastructure, and does an infrastructure for free-choice science learning currently exist?

During conference discussions, participants repeatedly returned to the notion of what an infrastructure is and whether or not one exists in the free-choice science learning community. In his paper, "Who Produces Science Information for the Public," Bruce Lewenstein set the stage by offering the first working definition of an infrastructure for conference participants: a pattern of connections that provides for interaction, communication, and especially progress. He went on to say that if no infrastructure exists, then each group interested in the public communication of science will have to create its own programs, materials, and systems for facilitating science learning. If, on the other hand, an infrastructure exists, then the creativity and energy of individuals in the field can be directed toward the development of new approaches and collaborations that will serve the ultimate goal of increasing public understanding of science. Lewenstein argued that there is indeed an infrastructure for free-choice science learning in place, and he cited evidence for the existence of this infrastructure (cf. Chapter 2).

Some conference participants challenged Lewenstein's assumption, focusing almost entirely on the nature of the connections between the myriad science learning resources available to the public. Participants argued that although there are connections and collaborations between these various resources, the connections are too dependent upon individuals and, as such, they are too ephemeral and ad hoc to be called an infrastructure. For instance, in summarizing the threads of discussion in her small group session, Jessica Luke, from the Institute for Learning Innovation, suggested, "We need to think about formal links rather than personal ones. We should be aiming for institutional links rather than ad hoc connections made through specific people."

On the whole, participants agreed that while an infrastructure may not currently exist, the present links within the science learning community do lay the necessary groundwork for the building of an infrastructure. Speaking for his small group, David Bibas, from the California Science Center in Los Angeles, acknowledged that although "there is not an infrastructure now, there is great potential for one; work is needed to help one emerge." Diane Perlov, also from the California Science Center, offered the following analogy that emerged from her group discussion: "What we currently have are trade routes. We are pioneers putting the routes across, but we do not yet have an infrastructure."

The majority of participants clearly felt that the time had come to build and consolidate the infrastructure. There were some, however, who offered a different perspective, suggesting that rather than a formalized infrastructure perhaps what was needed was more of a loose collaboration on a project-by-project basis. These participants felt that a more organic structure, one in which the level of coordination and communication varied according to the nature of the project, would be best suited to the current needs and realities of the free-choice science learning community.

What is the scope of the infrastructure for free-choice science learning?

Participants conversed about the various groups that make up the infrastructure. Summarizing discussion in her small group, Lynn Dierking, from the Institute for Learning Innovation, asked, "Does the infrastructure include federal agencies? Schools? Individual institutions? Funding agencies? What about health organizations and policymakers? Does it include the media?" Participants acknowledged that the infrastructure comprised a variety of divergent resources and institutions, and that many of these resources and institutions were unaware of their contribution to a larger whole. In the words of Donna Mitroff, from Fox Kids Network in Los Angeles, "The librarians and journalists did not come to this meeting, probably because they did not recognize [as a group] that they are part of the infrastructure and that what they do relates to our work. How do we get them to recognize the links that are out there?" A number of participants suggested that stronger and more abundant connections need to be built among the various components of the infrastructure.

Discussion also focused on whether the infrastructure should be science-based or more interdisciplinary in focus. Conference participants acknowledged that not all of the members of the free-choice science community were exclusively science-focused, suggesting that it may be beneficial to widen the lens to include all disciplines. Diane Perlov summarized relevant discussion in her group with the following questions: "What is the scope of the infrastructure? Informal education or science education or both? How broad is the infrastructure? If it is just science, how does that affect multidisciplinary organizations? Some of the groups absent from the conference, such as the Girl Scouts or libraries, may not be exclusively science-based. What kind of an infrastructure are we looking for?"

Repeatedly, participants returned to the role of the formal education system in the infrastructure for science learning, discussing whether the infrastructure includes links with the formal education system or whether it should be separate. Participants were divided on this issue. Some felt strongly that the infrastructure should involve distinct relationships with the formal system. Summarizing multiple voices within her group's discussion, Jessica Luke said, "Free-choice learning is only part of the science education infrastructure. What is more important is how we relate to the whole and how we relate to the formal education infrastructure." It was felt by many that one of the most important challenges for the infrastructure is to create links with the formal system, equal links with equal partnerships. Others felt that the infrastructure for free-choice science learning was entirely separate from the formal education system and should seek to facilitate awareness and understanding of science outside of the formal system.

What are the benefits of having an infrastructure for free-choice science learning?

Having talked about the need to build a better infrastructure, and bring together the various groups that are part of the infrastructure, conference participants took some time to affirm the perceived value and benefits of investing in the development of an infrastructure. One group, facilitated by David Bibas, offered the following explanation: "There is room to bring all the groups together. The whole is greater than the sum of the parts. Investment in an infrastructure will have greater returns. Each individual entity is otherwise limited by its own constraints." Participants agreed that the main payoff of having an infrastructure is that it enables the sharing and pooling of available resources, expertise, and professional development.

As a further strength, some suggested that an infrastructure would allow the reinforcement of messages by communicating them in multiple ways to multiple groups. There also was mention of the political and economic benefits to forging collaborations among members of the infrastructure. Although it can be argued that people learn much of what they know outside of school, most of the public money for education goes to the schools. By building a coalition of free-choice learning organizations that includes museums, libraries, print and broadcast media, the Internet, and community-based organizations, a powerful lobbying force is created for redistributing public education funds. Individually, these organizations have had little ability to compete with the powerful formal education lobby; collectively they would have a much greater chance of being successful.

What are the common terms and mental models for the infrastructure?

Perhaps one of the most critical discussion threads woven throughout the 2-day conference was the need to define common terms and create mental models for the infrastructure. In order to function effectively, the free-choice learning community needs a shared set of terms to describe their collective structure and their collective work. Participants sought greater clarification about the nature of the infrastructure for free-choice learning. Is infrastructure the best construct? What are the distinctions between free-choice learning and informal learning?

Although participants agreed on the need to develop an infrastructure, the infrastructure model was problematic for some. Summarizing discussion in his group, David Bibas commented, "We need to think about the metaphor of an infrastructure. What are the implications of choosing and using it and how do we make our choice explicit?" As an alternative, it was suggested that a web or network might serve as a more appropriate model, although it was acknowledged that a network metaphor has limitations as well:

> An infrastructure implies it is the framework on which something else can go. A network or web implies that there are nodes that are interconnected in some way. The infrastructure metaphor has the notion that we can build on it, that we do not have to reinvent each piece. Although nodes of a network or web can communicate, they are independent. The way a network functions is that some pieces can drop off but the whole keeps working. We need each piece so that we can build new things, like partnerships and collaborations. In order for that to happen, we need to

recognize the stability in communication between the different groups (Bruce Lewenstein, Cornell University, New York).

Another interesting and viable alternative suggested was that of a system, a complex whole formed from interacting and interrelated groups. Uncomfortable with the rigidity and permanence implied by the infrastructure model, supporters of the system model perceived it as more flexible, more organic, and more responsive to the changing nature of the free-choice science learning community. In the words of one group, facilitated by Lynn Dierking, "Consider the model that what we are right now is an ad hoc, nonhierarchical, decentralized system. The systems approach would allow connections to the infrastructure for formal education as well."

The mental models and terms used to describe the learning within the infrastructure were questioned. On a broad level, participants focused on the differences in meaning between the terms *learning* and *education*, emphasizing that these two terms are not synonymous and stressing the need for common terminology. Elsa Bailey, from Lesley College in Somerville, Massachusetts, commented, "The word learning means something different to the public than education. Education is something scary, but if they think of themselves as helping children grow and learn, they are more willing to enter the dialogue."

More specifically, the debate over the terms *informal learning* versus *free-choice learning* was particularly heated. Since the 1970s, museum professionals have been using the term *informal learning* to distinguish their activities from the activities of school-based formal educators (formal learning). And in the last two decades, informal learning increasingly has achieved recognition within the educational community. However, Falk and Dierking (1998) have recently suggested that free-choice learning might be a more appropriate way to characterize what goes on in the infrastructure. Falk and Dierking point out that although there is clearly an important distinction between formal and informal education settings, the problem arises when the terms formal and informal are used as modifiers of the word learning. Learning is influenced by many factors, they argue, including the physical context. However, the physical context alone is unlikely to influence the type of learning that occurs in any given place. Proponents of this term argue that "free-choice learning" focuses on the unique characteristics of such learning—freely chosen, nonsequential, self-paced, and voluntary—rather than on where the learning occurs.

In addition, there was a perceived political benefit to using the term *free-choice learning* to characterize what goes on in the infrastructure. In the words of John Falk, "Politically, there will always be barriers created by the term *informal learning* because it will always be considered by some as second best; it will always be pejorative. *Free-choice learning* will be viewed as a more positive term."

Conference participants were divided in their support for informal learning versus free-choice learning. Some felt that *informal learning* is a well-established term that is known and carries currency in the field. For instance, Barbara Butler, formerly at the National Science Foundation in Arlington, Virginia, pointed out that "there are dictionary definitions for both formal and informal learning and they are all exclusive. Informal education is voluntary, self-directed learning. It's been defined for some time now. Let's either agree on the definitions that are out there or agree to redefine them. What's the relationship between informal learning and free-choice learning? How are they similar and how are they different? What do each of those words actually mean?"

Other conference participants subscribed to the newer, and perhaps less well-known term, *free-choice learning*, arguing that it focused on the learner rather than on the setting in which the learning takes place. These participants acknowledged the inherent difficulty in redefining established terms but felt it could be done. Bonnie Van Dorn, from the Association of Science-Technology Centers in Washington, DC, commented, "I like the term *free-choice learning*. Just as the California Science Center changed its name, so we can change ours. But there has to be a reason for doing it. It's taken a long time to get 'informal education' known on the Hill [Capitol Hill, Washington, DC]. If we're going to change our name, let's not take it lightly. Let's conduct a public relations activity amongst ourselves to make it known."

What strategies can be used to encourage coalition building and collaborations across the infrastructure?

During the 2-day conference, individuals from disparate parts of the infrastructure were asked to strategize means for fostering collaborations. What resulted from these discussions was not a list of specific strategies but a broader acknowledgment of the many obstacles inherent in collaboration. Although conference participants recognized the benefits of working together to facilitate free-choice learning, they emphasized that collaboration was not always easy. The various obstacles to collaboration were listed, including difficulties in reaching consensus on a mission, frequent differences in the political agendas of collaborators, the need for multiple outcomes and strategies, and the amount of time and resources required to initiate and maintain collaborations.

Furthermore, collaboration was seen as something that was oftentimes mandated rather than desired. For instance, summarizing discussion in her group, Roxie Esterle from the California Science Center noted, "Most often we collaborate simply because funders demand it." It was suggested that external motivations for working together do not readily lead to successful collaboration. Instead, conference participants recommended the creation of specific, internally driven goals for collaboration.

Further complicating the issue, participants emphasized the diverse nature of the different groups within the infrastructure—from museums to television to print media to libraries. People wondered if the various parts of the free-choice science learning community share a common mission that could be translated into collaboration. It was also suggested by one group that rather than developing a formalized system for collaboration, perhaps what is more appropriate is a loose form of collaboration that happens on a project-by-project basis.

What are the overall goals of the infrastructure?

Conference participants agreed that for the infrastructure to come together as a functional and credible whole, common goals should be created for it. Many felt that one of the first orders of business should be to decide upon the outcomes, expectations, and standards to be used within the infrastructure and to agree how to assess and document the effectiveness of the infrastructure in achieving those outcomes. In short, there was overwhelming consensus on the need for a common agenda that would move the infrastructure forward with one strong, unified voice.

Much discussion concerned the nature of a common agenda for the infrastructure: Is the goal of the free-choice science learning community to get people excited about science and about learning? Or is the primary goal awareness and recognition that free-choice learning is a real part of people's everyday lives and has validity and meaning for both individuals and society? Is the free-choice science learning community "building a bridge to take science to the people and people to science"? Or is it most important to focus on scientific literacy, helping people to "understand what good science is versus what junk science is"?

After much debate, participants generally agreed upon the following agenda, first suggested by Carey Tisdal from Missouri's St. Louis Science Center and then revised by the group at large: *"To develop linkages for and communicate the value of free-choice science learning with the public and learners, policy makers, practitioners and professionals."*

To whom does the infrastructure need to be credible? Who is the audience?

In conversing about a common agenda, participants acknowledged that there are different goals for different audiences. In the words of Sholly Fisch from Children's Television Network in New York City, "Some of the ends of the infrastructure relate to the public and learners, some relate to policy makers, and some relate to practitioners." In particular, it was suggested by Jon Miller, from Chicago's International Center for the Advancement of Scientific Literacy, that preschool children and adults comprise the primary target audience:

We are trying to figure out how to portray ourselves relative to formal education, but once a person has finished formal education, science keeps
happening. Because of the pace of scientific change [free-choice science
learning] institutions play a particular role in enriching and enhancing
adult understanding of science, therefore we are not competing with formal education. Also, formal education is not affecting pre-school age, so
they are our key audiences—adults and preschool.

Family and societal issues also figured prominently in discussions about
the audience for the infrastructure. Emlyn Koster asked, "How do we address
ourselves to the needs of society? What are those burning needs? We need to
be relevant and address ourselves to matters at hand. In addressing social and
educational causes in society we have a unique role." It was suggested that what
distinguishes the free-choice community from the formal system is the social
relevance of the learning that occurs in the free-choice infrastructure. Ken Phillips from the California Science Center commented, "We can foster parent and
child relationships in a way that formal education cannot. What makes us unique
is that we can strengthen family and community connections."

FUTURE DIRECTIONS

The first Free-Choice Learning Conference brought together researchers, practitioners, and policymakers to discuss a number of fundamental and challenging
issues facing the free-choice science learning community: Is there such a thing
as an infrastructure for free-choice science learning? What would it look like to
step back and think about science learning more systemically, with each of us
contributing to a larger whole? How can we best integrate all the various components of the infrastructure to effectively facilitate free-choice learning?

Perhaps the most profound outcome of this national dialogue was the real-
ization that there are no easy answers to any of the above-mentioned issues.
Just as a research study often raises as many questions as it answers, conference
conversations oftentimes generated more questions than answers. The questions
and issues raised, however, serve as a rich and fertile seedbed from which we
can draw the next steps for defining and building a better infrastructure to facilitate free-choice learning.

Although the notion of an infrastructure for free-choice science learning
may not be firmly entrenched, it is generally recognized and accepted as a
loosely defined collective. Being part of a larger infrastructure offers clear benefits—the sharing of expertise, the pooling of resources, and the economic and
political clout that comes with a strong, unified voice. At the same time, an
infrastructure is a complex, multidimensional entity that is composed of varying

groups with diverse agendas. As Bruce Lewenstein points out in Chapter 2 of this book, the complexity of the free-choice science learning system should not lead us to expect simple answers to the "problem" of encouraging and facilitating free-choice learning. In order to move forward, it will be important to more clearly define the nature of the infrastructure, articulating its various constituents and clearly delineating its parameters. It will also be important to define and build the infrastructure from within, making its benefits explicit to each and every member in order to build consensus.

As further thought is given to defining the infrastructure, it may be more useful to regard the collective as a system rather than as an infrastructure. An infrastructure carries associations of permanence and rigidity, whereas a systems approach offers a model more flexible, more dynamic, and more responsive to the changing nature and needs of the informal science education community. In *Blueprints for Reform* (1998), the American Association for the Advancement of Science points to the need for understanding education as a system, emphasizing that this system includes both formal and free-choice learning and recognizes that what one "knows" is an ongoing process and the product of what occurs in both settings. It also recognizes the complexity of learning and that one cannot consider science learning by itself but must instead regard it as one part of the total interdisciplinary picture.

Whether it is an infrastructure or a system, a critical next step in building and consolidating the free-choice science learning community is establishing terms and mental models used by all constituents. Perhaps the most crucial issue to be resolved is the debate about the terms *informal learning* and *free-choice learning*. For some, *free-choice learning* is the more appropriate term, as it focuses on the learner rather than on the setting in which the learning takes place. For others, *free-choice learning* simply confuses matters—why introduce another term into the mix when *informal learning* is a clearly recognized and established term within the field? It will be important to come to some agreement on this terminology within the science learning community in order to move forward.

Equally important for future directions is the need to increase awareness and buy-in by all involved in free-choice science learning—that is, consensus building. This requires that participants step back from their individual perspectives and recognize that they are working toward the collective success of all. By doing so, they recognize that the whole is indeed greater than the sum of its parts, and that success of the whole also means success for individual participants. Fostering collaboration is another crucial step in consolidating the infrastructure. It will be important to brainstorm innovative ways for practitioners from various parts of the infrastructure to collaborate so that efforts are not seen as time- and labor-intensive mandates but rather as necessary ways to maximize strengths.

In addition to building consensus and fostering collaboration, common goals need to be created within the infrastructure as a whole. Perhaps the greatest benefit of a collective infrastructure is the ability to speak with one, strong, unified voice—the economic, political, and social benefits of one collective voice are staggering. It will also be important to define more specific goals of the various constituents of the infrastructure, including researchers, policymakers, practitioners, and the public.

CONCLUSION

This conference represented an important starting point in building a more inclusive, and ultimately more successful, infrastructure for free-choice science learning. Although many issues remain unresolved, the conference catalyzed discussion and started people down a path toward a stronger, more stable infrastructure. Building on the foundation of this first conference, we can look forward to continued efforts to forge collaborations between disparate parts of the science learning community.

REFERENCES

American Association for the Advancement of Science. (1998). *Blueprints for reform.* New York: Oxford University Press.

Falk, J. H., & Dierking, L. D. (1998, July). Free-choice learning: An alternative term to informal learning. *Informal Learning Environments Research, 2,* 2.

CHAPTER 10

The Free-Choice Education Sector as a Sleeping Giant in the Public Policy Debate

Diane B. Frankel

As executive director of the Bay Area Discovery Museum in Sausalito, California, from 1986 until 1993, I had the pleasure of seeing busloads of school children walk through our door, and watching as their eyes widened with wonder at the sights and experiences before them. Whether it was the exhibition that gave new meaning to the familiar San Francisco Bay, or the exhibition explaining the craft of architecture and design, the museum clearly made an impression on the young developing minds that visited us.

In those days, not so long ago, we made very little effort to quantify the learning that took place within our walls. Sure, the museum staff and I talked to the teachers, especially those who took the trouble to return with the same class again and again, taking pains to incorporate the museum and museum experience into their course work.

Those teachers told us that the children's learning took off after visits to the museum. It stimulated some of the children who had seemed disinterested in the classroom, and reinvigorated those who already were good performers.

And we'd walk away from those conversations, proud of the contribution we had made. Like many other museums at that time, we made little effort to systematically track our progress as an institution of learning and, not having that information, never thought about sharing it with the rest of the museum community or the public policy experts whose decisions would have such a tremendous effect on us. What a loss!

Today's museums and other members of the free-choice learning community involved in providing free-choice education experiences have a better understanding of the importance of collecting and sharing data that demonstrate an organization's effect on the community it serves. But this sector lags far behind where it needs to be in order to take its rightful place at the table when relevant public policy decisions are being made. However, the time has never been as auspicious for the free-choice education sector to make its mark and redefine itself as a proactive player in the making of public policy.

The history of museum public policy provides an enlightening backdrop to ways members of the free-choice education sector can play an active role in collaborating among themselves and in benefiting the communities they serve.

A BRIEF HISTORY OF MUSEUMS AND PUBLIC POLICY

The life of the arts, far from being an interruption, a distraction, in the life of the nation, is very close to the center of a nation's purpose—and is a test of the quality of a nation's civilization.
—President John F. Kennedy, 1962

Although the federal government took an active role in advancing the arts and humanities from the earliest days of our nation's history, direct grant-making support did not come about until much more recently. The first government-backed museums were formed with private gifts of money and art. James Smithson's monetary gift launched the Smithsonian Institution in 1846, and it was Andrew W. Mellon's major art collection and endowment that led to the establishment of the National Gallery of Art.

But even before the federal government became a direct grant maker, it affected cultural life through its programs and policies. Second-class postage rates encouraged what was then considered the rapid communication of ideas, and in 1917 Congress enacted a provision allowing tax deductions for contributions to educational, cultural, and social service organizations. The Works Progress Administration (WPA) programs of the 1930s gave money—and employment—to thousands of artists and researchers, stimulating cultural expression that is still appreciated today.

But it wasn't until 1965, when President Lyndon B. Johnson established the National Endowment for the Arts (NEA) and the National Endowment for the Humanities (NEH), that the government took a direct role in helping to improve public access to cultural institutions and to encourage individual acts of creativity.

The Institute of Museum Services (IMS) was established by a law enacted in 1976 to offer general operating support to qualified art, history, and science museums, botanical gardens, and zoos. And in 1996, the federal museum and library programs were joined together in one agency, creating the Institute of Museum and Library Services (IMLS).

WHY IS PUBLIC POLICY IMPORTANT?

Thirty years ago, the network of state arts and humanities councils, which now are prominent in every state, did not exist. Today, the network provides state and local support for a rich American cultural life that is difficult to imagine flourishing without such support. Since the creation of the NEA, the NEH, and the IMLS, there has been a marked increase in the number of cultural programs created, the number of historic sites preserved, and the number of creative works produced. As an ardent populist, I see federal involvement in culture as nothing less than critical.

I know that many stakeholders in the free-choice education sector have their own stories to tell of the influence federal support has had on their institutions—or how a federal grant made a tremendous difference in the existence of a project or the conservation of an artifact. And I also know that those in the museum community are all too aware of budget cuts that have been made in the field.

Although there was a brief period when learning institutions such as museums could take for granted that they would receive federal funding and that politicians would consider it their duty to insure that museum doors remained open, those days for the most part are over. The mood of public policymakers of the final decade of the twentieth century has been to privatize as much as possible. Essentially, the trend reduces the responsibility government has as funder and makes government smaller by decreasing its commitments. The NEA, the NEH, and the IMLS have seen their budgets cut—in fact, federal funds to these agencies have not grown, in real dollars, since 1979. During the mid- to late 1990s, the NEA was cut by 39 percent, the NEH by 36 percent, and the IMLS by 28 percent. The IMLS has been able to fund fewer and fewer museums that qualify for grants.

Cultural institutions, particularly museums, feeling those cuts would do well to ask themselves some important questions: How can we do a better job of communicating our importance to public policy makers? How can we take a more proactive role in the public policy debate?

The assumption that people learn by visiting museums and libraries, watching public television, and attending performances is central to any discussion pertaining to public policy and the free-choice education sector. Quite simply, the degree to which policymakers find the free-choice learning sector worthy of public funding is the degree to which this sector will be a place where people learn throughout a lifetime.

BUILDING BRIDGES TO CLOSE THE GAPS

Education is the number one priority of the public right now. Falling test scores, violence in the schools, the growth of home schooling and charter schools, welfare reform, adult education, and the technological revolution have all conspired to make this a great time for those involved in the free-choice education sector to become major players in public policy debates if they put the time and care into this effort.

Making the Connection

How can they do this? First, they must learn to connect what they are providing with bigger issues. For example, museums and libraries must begin to quantify their ability to teach and make the public aware of that ability. It is great that the free-choice education sector is taking a greater role in partnerships with schools, often filling important gaps in schools' curricula, but where are the partnerships with the Department of Education? Have these organizations worked at quantifying their influence as educators so that a strong case can be made that they are important partners in the educational process? It is great that museums and libraries are initiating after-school programs that give kids a safe and educational place to go in the dangerous afternoon hours. But where are the partnerships with the Department of Justice? Who is looking at the success this sector has had in keeping kids out of danger?

More and more research has proven that children learn from a variety of methods and that learning by doing—as so often is the way promoted in children's museums—can be most effective. More research has shown that learning in the preschool years, even stimulating the imagination of children under 3 years old, can be invaluable in expanding children's capacity for learning later in life. How has the free-choice education sector tried to capitalize on that information?

Another way to communicate better to public policymakers lies in redefining the problem to make it more sympathetic to them. The category into which one places a problem helps structure people's perception of it in many important respects and can define our way of looking at and talking about that problem. For example, the Department of Transportation found it easier to get needed funding every year if instead of asking for money for "highway maintenance" it asked for funds to arrest "infrastructure deterioration." This helped make the issue seem more urgent and was perhaps a more accurate way of defining the problem.

Identifying the Infrastructure

All of us would agree that there is an infrastructure for health care and for compulsory education, but we might debate that there is an infrastructure for free-choice learning. Perhaps this is because in the other sectors the infrastructure has distinct and clearly articulated parts. In the formal education sector, we have K–12, community college, college, and graduate school. We can see how they interrelate and build upon one another. In our sector this pattern is definitely more difficult to see because the relationships are not linear. Our sector is more amorphous and includes a spectrum from the for-profit to the nonprofit, from the voluntary to the professional, and from the nonformal to the formal. If we are willing to at least entertain that we are a sector with common interests and concerns, the first step is to identify ourselves as a public policy community.

A public policy community is a group of specialists in a given policy area, scattered within and outside of government, who share in common their concern with one area of public policy. They need to come together to share information and to see if creating a common agenda is possible, then force themselves to hammer out such an agenda. In the free-choice learning sector there are multiple goals, and a broad one might be creating enhanced public awareness about the roles that museums, libraries, public television, and the performing arts play in the lives of Americans. But what if the ultimate goal was to be a community that was given priority in the public policy debate? It is fine for the goal to be broad, but the message has to be narrow.

I am advocating for a broad coalition within the free-choice learning sector and for the different groups to identify themselves with that sector in order to give the public a sense of the sector's breadth. The size of the sector legitimizes the individual parts and assists each group in articulating a public policy agenda that encompasses all of them. There can be communities within communities and partnerships that cut across communities. However, sometimes it is beneficial to come together over an issue that influences the entire free-choice learning sector so long as the message is narrowly focused and tightly targeted. The broader and more diffuse the message, the more difficult it will be to get anyone to pay attention to it.

Defining the Message. Consider the library community, for example. If their message was simply and broadly, "Let's get people to read," no one would oppose it, but no one would know what to do about it either.

Even if the message was, "Increase funding for reading programs so we can stop people from being illiterate," it is still too broad. But what if they looked at specifics and selected the one or two successful literacy programs and asked for specific funding for those programs, citing the number of people who have been enabled to enter the work force? That would be a powerful message.

The free-choice learning community should not find it difficult to break down the larger issues into narrower ones that relate to public need right now. By creating interconnections and benefits between broad societal concerns and the free-choice learning sector's abilities and vision, the sector should become a player in the public policy debates.

When one is in the trenches doing the hard day-to-day work of running an institution, it is very difficult to even contemplate putting in the extra effort needed to formulate the sort of compelling story the public and the public policy community must hear about your institution's needs. When I was director of the Bay Area Discovery Museum, I struggled to find the time to reach out to public policymakers. But times have changed, and now this work simply must be done, no matter how difficult or time-consuming.

Setting the Agenda. Frank Lindenfeld (1972) identified four stages of agenda setting. The first stage requires Issue Recognition, whereby an issue is noticed and perceived to be a potential topic of research. The second stage mandates Issue Adoption, if the issue warrants enough legitimacy for government action. Issue Prioritization, the third stage, suggests that the existing agenda be reordered and redesigned to include the new topic. And stage four, Issue Maintenance, facilitates the process of maintaining such an agenda until substantive decision making can take place.

I use these four stages as organizational tools to describe how members of representative communities within the free-choice learning sector can gain more public policy recognition.

ISSUE RECOGNITION: WHERE THE PLAYERS STEP FORWARD

How can we use issue recognition to achieve our goals? First, by finding relevant issues in the public and demonstrating how we are tied to them. For example, the report from the National Commission on Excellence in Education, *A Nation at Risk*, identified significant problems within the public school system and listed a number of potential solutions to those problems. Museums, libraries, and other institutions in the free-choice education sector were notably left off the list. For those of us who care about the future of these institutions, that study, and others like it, indicated the magnitude of the problem that such institutions face in getting recognition for the work they do in education.

Documenting our Progress

One way to solve this problem would be simply to do a better job of explaining what this sector does and how it is important to the nation. But it is difficult to market a product without documentation. Despite the good reputation that museums and other educational sources within the free-choice education sector have, our failure to have conducted research and studies about learning outside of school has weakened our cause. *Creative America* (1997) and *Coming Up Taller* (Weitz, 1996) are two reports published by the President's Committee for the Arts and Humanities stressing that arts and humanities can make a major contribution to the education of our youth. For example, *Creative America* states:

> Researchers are demonstrating there are many ways that children learn; teachers can reach students through their spatial, musical, kinesthetic and linguistic intelligences. Educators observe that students develop creative thinking through the arts and transfer that capacity to other subjects. Studies also show that when the arts are a strong component of the school environment, dropout rates and absenteeism decline. (President's Committee on the Arts and the Humanities, 1997)

The report goes on to demonstrate that schools offering the arts in their basic curricula found measurable improvements in learning. Students who studied the arts did better on College Board tests, and first graders who participated in special art classes had their reading and math skills increase dramatically compared with those of other students.

Coming up Taller (Weitz, 1996), describing arts and humanities programs for children and youth at risk, is equally helpful. Besides listing impressive programs from all over the country, the report makes the point that the arts and humanities:

1. Provide children with different ways to process cognitive information and express their own knowledge.
2. Have the potential to enhance academic performance.
3. Spur and deepen the development of creativity.
4. Provide critical tools for children and youth as they move through various developmental stages.
5. Teach the value of discipline and teamwork and the tangible reward that each can bring.
6. Provide youth with a different perspective on their own lives, a chance to imagine a different outcome, and to develop a critical distance from everyday life.
7. Are a critical part of a complete education.

IMLS Documentation. For 3 years, from 1994 to 1996, the IMLS supported museum–school partnerships under the Museum Leadership Initiatives program. It was that experience that led us to fund a research project—in conjunction with the National Science Foundation (NSF), the NEA, and the

NEH—to find out more about the learning that goes on in museums. The 5-year study, begun in March 1997, is a good first step toward helping the museum community quantify the benefits they bring to the communities they serve.

IMLS recently has completed a survey about the status of museum and school partnerships. We found that museums spend a minimum of $193 million annually on K–12 programming and that the typical museum provides between 100 and 223 instructional hours annually to students, with a low estimate of 3.9 million hours collectively for all museums.

Studies such as these go a long way in making the point to the public as well as to policymakers that museums are more than amusing places to visit once or twice a year. They are important players in educating and lifting up entire communities.

ISSUE ADOPTION: WHERE THE PLAYERS JOIN ARMS

Events that happen naturally in the public arena can help promote issue adoption better than a planned strategy or marketing goal. However, a plan with specific steps can assist in making the case. These steps include the following:

1. Recognizing the need for creating a policy community.
2. Creating a policy community with a structure for meeting and communicating.
3. Agreeing on a common agenda.
4. Agreeing on prioritizing the agenda.
5. Agreeing on a plan to reach goals.
6. Working on the messages.
7. Making sure the message is specific, of interest, and clearly tied to the general public welfare.
8. Focusing on what unifies us in the free-choice education sector and what unifies us with the larger free-choice learning sector in general.

Likening the free-choice learning community to the economy might be helpful. Each part of the economy works better when the whole economy is healthy, even though there is competition within the parts. The economy that works best tries to foster healthy competition while finding as many ways as possible to forge links, to build compatibility, and to draw energy from each part's special strengths.

Certainly this involves a lot of work, but the labor is worth the effort. It will enable the entire sector to fulfill its mission of serving the public better. It will inform the public and policymakers that they depend on the resources of the free-choice learning sector throughout their lives and that these resources are necessities to sustaining a well-educated citizenry.

Making the Case

Several important trends make now a good time for the free-choice education sector to press its case in the public policy arena.

Falling Test Scores. As parents and teachers continue to see ways in which public schools are failing children, they will rightly search for alternative methods of teaching and learning. Museums and libraries are places they have looked and will continue to look.

Charter Schools. Since the first state charter law was passed in 1991, 24 states including the District of Columbia have joined the ranks of the charter school movement, with nearly 800 of the schools functioning. Those involved in charter schools (including museum schools, explained in more detail below) often are more open than those in traditional schools to finding alternative methods for teaching and learning.

Museum Schools. A form of charter schools, more than 16 museum schools have begun in the United States in the past decade. The schools operate from, and in conjunction with, art, history, and science museums. Museum schools are based on the premise that children learn in many different ways through different modalities, embracing different styles. The use of objects as well as interactive techniques available as enhancements to learning in all of these schools provides a variety of learning settings for students. Studies of the efficacy of these types of schools are just beginning to be conducted. Further studies will measure the teaching effectiveness of museum schools.

Home Schooling. Home schooling, recently a fringe movement like charter schools, has gained in popularity over the past 10 years as parents look increasingly for alternatives to traditional schooling for their children. According to the Home Education Research Institute, about 1.5 million American students are being home-schooled today, compared with approximately 300,000 in 1992. Most states allow home schooling, and 41 states have no minimum academic requirements for parents who want to home-school their children. That leaves parents searching for educational resources and partners. Increasingly, the free-choice education sector is being turned to for those partnerships.

Lifelong Learning. Institutions throughout the free-choice learning sector provide entertaining educational leisure time activities for people of preschool age through senior citizens. Increasing demand for engagement in learning opportunities presents this sector with a new and important role.

ISSUE PRIORITIZATION: WHERE THE PLAYERS CHANGE TACK

To make a difference in the public policy world, an issue must be not only deemed important but also given priority. There must be a sense of urgency about the issue. By giving the issue of free-choice education top priority, other activities would be encouraged: The research community could continue to do research in this arena; the research community could talk formally and informally about the relationship of free-choice education to formal education issues and continue to explore ways to gather data; and private funders would be encouraged to continue to provide funds or initiate new programs to support the kind of research that focuses on the relevance of free-choice education to formal education.

The Importance of the Research Community

Although it is often difficult for directors of institutions to make the time and exercise their ability to influence public policy, those in the research community are in a powerful position to do so, even though they rarely realize this potential. The research community concerned with education in museums and libraries can establish the mechanisms for exploring and studying the issues critical to the free-choice education sector in making a stronger case to the public policy community.

ISSUE MAINTENANCE: WHERE PLAYERS PROTECT THEIR INTERESTS

A key element in maintaining public policy is the development of core policy with equally powerful supporting ideas that create connections with the values of the special-interest community concerned and with basic political values. Definitions and policy proposals must be compatible with values of specialists and interests directly involved. Connections with larger concepts that are of importance to decision makers help insure a hearing in the court of public policy. Such community values are then incorporated into relevant public policies.

CONCLUSION: THE SLEEPING GIANT

The research community is much like a sleeping giant in that it has already amassed a great deal of research about how people learn in free-choice learning settings, but it has not yet awakened to the task of pulling these materials together to create a coherent argument for the value of free-choice education.

Policy communities work in a variety of ways to bring their issues to the attention of policymakers, using power, influence, and pressure. By using these mechanisms within the four stages of agenda setting, the research community could help raise awareness of the need to gather and compile data and to conduct additional research. By organizing their resources and marshaling their forces, they could approach public and private funders and indicate that they would like to tackle this important topic as a group.

The research community, if it wants to be taken seriously in the public policy world, needs to come together and discuss the role of free-choice learning sector issues, to arrive at ways to talk about these issues in such a manner that policymakers find them relevant. It is the responsibility of the research community to keep the policymakers engaged. The work is tough and proactive, but the cost of ignoring this duty will be high, whereas the benefits that will come with doing it right will be tremendous.

More than three decades ago, the Congress inaugurated an unprecedented program of federal funding for the arts, humanities and sciences. At that time, Congress recognized that the free-choice learning sector provided important voluntary educational opportunities for all citizens.

At my swearing-in ceremony as director of the IMS (now the IMLS), I said that not one institution could afford to remain on the sidelines when so many important issues face our communities. I believe that more than ever today; members of the free-choice learning sector have a duty, as institutions of lifelong learning, to make a commitment to the communities in which they serve.

Within today's reality, this sector must strengthen its message and articulate why it is more than an important addition to its community. The sector must be able to communicate about the significance of its role to the broader, national community. As a nation of learners, we depend on the resources of museums, libraries, public television, and the performing arts throughout our lives. To insure that these sources will be there for us and will receive the support they need, they must become better advocates for themselves.

REFERENCES

Lindenfeld, Frank. (1972). *Radical perspectives on social problems; readings in critical sociology* (2nd ed.). New York: Macmillan.

National Commission on Excellence in Education. (1983, April). *A nation at risk: The imperative for educational reform.* Washington, DC: U. S. Department of Education.

President's Committee on the Arts and Humanities. (1997). *Creative America: A report to the President.* Washington, DC: Author.

Weitz, Judith Humphreys. (1996). *Coming up taller.* Washington, DC: President's Committee on the Arts and Humanities and Americans for the Arts.

CHAPTER 11

Supporting Systemic School Science Education Reform in Partnership with Free-Choice Science Learning: A Texas Case Study

Charlie Walter and Vanessa Westbrook

In January of 1999, the board of directors of the Science Teachers Association of Texas (STAT) voted to accept the Informal Science Education Association of Texas (ISEA) as an affiliate member to the organization. STAT is a statewide organization with a membership of over 5,000 elementary through college teachers and supervisors in science education dedicated to maintaining the highest levels of science education in Texas schools. The vote to accept ISEA marked the first time a nonteacher group had been granted affiliate status by STAT. For the first time, institutions of free-choice learning had been formally recognized as important stakeholders in the Texas science education system. This affiliation was a step in a sequence of events that began in 1995 as part of a project initiated by the Texas Statewide Systemic Initiative (SSI).

The goal of improving science, mathematics, and technology education for all Texas students is a formidable task. As of 1998 there were 1,061 school districts, 7,053 schools, and 3,891,877 students in Texas. The Texas SSI took on this challenge in 1994 and set out to develop policy and public support, redefine curriculum frameworks, connect decision makers, and create new infrastructures to support improvements in the Texas education system. During its initial years of development, the Texas SSI identified "science rich" institutions outside of the formal, grades K–12 education system as an important component of the state's educational infrastructure. The SSI invested in and nurtured the involvement of these institutions as important stakeholders in the state's education improvement enterprise.

BEGINNINGS

The initial step in developing a relationship between the Texas free-choice science learning community and the SSI began at a 2-day conference at the Fort Worth Museum of Science and History in September of 1995. The goal of this meeting, as described by participants, was to "focus on the role Texas's informal science education community can play in supporting and effecting positive change in education in the State." Of the 48 delegates invited, 21 were from museums, 21 represented formal education, and 6 were business and community leaders. The fact that only museum educators were invited to this initial conference (science museum staff planned the conference) is symptomatic of the nature of free-choice science institutions in the state at the time. No mechanisms were in place to facilitate the crossover of ideas among institutional communities—for example, museums, zoos, nature centers, media and other community-based organizations.

Evaluations of this initial conference indicated that delegates were enthusiastic about the potential of free-choice science learning institutions as partners in Texas school improvement. Ultimately, the SSI leadership agreed to create an Informal Science Action Team (ISAT) as part of its statewide efforts. This ISAT consisted of formal and free-choice educators and community leaders. Other Texas SSI "action teams," which focus on education improvement, included Elementary Science, Algebra, Preservice, and Professional Development.

It is important to note here that this initiative purposefully focused on school improvement by bridging the "science rich" resources of Texas's free-choice science education community to schools. Free-choice science learning institutions have much to offer formal education but can be most effective in this area when connected and aligned with state and national goals for our schools. It is as simple as the metaphor of all oars rowing in the same direction. It is complex in that non-school science institutions must preserve their identity as "free-choice" institutions with a much broader mission. Supporting education improvement is an extremely high priority in most communities. Thus if a free-choice science learning institution is truly being responsive to its community, systemically supporting formal education improvement must be a priority of that institution. The philosophical conundrum is that if a free-choice learning institution systemically weaves itself into the infrastructure of formal education, it is no longer fully free-choice.

The philosophical danger here is that by supporting school improvement, an institution of free-choice learning must support the goals of school improvement. This comes with the baggage of standards-based education, standardized testing, teacher certification, and the politics that come with text and curriculum adoption. A free-choice learning institution can find itself immersed in the world of schooling and less so in the business of learning.

CREATING A LEARNING COMMUNITY

In the months following the initial Texas conference, a broad list of possible Action Team members was developed. The goal was to create a team that was representative of Texas's cultural and geographic diversity and was a well-rounded mix of teachers from both the K–12 classroom and university, school administrators, and science educators representing museums, nature centers, botanic gardens, zoos, and aquariums. In an examination of the many well-qualified individuals on the list, it became apparent that this initial Action Team would have to be limited to be manageable, and that ultimately it could face criticism from those not included in these initial discussions. This became an important priority concern as the team looked to the future.

Action Team

Veena Kaul, an SSI science education associate, and I [CW], senior vice president of the Fort Worth Museum of Science and History, shared team leadership. Veena and I felt that it was critical to the effort's success that we create a true learning community among the team members. Building a successful team became as important as its recommendations. Initially, the management writings of Senge (1990), Senge, Kleiner, Roberts, Ross, and Smith (1994), McGill and Slocum (1994), and, at a later time, those of Collins and Porras (1994), provided a great deal of help in developing a framework for the team's strategy and structure as a learning community.

"Facilitating the Work of a Learning Community: Shared Values and Expectations" (see Table 11.1) was utilized as an outline for building a team philosophy in the Action Team's first meeting in June of 1996. The group was also told that most work would be done in team meetings, with very little required of them between meetings. This expectation was set out of respect for their time, knowing that each member had a pressing "day job" and that this work was far above and beyond.

Action Team Year 1. During its first year of activity, the team met seven times, each time at a different location in Texas, expanding its network and

Table 11.1. Facilitating the Work of a Learning Community: Shared Values and Expectations

A learning community is about:	A learning community is not about:
Positive advocacy	Personal agendas
Teams	Hierarchy
Systemic thinking	Narrow orientation
Networks	Bureaucracy
Openness	Control
Creativity	Conformity
Continuous improvement	Best way
Experimentation	Get it right the first time
Seeking input	We know best
Constructive dissent	"Don't ask why"

Note: Adapted from the writings of John W. Slocum and Michael E. McGill by Charlie Walter.

building advocacy. The team's first four meetings were a combination of business and touring of regional sites. The business portions of the meetings included updates on the work of the Texas SSI, review of model programs and the literature targeting linkages between formal and free-choice science education, and discussions of action steps the team should take. Touring regional sites gave the team glimpses into the unique institutions and communities around Texas and provided important information on the programs offered regionally.

In October of 1996 a subgroup of the Informal Science Action Team attended the Association of Science and Technology Centers (ASTC) annual meeting in Pittsburgh. An important dynamic occurred at this meeting. Approximately 12 team members were sitting in a hotel lobby discussing the day's sessions. Members realized that there was not a venue in Texas that supported the work of free-choice science education at this level. The only reason the team was at the ASTC meeting was because the Texas SSI had supported their travel, and this support would ultimately go away. A majority of free-choice science institutions in Texas did not have the financial resources to send staff to national meetings, and if they did, it was to the particular free-choice "niche" that institutions represented. The dynamic of outstanding ASTC sessions combined with the diversity of the group produced new conversations on science education. At this point, one of the group's goals became to create that same ASTC dynamic for colleagues back home in Texas.

Toward the end of its first year of activity, the team spent 2 days in a retreat to summarize lessons learned to date and make recommendations based on these lessons. The team sifted through its options and priorities and broadly identified the focus areas it would address. Its goal for the remainder of that first year was to develop guidelines in the areas of (a) institutional capacity building, (b) family learning and public engagement, and (c) preservice and teacher professional development.

Throughout the rest of this year, the team refined guidelines pertaining to the three focus areas identified and began a statewide survey of "science rich" institutions. The publication *Directory of Science-rich Resources in Texas* published by the Southwest Educational Development Laboratory provided invaluable information for this effort. Ultimately over 200 "science rich" institutions were identified by the team, and respondent survey information was used to facilitate expansion of the action team's efforts.

A leadership change also occurred toward the end of year one when Veena Kaul left Texas to pursue a doctorate at Stanford. SSI Science Specialist Vanessa Westbrook took her place. As the team started year 2 of its effort, Westbrook, a veteran teacher before being recruited by the SSI, introduced a new consensus-building plan to the group. At each host meeting site, area teachers and regional education agency representatives along with members of the local free-choice science learning community were invited to an evening reception. This ongoing activity continues to create good will and better understanding between the formal and free-choice community sources in Texas.

RECOMMENDATIONS—EXPANDING THE COMMUNITY

In February 1998, 20 months after the team had its first meeting, a statewide conference was held at a retreat setting in East Texas. The purpose of this conference was to present a draft copy of *Texas Informal Science: Guidelines for Supporting the Improvement of Science, Mathematics, and Technology Education in Texas* (1999) to a broader group of free-choice science educators for feedback. The guidelines represented what the action team considered to be the most important and effective ways free-choice science learning institutions could systemically support the improvement of science, mathematics, and technology education in Texas. Conference sessions would allow for small group discussions around the guidelines. By the end of the 2 days, the team hoped they would have enough feedback to merit the release of the guidelines and also have broader buy-in from conference delegates.

A retreat setting was selected to help create an informal atmosphere of collegial learning. The meeting featured as speakers Mark St. John, president of Inverness Research Associates, David Hill, director of the Texas SSI, and Steve

Rakow, professor of science education at the University of Houston at Clearlake and, at the time, incoming NSTA president. Evaluations from the conference indicated that delegates felt very positive about the guidelines and looked forward to joining as part of the expanded network. In effect, the team had created a dynamic conversation around science education that replicated the ASTC experience from year 1.

The publication, *Texas Informal Science: Guidelines for Supporting the Improvement of Science, Mathematics, and Technology Education in Texas* (1999), recommends three major areas of focus. These deal with organizational quality (capacity building), family learning and public awareness, and teacher preparation and professional development. The 28-page booklet was published in outline form with model programs and additional information published in its margins. Its brevity was by design. The following is an outline of the guidelines developed by the action team:

Free-choice Science Guidelines

Organizational Quality. Free-choice science learning institutions must build their ability to connect and align with all the community's educational partners to improve science, mathematics, and technology education. To accomplish this goal, we suggest several action steps.

1. Science rich institutions collectively have vast resources for expanding the experiential background of all citizens. These resources are optimized when the community recognizes collections, exhibitions, unique environments, and staff of institutions as opportunities for firsthand learning.

2. Strong partnerships lead to systemic improvement in education. Free-choice science learning institutions provide a "neutral ground" to bring together diverse constituencies, and long-term partnerships utilize each partner's particular strengths.

3. Inquiry experiences are the basis of learning and are provided by free-choice science learning institutions. Inquiry learning opportunities are strengthened when free-choice science institutions stimulate curiosity beyond the visit, and when learning research is utilized in developing programs and exhibits.

4. Free-choice science learning institutions must preserve their unique identity in order to maintain their strength as they undertake collaborative projects.

5. Networking creates important information sharing opportunities.

6. Free-choice science exhibition materials and program-support materials are developed in collaboration with formal educators and link the exhibits and programs to the Texas Essential Knowledge and Skills for Science, a state grades K–12 standards document of the Texas Education Agency.

7. Efforts must continually be evaluated in order to develop effective programs.

Family Learning and Public Awareness. Free-choice science learning institutions provide opportunities for family learning and public awareness to help all children and adults become more literate in science, mathematics, and technology. To accomplish this, we suggest several action steps.

1. Free-choice science learning institutions benefit when the entire community is involved in promoting science, mathematics, and technology literacy. The community is engaged when school, community, and free-choice science learning institutions collaborate to conduct family learning and public awareness events.

2. Free-choice science learning institutions provide families with rich learning environments for science, mathematics, and technology. These environments should give families opportunities to make personal connections to everyday science, increase the families' desire to learn more, and provide additional materials for further learning when possible.

3. Equitable access to programs is possible when barriers are removed. Access is improved when staff and boards reflect the diversity of the community, events and programs are held in a variety of locations, operating hours allow for varied visiting times, communications strategies are sensitive to varied needs, and facilities are designed to accommodate all age groups.

Teacher Preparation and Professional Development. Free-choice science learning institutions utilize their rich resources to improve preservice teacher preparation and teacher professional development in science, mathematics, and technology. To accomplish this goal, we suggest several action steps.

1. Free-choice science learning institutions are recognized as an important stakeholder in teacher education preservice programs and are utilized as an integral resource in preservice programs.

2. Free-choice science learning institutions provide opportunities for preservice teacher learning. Preservice learning is enriched when preservice providers acknowledge, value, and utilize the capability of free-choice science institutions. This opportunity is maximized when preservice teachers observe children learning in a free-choice science environment.

3. Free-choice science learning institutions offer experiences and resources that enhance the understanding of science, mathematics, and technology. Teacher professional development is enriched when information about free-choice, science rich resources are available for educational institutions, a part-

nership with formal educational institutions is established to give teachers experiences outside the classroom and within a free-choice setting, and successful collaborative programs are identified to exemplify positive impact. Teacher professional development opportunities are also enriched when free-choice science learning institutions provide opportunities for inquiry learning and support teachers as lifelong learners.

CREATING AN OPERATING STRUCTURE—IN FOR THE LONG HAUL

After the initial conference and subsequent release of the guidelines booklet, the Informal Science Action Team began looking for ways to incorporate a growing body of proponents into its efforts. Dr. Steve Rakow recommended a strategy. The Action Team could transition into a statewide association, and eventually apply for affiliation status with the Science Teachers Association of Texas. The group's final project under the Action Team status was to facilitate a metamorphosis of itself into the Informal Science Education Association of Texas. The plan included the development of a constitution and bylaws. Action Team members became ISEA's first governing body. One very important early step was to outline the turnover of seven members of the original Action Team from this governing body each year for 3 years.

The Informal Science Education Association

The first "members" of the Informal Science Education Association were individuals who attended the group's second annual conference in February of 1999. These 80 charter members voted in the initial seven new ISEA board members in September that same year.

ISEA has linked a diverse free-choice science learning community in Texas and created a very positive and visible force to support education improvement issues. Key state and national leaders have taken notice and have supported the effort. ISEA members, who had earlier expressed feelings of isolation and a lack of credibility within formal school settings, have begun to consider themselves important partners in the improvement of formal science education.

As the association continues to grow, it utilizes its own guidelines as a framework for expansion. Important capacity building experiences for members are a focal point of its work. To support its members, ISEA hosts an annual meeting that features keynote speakers and presentation of model programs related to guideline priority areas. ISEA also has expanded its presence at the state's Conference for the Advancement of Science Teaching by presenting sessions, hosting an annual reception at a local free-choice science learning institution, and staffing its booth along side other STAT affiliate organizations. ISEA leaders also have begun regional efforts to support year-round dialogue with other free-choice science educators in their region of Texas.

Program outcomes and professional reflections demonstrate how systemic partnerships between formal and free-choice education have strengthened Texas's educational infrastructure and increased the state's capacity to promote lifelong learning to all its citizens. Several specific examples of these outcomes are:

1. The Science Center for Educator Development, a part of the Texas SSI, has included free-choice science in its Science Toolkit for teachers. The toolkit is an on-line resource for helping teachers implement state science standards. Free-choice science resources are listed by region, and examples of how to utilize free-choice science resources to improve science education in the classroom are included in sample lesson plans. (http://www.tenet.edu/teks/science/stacks/resources/general_res.html)

2. In Houston, the Informal Science Coalition is a strategic partner of the newly funded Urban Systemic Initiative. The coalition has developed a pilot program of family learning events at free-choice learning sites to promote parental involvement in their children's education. Educating families about national and state shifts in science education is another goal of the program. The partnership with the Houston Independent School District has allowed many families who have not visited a free-choice science learning institution access for the first time. The Children's Museum of Houston hosted 1,500 individuals at its pilot family learning events associated with this effort. It was estimated that a minimum of 70 percent of these individuals had not been to the museum before.

3. In addition to the Houston area, regional groups have formed in Austin, San Antonio, Galveston, and El Paso with the goal of systemically working with the formal education community in the region to improve science, mathematics, and technology education.

4. At the 1999 Conference for the Advancement of Science Teaching sponsored by the Science Teachers Association of Texas, a session block on free-choice science learning opportunities for teacher professional development highlighted 16 institutional offerings ranging from teacher camp-ins to institutes to internships. ISEA plans to make this "Informal Science Showcase" a regular feature at the yearly STAT conference.

5. Four out of seven pilot grants awarded by the Texas SSI in 1997 to improve preservice science education in Texas went to projects that included a free-choice science learning partner.

Evaluations and anecdotal feedback of ISEA programs indicate that the association is providing valuable networking and capacity building activities for members:

It is very motivating to be a part of a diverse group that is working toward a common goal (increasing science learning outside the classroom), yet encourages each institution to maintain their individual strengths and focus. . . . I have been able to bring a sense of statewide and national trends to my staff. (Tara Schultz, Texas State Aquarium)

My involvement in ISEA has greatly influenced and shaped my own professional development over the past three years. . . . My affiliation with the group has lead to an overhaul of programs at the Austin Nature Center. (Janice Sturrock, Austin Nature Center)

I like feeling that what I am doing fits into a larger picture. I have been in the field of informal science education for years, but felt as if we were in little pockets rather than parts of a larger picture. (Margaret Bamberger, Bamberger Ranch)

Most importantly, a sense of community has emerged in the informal education community that has been unprecedented in my experience. Staff of smaller institutions without the scope or breadth of larger ones have been included in something more than a professional organization. They have been supported and included in the discussions of relevance and future of informal education. . . . It is this intangible sense of community that has broadened my opportunities to work with informal sites, both large and small, to improve the education efforts of Texas Parks and Wildlife. (Bob Murphy, Texas Parks and Wildlife Department)

My experience with the Texas SSI's Informal Science Education Team has helped to develop my efforts to seek out and collaborate with some of the science-rich institutions in the Houston area. My collaborations are far more then just a field trip, but a component of the learning experience which actively involves students and experts from a variety of areas. (Dorian Reynolds, Teacher Houston ISD)

THE FUTURE—CLOSING THE FIRST CHAPTER OF A LONG BOOK

The Texas Informal Science Education Association has been successful in linking together a diverse constituency and focusing efforts on the improvement of science education in Texas. Although its focus has been on bridging the rich resources of free-choice science learning institutions appropriately to formal education, ISEA is also helping to build stronger free-choice science learning institutions. Family learning activities at free-choice learning sites are serving schools by emphasizing the important role parents play in their children's education, but at the same time they are introducing many underrepresented families to free-choice science learning institutions for the first time. Staff are less isolated and are able to share ideas with colleagues through networks fostered by ISEA. Model programs provide new strategies for adaptation at other free-choice sites. Teachers have greater opportunities to utilize free-choice learning sites through greater awareness of program offerings and greater support from state science education leaders.

When we started our effort in Texas, our definition of free-choice science learning institutions included science museums, science centers, children's museums, nature centers, aquariums, botanic gardens, zoos, public television, and community organizations. This community has now been expanded to include federal agencies, professional organizations, state agencies, and university agencies. All of these organizations are rich in resources that can improve education in the state. ISEA has provided an arena in which these diverse groups can learn how to be a better systemic education partner and given free-choice science educators a sense of professional efficacy.

Today ISEA has over 100 individual members that represent a diverse array of institutions. ISEA leadership will continue to work with state science education leaders to keep the free-choice science learning community actively involved in the formal education arena. It is hoped that ISEA will be able to weave free-choice science education intricately into the very fabric of formal education in Texas. Maintaining the free-choice science learning community's unique identity as institutions of lifelong learning is critical as more partnerships are formed with formal education. This work is important though, and free-choice science learning proponents cannot stand "outside the fray" as communities struggle to improve formal education.

Free-choice science educators must expand their thinking and consider themselves and their institutions as important stakeholders in the systemic improvement of science education in their communities. In Texas, there has been incredible support for this idea. National debates over the appropriateness of free-choice learning institutions' using resources to support formal education have not surfaced here. ISEA promotes the view that the free-choice science learning community must support all stakeholders: children, adults, families, students, and teachers of every cultural ethnicity and in every region of the state. How this support will play out at each free-choice science learning institution will be different, based on each institution's unique community, funding streams, resources, and strategy.

Free-choice science learning institutions provide opportunities for all stakeholders to deepen their relationship to their world. The one thing ISEA does not promote is trying to be all things to all stakeholders. A nature center with two staff members should focus its efforts on interpreting that unique natural resource to its visitors. It should not try to address all elements of the Texas Essential Knowledge and Skills for Science.

ISEA has closed the first chapter of its existence. Chapter 1 highlighted the beginning of an organization. Future chapters should continue to tell the unique stories of partnerships between formal and free-choice learning institutions, each contributing in appropriate ways to an improved system of teaching and learning in Texas.

Note: The authors wish to thank the Charles A. Dana Center at the University of Texas at Austin for its encouragement and support in making this effort a reality.

REFERENCES

Collins, J. C., & Porras, J. I. (1994). *Built to last: Successful habits of visionary companies.* New York: HarperCollins.

McGill, M. E., & Slocum, J. W. (1994). *The smarter organization: How to build a business that learns and adapts to marketplace needs.* New York: John Wiley.

Senge, P. M. (1990). *The fifth discipline: The art and practice of the learning organization.* New York: Doubleday.

Senge, P. M., Kleiner, A., Roberts, C., Ross, R. B., & Smith, B. J. (1994). *The fifth discipline fieldbook: Strategies and tools for building a learning organization.* New York: Doubleday.

Texas Statewide Systemic Initiative, Informal Science Education Action Team. (1999). *Texas informal science: Guidelines for supporting the improvement of science, mathematics, and technology education in Texas.* Austin: University of Texas at Austin, Charles A. Dana Center.

CHAPTER 12

Free-Choice Science Learning: Future Directions for Researchers

Laura Martin

Learning science outside of school happens as we read magazines, watch television, run our households, and enjoy ourselves in our leisure time. The first conference on "free-choice" learning, Free-Choice Learning: Assessing the Informal Science Education Infrastructure, convened by the Institute for Learning Innovation was a terrific opportunity for individuals working in many of these sectors to compare thoughts on science learning that takes place outside of formal school settings. Participants represented policymakers, the general public, economic and intellectual interests, and entrepreneurial interests. Representatives from science centers, the Institute for Museum and Library Services, and public broadcasting as well as academic researchers and exhibit designers were some of those gathered. As a cognitive psychologist working in a science center, I was particularly interested in the mix. I have studied media and science learning for a number of years and have also had opportunities to apply research findings in developing programs. Working with both theory and practice, I was eager to learn about the perspectives of these various stakeholders in science learning.

The conference group was heterogeneous in several key respects. Most important, people held quite different views of what they considered to be science learning. Some argued for defining science learning as a mastery of school subject content whereas others argued that motivation, appreciation, and imagination about science are key outcomes of free-choice science learning. Right away, then, we had fundamentally different starting points because of what our respective work environments had led us to focus on: science fact and processes or attitudes toward science. In fact, both views of learning are important, as I argue here, but as the outcome of an enculturation process, for we pass on and extend the working knowledge of our society through our institutions, routines, discourse, and habits of mind—cultural practices, in short. What we need to explicate, then, are the general cultural practices of our society concerned with understanding the natural world.

Participants at the free-choice learning conference also held different views of the learner. Some, in the tradition of educational psychology, focused on the individual mind, using, in part, constructivist arguments that claim the individual uses experiential building blocks to formulate conceptual knowledge. Others defined the learner in terms of a learning community or exchange. For them, the conceptual building blocks are put together in interaction with others and the construction of understanding is detectable in dialogue or activity with others.

At the same time, attendees were a consistent group of "do-ers," not just talkers. Everyone was energized by the prospect of moving ahead with actions to promote awareness and opportunity in the free-choice science learning sector.

We agreed on the need for advocacy in legislation, and for developing research topics in ways that will improve practice. Interestingly, research was the one arena where there was clear consensus: We agreed that there is a definite need for further research into learning outcomes and institutional impact, so that claims about the value of free-choice learning experiences can be substantiated and areas of murkiness about exactly what the experiences lead to can be clarified.

Conference participants wanted to move beyond theory to an action agenda backed by research that addresses concrete questions. Yet research on free-choice science learning is in its infancy, both definitionally and theoretically. It will be critical to continue building in these directions as we pursue our respective projects, because part of what we are all looking for cannot be identified adequately without a theory of free-choice science learning. Here, then, is a modest contribution to that effort.

THE PARADOXICAL NATURE OF FREE-CHOICE SCIENCE SETTINGS

The concept of science being learned in a relatively untutored fashion at first appears to be paradoxical. First of all, science is about abstract knowledge: It is not the visible, the everyday, the intuitive. Vygotskian developmental theory, for example, would assert that scientific thinking is, by definition, schooled. Vygotsky (1987) himself demonstrated, furthermore, that concepts that are developed intuitively are incomplete.

Science is about abstract, general understandings and explanations of phenomena. Science is communicated through mathematical and other formal description, categorization, prediction, and theory. Science itself is not intuitively perceived, like beauty in nature. It is, rather, an area of study, accessible through complex tools—including lenses, calculators, and equations—that have developed in our culture over time. The goal to adopt and master esoteric tools and practices to study the natural world, beyond a certain level, needs to be inculcated in individuals. When the culture agrees on a set of procedures for doing this, we call it formal education (Scribner & Cole, 1973).

Paradox 1: The Free-Choice Dilemma

The first paradox here is that, in contrast to nature and what is noticeable on the surface of things, science and its principles have to be taught and cannot be self-taught intuitively through free-choice encounters, and yet, free-choice learning assumes self-direction and self-discovery. Proponents of free-choice learning are generally aware of this. Their environments and materials are deliberately engineered for learning encounters but without traditional teachers or obligatory curricula. Educators in more formal, curriculum-based programs, however, do not always perceive the educational engineering behind science centers, TV programs, hobbies, and so forth. For that reason, they may be uncomfortable with the apparent informality of these settings. This results in free-choice learning's being viewed as somehow lesser than formal learning.

Paradox 2: Alienation by Association

A second paradox follows from the first, that is, the fact that science needs to be taught: Free-choice appears to exclude the teacher and our traditional notion of science teaching and yet we associate science learning with *how* science is usually taught. Our school system, in subtle and not-so-subtle ways, discourages most people from scientific pursuits and so can be characterized as alienating and exclusionary for the learner. This was apparent to us, for instance, when we interviewed 45 professionals from multiple cultural backgrounds about their associations with science. Virtually all of the nonscientists reported having had personally alienating school experiences with science (Martin & Leary, 1996). Furthermore, these associations generalized negatively to scientists, to laboratories, as well as to specific content and processes. Free-choice learning, then, may require unlearning some fairly strong negative associations.

Paradox 3: How Free Is Free?

The third paradox is that if science must be taught and if it might mean unlearning negative associations, can anyone accomplish this purely as a free choice? How free is free choice really? As carefully as we try to define what counts as science and learning, for example, as acquiring content, procedural skill, good attitude, or accurate mental models, we must also carefully delineate what the term *free* means.

For researchers, the analytic boundaries we draw define what constitutes free choice. By defining free choice in one particular way, however, we risk losing the richness of meaning inherent in the term *free-choice learning*. For example, we could decide that what we count as free choice is what occurs during a single encounter, at what is called the microgenetic level (Wertsch, 1985). An example might be a child's decision to play an educational game one afternoon. Or, free choice might be what is inferred from the context of an activity, as when a child spends considerable leisure time manipulating some materials in play. The issue of analytical boundaries is further confusing because free-choice learning is found in schools: Students, for instance, may elect certain science courses over others or have options in selecting a science project for a fair. Conversely, requirements can exist in nonschool settings like camp, where children must participate in nature hikes, stargazing, or pond projects, perhaps. What is clear is that freedom is not absolute but is itself contextual.

GETTING ON THE SAME PAGE IN DEFINING FREE-CHOICE LEARNING: METHODS AND DEFINITIONS

These definitional points matter because if those of us interested in science education want to understand the interface of scientific and untutored learning in everyday settings, both in educational practice and research, we need to frame some common understandings so that we are all on the same page.

Terms and Meanings

This is where I encounter a bit of a postmodernist crisis. It is not clear whether, in research, the various stakeholders should agree on technical definitions for variables or should use a variety of definitions, instruments, and analytic schemes. The underlying question is, Do our research practices create what we mean by those terms as we conduct our studies, or do we have a foundation of shared meanings for which we simply have to work out the methodological issues? For instance, free-choice learning could be defined in a technical way as learning that is not negatively reinforced, as is much learning in school: done to avoid bad grades but positively reinforced by the outcome it produces, notably, personal satisfaction. If we use this technical definition, we can study learning and even unlearning fairly specifically. But what becomes of the methodological "noise," or data, that is not traditionally analyzed in formal learning settings? Noncognitive factors such as the presence of particular colearners, one's past experiences with a learning setting, and the social goal of the learning, to name three, have been found to have an effect on learning (Cole, Griffin, & LCHC, 1987).

There is evidence, too, that free-choice learning environments, if not the learners themselves, are not treated sui generis with their own outcomes and value. For instance, a recent book published by the National Research Council (1999) discussing "community based learning environments" simply states that the family is a key part of the learning environment; family learning models have been imported to schools; classrooms benefit from community connections; parents and business representatives can have impact on schools. The fact that there is little elaboration about these points implies that the benefits of free-choice learning institutions are of second-order value compared with those of formal learning. The value of free choice as an educational event in itself is not considered. Surprisingly, too, the large body of research showing the effects of physical setting on thinking is not referenced. The familiarity of learners with a setting is an important factor in their choosing to learn.

Perhaps, then, we need further conversations about definitional and methodological issues. A postmodernist would say that there are many sorts of free choices, but we want to avoid the problems that multiple definitions could bring—again, the challenge is to get to the same page.

ORGANIZING A COMMON RESEARCH AGENDA

How we measure learning is a critical point for organizing a common agenda. Some people attending the free-choice learning conference like to measure learning by looking at individual performance on standardized measures. Others evaluate individual responses with "ecologically valid" (Cole, Hood, & McDermott, 1979) instruments or indicators, which take into account the setting, its norms, and the participants' goals. Still others regard group behavior (for instance the family group) as an independent variable and "knowledge" that emerges during interpersonal interactions as the dependent measure (e.g., Borun, Chambers, & Cleghorn, 1996).

The Activity Theory Framework

To avoid having many sciences, many learnings, and many free choices, it would be useful to adopt a general theoretical framework that allows many units of analysis but does not leave us hopelessly relativistic. If we adopt what is called an *activity theory* framework, units of analysis are allowable at many levels. In this framework, the context of learning, the learners' objectives, the learners' immediate tasks for fulfilling that objective, and the mental operations they apply to complete the task are all of significance but what constitutes "activity" is not defined structurally. It is, rather, defined functionally and so its appearance can shift at any time. Thus, for example, playing the same board game might prompt strategic thinking in a competition yet silliness in a rainy-day setting. What distinguishes activity theory as a learning theory is the axiom that learning cannot be separated from the conditions that foster it. By ignoring the conditional and situated nature of learning, traditional learning research has created problems for the free-choice learning sector, because learning outcomes in the free-choice learning settings were compared to school outcomes without taking into account the different social structures of the settings.

METHODOLOGIES FOR MEASUREMENT

In the interest of developing flexible, developmental, analytic models for looking at free-choice science learning, two analytic models based on activity theory are presented briefly below. Each has been applied in free-choice learning settings.

The "Meso-Genetic" Approach

One approach, useful for analyzing the impact of a program or project, has been called a "meso-genetic" analysis (Cole, 1995). Cole used it to study a multiyear after-school computer program for children.

A meso-genetic approach involves keeping records of an educational project that describe the project's evolution at several points over time. The records track how the practitioners or producers accounted for certain developments as they were happening. What steps were taken with what result? What happened in the end? At the conclusion, the researcher has a story that looks both back and forward and thus can see which threads could account for the outcomes. Sometimes threads are tracked through linguistic evidence (Wertsch, 1991) sometimes through mapping of events in a project's history (see Cole, 1995). It is worth repeating that the advantage of this approach is that it does not separate the development of learning from the intervention used to foster it. Cole and his colleagues were careful to include analysis of the experimenters' actions and expectations in evaluating the project's history. In fact, the project work became a practicum for undergraduates and a model for university–community relations.

The Practice Approach

Another approach that is useful when specific kinds of mental activity are under investigation involves identifying variables influencing thought in complex social settings. The variable identification approach is a rather extended one. Scribner (1984), who studied thinking in workplaces, proposed a refined methodology that also might be useful to apply to free-choice science learning settings.

The first step in Scribner's approach is to generate rich descriptions of people learning in normally occurring situations using the tools of ethnography and sociolinguistics as well as cognitive psychology. These look at speech and gesture, at status relations and cultural norms, at symbols and signifiers. Looking at these in a specific cultural setting, the researcher can begin to discern patterns and alterations in patterns related to educational moments. The method allows the researcher to formulate hypotheses about what is motivating the participants and the action, about what the task is, and about the mental tools the learners may be applying. Observations are then usefully supplemented by interviews with the participants to probe whether the researcher's hypotheses are on the mark.

The second step of this kind of activity theory methodology is to identify cognitive tools that might come into play in the natural setting. What are the patterns of language, gesture, tool use, and other actions that are of psychological, or mental, consequence? How might these differ in another setting or when other people get involved? In the final phase, the researcher designs experimental tasks that require the application of the hypothesized cognitive tools, allowing a test of the hypotheses about what mental tools have been activated by the learner as they worked and with what consequences.

So, for example, through observations and interviews, Scribner (1984) identified a unique system of multiple-base arithmetic calculation in use among experienced workers in a dairy who had to load cases of milk products to fill orders as efficiently as possible. She then developed arithmetic tasks based on the dairy problems and tested college students and dairy workers in a laboratory setting. Noting that the dairy workers outperformed college students on the dairy task analogies, she concluded that the work practices support a specific kind of mental activity that is not automatically acquired through the mastery of school-based math. This pathbreaking work challenges traditional claims about the abstract and generalizable nature of formal education and highlights the fact that learning practices and outcomes are different in the workplace than they are in school. This finding suggests that the systematicity of "lessons" is related to the motivation of the learner.

CHARACTERISTICS OF FREE-CHOICE THINKING

The problem of studying an uncontrolled environment as well as the problem of identifying mental tools people bring to bear in those settings can also be extremely different from those in schools, which have been well-studied. Research tells us that free-choice learning does appear to have certain distinct characteristics that would be missed if we applied only traditional methods of research.

Studying Free-Choice Learning

There already are clues to some of the special features of science learning outside of school. Although comparative observations across types of settings have not been done in the free-choice science learning field as a whole, there are some possible starting points for doing so. Specifically, a lot of research in the literature details interactions in the science museum setting that include observational and interview data (e.g., Borun et al., 1996; Crowley & Callanan, 1998; Stevens & Hall, 1997). Such studies have shown the impact of parents' interactions with children, the activity structures fostered by exhibits, and the purpose of a group's visit.

Those who have studied learning and problem solving in nonschool settings have identified characteristics of problem solving in these settings (Martin, 1997). Among other things, they found that in their daily life people think about and find problems within a broader societal goal structure in a way that is integrated with their actions. People use numerous cognitive supports (mneumonics, concrete manipulables, visual aids, etc.) and they work in collaboration with others or in distributed patterns. These insights and the research already available about science centers suggest that we need a more complete theory about the tools of the free-choice settings, their actual use, and the value of the mediational experiences for the learner.

Questioning Free-Choice Learning. We can certainly expect, then, that free-choice science learning happens in ways that do not resemble school learning because the activity is different. And, yet again, we return to our paradox that science content is quintessentially a "tutored" knowledge system. Can systematic, conceptual growth evolve from everyday, unschooled activity? Should science concepts be the area of focus? The free-choice world doesn't always mark right and wrong ideas as such. Does it instead create weightings by positive attention and by the structure of information? How does it engage mental operations?

We don't quite know enough yet about how free-choice science learning activity influences the mental matrix on which truly scientific concepts ultimately are built. We do know many of the pieces to the puzzle, but a complete model eludes us.

We know, for instance, that children develop "naive theories" (Carey, 1985) of physics, biology, and psychology. These are incomplete and at times erroneous. We collected examples of science beliefs held by our volunteer staff as children. These were among them: from TV, that cats are girls and dogs are boys, and, from a playground pal, if a raindrop lands in the center of your eye, you will go blind. These beliefs were all influenced by someone credible to the child. Sometimes an actual experience is deceptive (for example, a 5-year-old's recipe says to "cook the beans until Daddy gets home") or language misleads (for example, one staff member knew her father worked in a plant, which she imagined was a forest) or an adult misleads (several staff were told if they swallowed a watermelon seed, a melon would grow in their stomach). If we wanted to see how a specific concept developed or deepened, then we would want to know what cultural practices constitute a child's belief system, credible sources, confusions, and novelty.

ENCULTURATION AND IDENTITY

In studying free-choice learning, I believe we should look at science content, but as a cultural tool, not as structures of knowledge. In that way, the outcome questions we want to research might be very different.

What would it mean to look at science concepts as cultural tools? We can agree with Bruner (1996), who wrote that educational institutions are about enculturation. Certainly, our museums and science centers, our media diet, and our amusement choices all serve this important function. Enculturation, in turn, is about learning one's identity in society—how what you are and do fits into broad social practices. It is essential that an analysis of learning take into account the available tools of enculturation.

Culture in Free-Choice Learning

One question this view might entail is whether the free-choice arena is reflective and constructive of characteristics of the science learner we'd like to see, such as curiosity, persistence, and flexibility. Equity of access to free-choice experiences, for a start, is important to strive for if we want to promote a democratic sense of identity in our society. Ownership of the tools and language of science also is something we would hope to see fostered. Getting science to speak to people in a way that engages their imagination also is a goal.

The goal of full participation in science learning asks us to bridge the gap that already exists between most people's everyday experiences and a scientific analysis of the world. We should reflect on whether we are not reinforcing some of the barriers to positive experiences with science when we imitate formal education in the structure of free-choice learning activities. We mentioned that the term science and its associations are often reacted to negatively even by educated people. At this time, we should be careful about unwittingly reproducing the voice of school in our free-choice projects.

NEW DIRECTIONS FOR RESEARCH

Looking at free-choice activity as enculturation, then, suggests several directions for research. One outcome we may want to pin down is the kind and level of support needed to get people to explore science. The data are there and could be compared using meta-analysis, in which results across different studies are equated. We could usefully attempt analyses of instructional "scaffolding," or other kinds of interpersonal support for learning, in free-choice settings. More studies of interpersonal interactions around science in free-choice settings would be valuable because although the landscape is becoming clearer, it is not fully mapped and if, as it has emerged elsewhere, the interpersonal is the medium of transfer for learning (Martin, Shirley, & McGinnis, 1988), then studying interpersonal actions more systematically could be a fruitful avenue for developing tests of free-choice learning outcomes.

Interestingly, one of the focal questions asked at the conference had to do with whether or not an infrastructure exists for free-choice science learning. By taking an activity theory approach we actually build and reinforce such an infrastructure. Through reflexivity we discover the infrastructure by building it. All research becomes action research.

THE DIFFERENT AXES

Adopting the issue of enculturation might be useful for getting us to the same page. Perhaps our interests are not so divergent as we imagined. Let's look at some examples. Several orthogonal dimensions of concern or axes were distinguished by conference participants that should be addressed if we want to strengthen the theory and practice of free-choice science learning through research. If we look at each axis with the idea of enculturation in mind, some common ground for conducting research may become apparent.

Axis 1: The Science/Humanities Continuum

The question was posed about whether science should be studied along with other free-choice domains such as art. Some conference attendees argued yes, some no. If we regard free-choice learning as a cultural practice, we would want to look at practices as they occur in relation to different contents. For instance, we would look at how museum activity in the richest sense differs with different exhibit content.

Axis 2: The Formality of Education

Again, we have many reasons to believe that free-choice learning settings work very differently from formal ones. But if we add a cultural element to the definition, we can look at the distinction in another way. Scribner and Cole (1973), for example, distinguished formal from informal not based on whether learning occurred in school but on whether a culture organizes a learning experience systematically. By this definition apprenticeships and initiation rites are considered formal learning settings. A useful question for us is whether, in our culture, museum-going, travel, or family TV viewing are ritualized, at least for certain groups of people. Activity theory can accommodate the fact that museum-going or television-watching behavior may look the same but are actually not functioning the same, or that the same content may function differently in different cultural contexts, for instance, TV watching at home or in school. This is something that I have not seen considered widely in our research projections because of our tendencies to focus on structural units of analysis (e.g., family groupings, zoo visits) rather than functional ones (e.g., tool use, goals).

Axis 3: Integrating Entertaining Features With Educational Material

At this time, cultural boundaries of our society are blurring, or shifting in unfamiliar ways. One can watch *Nova* at a laundromat. One can have coffee at a bookstore. One can talk on the phone to someone in one's own kitchen while walking through the grocery store. What does it mean that different environments are borrowing each other's characteristics? There is no single answer. There is room, however, for systematic experimentation in creating meaning. It is up to us to try out new forms and see how we can combine them in ways that tell people something about their relation to science. In the meantime, we do have some excellent experimental data to support the effectiveness of combining education and entertainment for promoting learning (Hall, Esty, & Fisch, 1990; Wright & Huston, 1995).

Axis 4: Interpreters of Science in Free-Choice Settings

Another interesting dimension focused on staff at science centers and whether their voluntary or professional status has an effect on their work. Who are interpreters of science in free-choice settings? Producers? Docents? Camp counselors? Do we want to professionalize the field to insure quality, and is that possible? Would it change the free-choice nature of our projects? For instance, how much knowledge does the docent or instructor need to have? Free-choice learning contexts are likely to make use of expertise at many levels and this needs to be acknowledged.

Axis 5: Support for Nonprofit versus For-Profit Sectors

Clearly, free-choice institutions have to think about marketing, sponsorships, tie-ins, merchandise, capitalization, and so on. How do we distinguish nonprofits from for-profit institutions in handling these aspects of our work? Here, the issues are most complex because, by adapting the tools of the marketplace, nonprofits may be recreating inequalities of the economic sector socially. Free choice may actually not be literally free. We may therefore be changing the distribution of choices in ways that end up restricting science learning for some. The question has fewer implications for learning research per se but is of great import for any cultural description of free-choice learning options and opportunities.

CONCLUSION

In sum, what is important is to look at the functional, rather than structural, elements of a learning setting. If we agree that the consequence of free-choice learning activity is acquiring a set of practices, there are precedents in both the formal and free-choice domains to help us identify factors that influence this enculturation process. It also suggests that we will have to build a model upon a convergence of methods. Following an activity theory approach, we might want to begin by summarizing evidence of activity and interactions in free-choice settings that enculturate: actions, language, physical tool use, and mental operations, each of which tells learners they are a part of a pattern of learning that they can appropriate.

Probably the most important thing to look at is whether the learner is in on the learning. Letting the U.S. public know that such a thing as free-choice learning activity takes place and that they are part of it will create a coherent message, practice, and culture of free-choice learning.

REFERENCES

Borun, M., Chambers, M., & Cleghorn, A. (1996). Families are learning science in museums. *Curator, 39*(2), 123–138.
Bruner, J. (1996). *The culture of education.* Cambridge, MA: Harvard University Press.

Carey, S. (1985). *Conceptual change in childhood.* Cambridge, MA: MIT Press.

Cole, M. (1995). Cultural-historical psychology: A meso-genetic approach. In L. Martin, K. Nelson, & E. Tobach (Eds.), *Sociocultural psychology: Theory and practice of doing and knowing.* New York: Cambridge University Press.

Cole, M., Griffin, P., & The Laboratory of Comparative Human Cognition. (1987). *Contextual factors in education.* Madison: Wisconsin Center for Education Research.

Cole, M., Hood, L., & McDermott, R. (1979). *Ecological niche-picking: Ecological invalidity as an axiom of experimental cognitive psychology* (Tech. Rep.). New York: Rockefeller University, Laboratory of Comparative Human Cognition.

Crowley, K., & Callanan, M. A. (1998). Describing and supporting collaborative scientific thinking in parent–child interactions. *Journal of Museum Education, 23*(1), 12–17.

Hall, E. R., Esty, E. T., & Fisch, S. M. (1990). Television and children's problem-solving behavior: A synopsis of an evaluation of the effects of Square One TV. *Journal of Mathematical Behavior, 9,* 161–174.

Martin, L. (1997, March/April) Learning in context. *ASTC Newsletter, 24*(2), 2–5.

Martin, L., & Leary, R. (1996, September). *Using narrative to introduce science concepts to diverse audiences in a science center.* Paper presented at the second annual Conference for Socio-Cultural Research, Geneva, Switzerland.

Martin, L., Shirley, M., & McGinnis, M. (1988). Microworlds to macroworlds: An experiment in conceptual transfer. *Children's Environment Quarterly, 5*(4), 32–38.

National Research Council. (1999). *How people learn: Brain, mind, experience, and school.* Washington, DC: National Academy Press.

Scribner, S. (1984). Cognitive studies of work. *Quarterly newsletter of the Laboratory of Comparative Human Cognition, 6*(1, 2).

Scribner, S., & Cole, M. (1973). Cognitive consequences of formal and informal education. *Science, 182,* 553–559.

Stevens, R., & Hall, R. (1997). Seeing Tornedo: How video traces mediate visitor understandings of (natural?) phenomena in a science museum. *Science Education, 81*(6), 735–747.

Vygotsky, L. S. (1987). Thinking and speech. In *The collected works of L. S. Vygotsky: Vol. 1* (pp. 121–166). New York: Plenum Press.

Wertsch, J. V. (1985). *Vygotsky and the social formation of mind.* Cambridge, MA: Harvard University Press.

Wertsch, J. V. (1991). *Voices of the mind: A sociocultural approach to mediated action.* Cambridge, MA: Harvard University Press.

Wright, J. C., & Huston, A. C. (1995). *Effects of educational TV viewing of lower income preschoolers on academic skills, school readiness, and school adjustment one to three years later: A report to the Children's Television Workshop.* Lawrence: University of Kansas, Center for Research on the Influences of Television on Children.

CHAPTER 13

A Practitioner's View on the Value of an Infrastructure for Free-Choice Science Learning

Ann M. Muscat

The importance of science education is at the center of worldwide conversations on global competitiveness, social justice, human health, and environmental sustainability. Improved science education and understanding are critical as science and technology affect almost every aspect of daily life. In addition, through the mass media of television, radio, print, and the Internet, there has been a proliferation and distribution of vast quantities of science and technology information.

THE VISION

Although many look only to the formal setting of the classroom to build a solid foundation of science understanding, multiple opportunities for deepening and refreshing the base of scientific knowledge among the public are provided through science programming on television and radio, exhibits and programs in science centers, natural history museums, zoos, and aquariums, and science presented in popular books, magazines, newspapers, and on the Internet. As a result, the importance and availability of these free-choice learning venues to help sort through and explain scientific information have increased significantly in the last half of the twentieth century (cf. Chapter 6).

FULFILLING A ROLE

Do the many organizational entities that make up the free-choice learning community coordinate their activities and messages, and should they? Do members of the American public perceive the existence of an educational infrastructure for free-choice learning dedicated to improving their science literacy on a variety of subjects over a lifetime of learning? And do practitioners at free-choice learning institutions desire and promote the idea of an infrastructure that could support and enhance their individual ability to achieve their respective missions?

What might it be like to hear a single message articulated by multiple and diverse voices, extolling the necessity, pleasure, and joy of lifelong learning about the world in which we live? The ability to create awareness of a network of constantly available and changing science education resources in the broader community would contribute significantly to the creation of an educated citizenry so vital to the maintenance of environmentally sustainable and democratic societies. A functioning infrastructure of electronic media, print media, community organizations, libraries, museums, zoos, botanic gardens, aquariums, and science centers would open up endless and exciting opportunities for interpretation to a broad and diverse audience of learners.

COLLABORATION VERSUS INFRASTRUCTURE

Many free-choice science education practitioners seem skeptical about the existence and value of an infrastructure. Others question the terminology—both infrastructure and free-choice. Still others are eager to discuss the value of and need for structure within what they sense is a loosely defined field.

Most free-choice science education practitioners collaborate with colleagues from similar institutions and are aware of the benefits of such efforts. These collaborations can take place at the local or national levels. And they often are ad hoc and dependent on individuals. Some involve the sharing of traveling exhibits and educational programs; others are formed to reach out to new and nontraditional audiences; and still other collaborations are intended to broaden audience reach. For the most part, under all the various challenges of collaboration, these efforts are of fixed duration and focus on specific topics. Lack of clear mission, different vocabulary, no established mechanisms for frequent interactions, different organizational structures and cultures, varying resource bases, and confused role definition have limited the success of many a collaborative effort.

However, the concept of infrastructure is different from that of collaboration. Whereas collaboration implies working together for mutual benefit, infrastructure implies a substructure that supports the continuance and growth of a community, as do our highways and communications networks. An infrastructure would provide consistent and well-maintained lines of communication that would allow innovative collaborations to develop. It would speak loudly and with a single voice about the value of lifelong learning and the institutions that provide multiple access points to current knowledge, real objects, and authentic experiences, all valuable commodities in today's rapidly changing world. Certainly in the competitive environment of today's experience economy, the incentive for institutions to contribute to and maintain an infrastructure could be great.

THE BENEFITS OF AN INFRASTRUCTURE FOR FREE-CHOICE SCIENCE LEARNING

A strong and vital infrastructure would allow practitioners to more effectively communicate the value of free-choice learning, and increase the importance and respectability of its sponsoring institutions. But practitioners, such as administrators, educators, authors, filmmakers, marketers, and fundraisers, need to shape the nature of the infrastructure for free-choice learning and contribute to its existence. It does not presently exist in the way the formal educational infrastructure does, with its established public image and clout. Many benefits could emerge from such an effort. It would allow institutions to promote a common agenda, broaden and deepen the impact of their educational messages, and emphasize the importance and joy of lifelong learning. More coordinated efforts could lead to significant extensions in audience, both in numbers and type. The ability to refresh the experience will become critical to audience retention, and different strategies will need to be employed. Increasing the number and type of access points to information is critical to reaching today's diverse audience of learners.

The presence of a functioning infrastructure could enhance and extend limited resources, both financial and human, by influencing public policy, voters' perceptions, and private funding sources. It also could facilitate the sharing of expertise garnered through years of experimentation so that scarce resources can be used more effectively. And it could support the creation and sharing of models of professional development that will produce the next generation of practitioners vital to the long-term health of institutions. The various sources within an infrastructure for free-choice learning could work together with the scientific establishment to promote the values and beliefs of science, and present different perspectives on the complex science and technology underpinnings and issues that affect every form of life on Earth.

The Role of the Practitioner

To the extent that these are viewed as worthy objectives and provide more than adequate incentive to institutions and individuals, it is critical that practitioners engage in discussions on how to operationalize and sustain an infrastructure for free-choice learning. Such an endeavor will be well served by the ability to be flexible and entrepreneurial as compared with the formal education infrastructure. Practitioners need to work together to communicate clearly about who they are, what they do well, and why it is important. In addition, the case for a vital network of lifelong, free-choice learning opportunities needs to be stated in the context of societal issues.

Practitioners must continue to quantify the affective and cognitive impact of free-choice models of educational practice and conduct research that examines learning in a broader context. Longitudinal and comprehensive studies need to be developed by practitioners across disciplines (e.g., educators, exhibit developers, curators, marketers, writers, media producers, etc.) to assess overall institutional impact on the community (cf. Chapter 7). And the results of these efforts need to be more widely reported and discussed within the free-choice and formal educational community.

Understanding the Consumer. For free-choice learning institutions to continue to grow and be sustained, practitioners must broaden and deepen their understanding of the consumer of free-choice science education within its greater variety of categories. At the same time, practitioners are competing for limited resources that require greater accountability. They need to understand that people make choices about how to spend their leisure time, and free-choice learning environments are competing for people's leisure time alongside television, as well as entertainment and recreation venues. Practitioners from administrators to marketers, educators, exhibit developers, curators, writers, media producers, and fundraisers will be more effective if they have an understanding of the following questions:

1. What constitutes the free-choice science education infrastructure?
2. How does their particular institution fit into this infrastructure?
3. How does the pubic perceive and use different parts of the infrastructure, such as print, media, the Internet, and museums? In other words, where does the public spend their educationally oriented leisure time?
4. How does the public perceive its interest in and knowledge of science and technology?
5. What perceptions does the public have about free-choice learning institutions, both positive and negative?

6. What are the common characteristics of individuals who embrace free-choice learning institutions and those who *do not?*
7. What is the perceived value of the programs and/or services offered by such institutions?
8. What is the actual affective and cognitive impact of individual programs on audiences, and how best to measure it?

Trends of Significance. Practitioners need to examine these questions in light of long-term trends that have great significance to free-choice learning institutions. For example, it is important to understand the implications of demographic trends such as the graying of America, increasing ethnic and cultural diversity, baby booms and busts, and the changing nature of employment. Lifestyle trends that can be taken advantage of include the increase in travel and tourism, the concern about safe places, the desire to have new and different experiences, and the need to counterbalance technology with a deeper appreciation of the beauty of the natural world. Pine and Gilmore (1999) have cited experiences as a new economic offering and state that the experience economy is replacing the service economy. This notion of memorable events that engage individuals in personal ways has been at the heart of most free-choice learning experiences for many years.

Operational Implications

What implications does all this talk of free-choice learning have for day-to-day operations? Practitioners need to better understand the different segments of their audiences and develop effective programming and marketing strategies for those segments. Staff and programs must mirror the diversity of an institution's community. Interest must be developed in the concept of lifelong learning, as distinguished from the appeal of children's programming. More packaged educational experiences should be developed that contain the necessary appeal of change and also allow more in-depth and meaningful interactions. And institutions must build brand recognition, as they become more successful at marketing. All this must be done without sacrificing institutional authority, credibility or trustworthiness.

AGENDA CENTERED ON LIFELONG LEARNING

Perhaps the time is right to form a national advisory panel to further define and strengthen an infrastructure for free-choice learning dedicated to developing and communicating a common agenda centered on lifelong learning. Funding agencies and foundations could and should provide the catalyst for such discussions. Institutions, and the professional associations that represent them, should begin discussions on common goals and create focus on a more expansive vision of public education and outreach. Workshops bringing together individuals from different parts of the free-choice learning community should begin developing a common vocabulary (e.g., how learning is defined in free-choice environments) as well as opening the flow of information. A more strategic, coordinated, and successful infrastructure for free-choice science learning would be a powerful partner with formal education and the scientific establishment in promoting science literacy in the next century.

REFERENCE

Pine, B. J., II, & Gilmore, J. H. (1999). *The experience economy: Work is theatre and every business a stage.* Boston: Harvard Business School Press.

APPENDIX

Free-Choice Learning: Assessing the Informal Science Education Infrastructure, 1998 Conference Participants

(*Editor's note*: names and affiliation are current as of 1998 conference registration.)

Linda Abraham
Natural History Museum of Los
  Angeles County

Roxana Adams
American Association of Museums

Steven Allison-Bunnell
Natureboy Media

Rinoti Amin
Institute for Learning Innovation

Paula Apsell
NOVA, WGBH-TV

Elsa Bailey
Lesley College

Julie Bank
Arizona Humane Society

David Bibas
California Science Center

Carla Bitter
California Science Center

Barbara Butler
Private Consultant
(Formerly with National Science Foundation)

Rodger Bybee
National Academy of Sciences

Betty Dunckel Camp
Florida Museum of Natural History

Stephen Carlson
University of Minnesota

Dave Combs
California Science Center

Al Desena
Exploration Place

Lynn Dierking
Institute for Learning Innovation

Catherine Eberbach
New York Botanical Garden

Roxie Esterle
California Science Center

John Falk
Institute for Learning Innovation

Sholly Fisch
Children's Television Workshop

Lorenza Fong
National Park Service

Diane Frankel
Institute of Museum and Library Ser-
    vices

Anne Gilliland-Swetland
University of California at Los Angeles

Geoffrey Godbey
Pennsylvania State University

Deann Gould
California Science Center

Todd Happer
Scientific American's "Explorations"

David Heil
David Heil & Associates, Inc.

Mark Hertle
Howard Hughes Medical Institute

Craig Howard
James Irvine Foundation

Warren Iliff
Aquarium of the Pacific

Janet Kamien
Franklin Institute

Judy Kass
American Association for the Advance-
    ment of Science

Beth Kirsch
WGBH-TV

Emlyn Koster
Liberty Science Center

Robert Lebeau
Temple University
Laboratory for Student Success

Patrice Legro
National Academy of Sciences

Sally Lew
James Irvine Foundation

Bruce Lewenstein
Cornell University

Jessica Luke
Institute for Learning Innovation

Gina Macias
California Science Center

Laura Martin
Arizona Science Center

Paul Martin
Science Museum of Minnesota

Dale McCreedy
Franklin Institute

Jon Miller
International Center for the Advance-
    ment of Scientific Literacy

Donna Mitroff
Fox Kids Network

Ann Muscat
California Science Center

Terri Olson
California Science Center

Ursula Pearce
Institute for Learning Innovation

Diane Perlov
California Science Center

Ken Phillips
California Science Center

Rick Piercy
Lewis Center for Educational Research

Mary-Beth Prokop
Institute for Learning Innovation

Barbara Punt
California Science Center

Shirley Radcliff
California Science Center

Linda Robinson-Stevens
California Science Center

Mark Slavkin
Getty Education Institute for the Arts

Billy Spitzer
New England Aquarium

William Tansey
Liberty Science Center

Carey Tisdal
St. Louis Science Center

Bonnie VanDorn
Association of Science-Technology
Centers

Bettye Davis Walker
African-American Male Achievers
Network

Cindy Wallace
Los Angeles Zoo

John Wright
University of Texas
Department of Human Ecology

About the Contributors

Rinoti Amin is a graduate student at San Francisco State University, San Francisco, California.

Dr. Daniel R. Anderson is a professor in the Department of Psychology at the University of Massachusetts, Amherst.

Dr. Pauline Brooks is an independent consultant, Los Angeles, California.

Dr. Rodger W. Bybee is Director of the Biological Sciences Curriculum Study, Colorado Springs, Colorado.

Dr. Betty Dunckel Camp is Director of Education at the Florida Museum of Natural History at the University of Florida, Gainesville, Florida.

Dr. Patricia A. Collins is Senior Lecturer and Senior Research Scientist of Human Ecology and Radio, TV, Film, University of Texas, Austin.

Dr. Lynn D. Dierking is Associate Director of the Institute for Learning Innovation, Annapolis, Maryland.

Dr. John H. Falk is Director of the Institute for Learning Innovation, Annapolis, Maryland.

Diane B. Frankel is the Program Director of Children, Youth and Families programming at the James Irvine Foundation, San Francisco, California.

Dr. Geoffrey Godbey is Professor of Leisure Studies in the College of Heath and Human Development at the Pennsylvania State University.

Phyllis Gyamfi is a Graduate Research Fellow at the Center for Young Children and Families and a doctoral student at Teachers College, Columbia University, New York, New York.

Dr. Aletha C. Huston is the Priscilla Pond Flawn Professor of Child Development, University of Texas, Austin.

Dr. Emlyn H. Koster is Director of the Liberty Science Center, Jersey City, New Jersey.

Dr. Robert B. Lebeau is Assistant Research Professor in the Department of Educational Psychology at Rutgers University Graduate School of Education, New Brunswick, New Jersey.

Dr. Bruce V. Lewenstein is Associate Professor of Communication and Science & Technology Studies at Cornell University, Ithaca, New York.

Dr. Deborah L. Linebarger is Assistant Research Professor at the University of Kansas, Kansas City.

Jessica J. Luke is Senior Associate at the Institute for Learning Innovation, Annapolis, Maryland.

Dr. Laura Martin is Director of Education and Research at the Arizona Science Center, Phoenix, Arizona.

Dr. Jon D. Miller is Professor and Director of the Center for Biomedical Communications, Northwestern University Medical School, Chicago, Illinois.

Dr. Ann M. Muscat is Vice President for Special Projects at the Natural History Museum of Los Angeles County, Los Angeles, California.

Ursula J. Pearce is Administration Coordinator at the University of East London, Careers Advising Service, London, England.

Dr. Kelly L. Schmitt is Assistant Director of Education and Research at the Sesame Workshop, New York, New York.

Charlie Walter is Senior Vice President of the Fort Worth Museum of Science and History, Fort Worth, Texas.

Vanesa Westbrook is Informal and Elementary Science Education Specialist at the Charles A. Dana Center at the University of Texas, Austin.

Dr. Karen Wizevich is Director of Exhibits at the Paleontological Research Institution, Ithaca, NY.

Dr. John C. Wright is Senior Lecturer & Senior Research Scientist of Human Ecology and Radio, TV, Film, University of Texas, Austin.

Index